Diagnosis is just the beginning.

The Lyme Book

The Lyme Book
for family, friends, and caregivers.

A primer for those diagnosed with *Borreliosis* and co-infections.

DAVID KENT, Ed.D.

Pedagogy Press

Copyright © 2018 David Kent, Ed.D.
All rights reserved.

No part of this publication may be reproduced, distributed, or transmitted in any form or by any means, including photocopying, recording, or other electronic or mechanical methods, without prior written permission, except in the case of brief quotations embodied in critical reviews and certain other noncommercial uses permitted by copyright law.

Trademark Notice: Product or corporate names may be trademarks or registered trademarks, and are used only for identification and explanation without intent to infringe.

Cover Artwork: © Can Stock Photo / NLshop
Infographic Artwork: openclipart

Grateful acknowledgment is made to the following, who granted permission to reprint material in this book: The Lyme Disease Association of Australia, www.lymdisease.org.au

A portion of the proceeds of this work will go towards Lyme disease research and advocacy.

A catalogue record for this book is available from the National Library of Australia

ISBN: 9781925555172 (paperback)

Pedagogy Press
www.pedagogypress.com
Sydney, Australia.

First Edition.

Disclaimer

Although every precaution has been taken to verify the accuracy of the information contained herein, the author and publisher assume no responsibility for any errors or omissions. No liability is assumed for damages that may result from the information, or use of information contained within.

Organizations, websites, articles, videos, or any other information or work referred to as a citation or possible source of potential further information in this book does not mean the author or publisher endorses any of those organizations, articles, websites, videos, or other sources, or the recommendations that they may make. Readers should be aware that any sources and citations, if internet-based, may change or disappear between when this book was published and when it is being read.

In line with recommendations from the Australian Association for Research in Education,[*] quotations from publicly available data (such as posts on social media) are entitled to be presented with anonymity in this and any other publication, with permission for use not requiring consent.[**] All such quotes used in this book have been paraphrased so that any similarity to the words or situation of any actual persons, living or dead, or any actual events is purely coincidental.

The information presented in this book is not a substitute for medical advice, or a diagnosis or consultation with a trained medical professional. It is intended for general information only, and is not to be relied upon to make determinations related to treatment of a medical condition. Recommendations of any specific treatment options or protocols are not intended to address any particular reader's medical situation, and the reader should always contact their own physician before considering or undertaking any new treatment. The information presented herein is not intended to treat, prevent, or cure any disease, nor to endorse any doctor, drug, supplement, product, or treatment modality that is referred to or discussed. Information is provided entirely for educational purposes, and is not intended to treat or diagnose any individual or serve as a prescription or cure for any disease or health condition. Use of the information in this book is entirely at your own risk. This book was not written to replace the advice or care of a qualified health care professional; it is only intended to perform as a sharing of knowledge and information. You should make your own health care decisions after conducting your own research, and in partnership with a qualified medical or healthcare professional.

---

[*] AARE. (2016). Code of Ethics. Retrieved from http://www.aare.edu.au/pages/aare-code-of-ethics.html

[**] AERA. (2011). Code of Ethics. *Educational Researcher 40*(3), 145-156. doi: 10.3102/0013189X1141 0403

*For those with multi-microbial systemic infections,
the people who love and care for them,
the doctors who treat them, and
the associations who support them.*

CONTENTS

	Acknowledgements	xv
	Foreword	xvii
	Prologue	xxiii
	Preface	xxxiv
	Who is this book for?	
	Layout of the text	
	How to use this book	
1	**Why this book?**	1
	Why now?	
2	**What is Lyme?**	7
	Lyme Today	
	Identifying Lyme – Borreliosis	
	Lyme Borreliosis	
	Classification – types of Lyme	
	A view from the field – terminology and global Lyme	
3	**What are the co-infections that can come with Lyme?**	36
	Common co-infections	
	A view from the field – co-infections	
4	**How do you get Lyme and/or its co-infections?**	42
	Transmission	
	A view from the field – what makes a tick, tick?	

5 How can you prevent getting bitten by a tick? 55
Prevention
A view from the field – rash, what rash? Bite?

6 How do you remove a tick? 63
Tick removal
After removal
Things to avoid
Allergic reaction
A view from the field – time to Lyme infection

7 What are the symptoms of Lyme and its common confections? 71
Indicators of Lyme and its co-infections
The great imitator
Lyme Borreliosis symptoms
Symptoms of common co-infections
A view from the field – symptoms surveys, questionnaires, and checklists

8 What can tests tell you if you have Lyme and/or its co-infections? 86
Available tests
Accuracy of tests
Testing for Lyme
Testing for co-infections
A view from the field – reading example test results and preparing for tests

9 How can you approach the treatment of Lyme and/or its co-infections?   108

    Treatment options
    A view from the field – alternative treatment approaches for late Lyme

10 How can you support your health when fighting Lyme and/or its co-infections?   127

    Methods of immune support
    A view from the field – the environment: metal toxicity; combating mold exposure; and, minimizing the impact of man-made electromagnetic fields (EMF) and radio frequency (RF) radiation

11 How do you detox from the treatment of Lyme and/or its co-infections?   193

    Detoxification
    A view from the field – additional detoxification methods and Jarisch-Herxheimer reaction relief

12 What should(n't) you eat when you have Lyme and/or its co-infections?   230

    Diet
    A View from the field – fasting

13	**What does it feel like to be chronically ill with Lyme and/or its co-infections?**	255
	Traits when suffering from early disseminated to late disseminated or chronic Lyme and/or its co-infections	
	A view from the field – the spoon theory	
14	**Frequently asked questions about Lyme and/or its co-infections**	299
15	**Resources list**	318
16	**Appendices**	344
	A. Signs and symptoms of *Borreliosis* (Lyme Disease)	
	B. Signs and symptoms of *Babesia, Bartonella, Ehrlichia/Anaplasma, Rickettsia,* and *Mycoplasma*	
	C. Signs and symptoms tracker – example checklist	
	D. Western blot – bands and explanations	
	E. Infographics – data and tables	
	Glossary	380

Acknowledgements

I extend my sincere and deepest appreciation to:

Dr. H, the best, most caring, and dedicated medical professional that I have ever had the pleasure to meet, although I wish it had been under other circumstances. Providence could not have provided a better doctor.

I also extend a great debt of gratitude to *Noel David* (intish.com) for his continued encouragement and support in all matters. For *Mike* for not forgetting, and for *Christopher*, *Jake*, *Joy*, *Judy*, *Mandy*, *Matthew*, and *Warwick* for simply being who they are.

Appreciation to *Kim* for accompanying me on my journey, and for taking the time to talk.

Thanks also, to the *Lyme Disease Association of Australia* (LDAA), and all other associations, for their assistance and support for those who are ill and all those who this disease and its co-infections affect.

Special appreciation also needs to be attributed to my wife *HyunHee*, for without her love, tolerance, sacrifice, unyielding support, and perseverance, this book would most definitely not exist.

Foreword

David has bought his considerable intellect and advanced University training to the task of objectively summarizing disparate views from a field that is incompletely understood by medical scientists and clinicians. That he has done this as a non-medically trained researcher, and whilst recovering from his own experience with Lyme and co-infections, is a testament to his abilities. His desire to share his experience and research with others to assist them in their Lyme journey speaks to his altruistic humanity.

This book provides an easy to read summary of the science as we know it, and describes what it's like to live with 'Lyme Disease' by someone who has been there and done that. The struggles of the sufferer and their need for understanding and support are very clearly explained. The assistance that family and friends can provide to the sufferer, especially in the emotional and spiritual realm, are well described.

Understanding that there is much that we don't know about Lyme Disease, and that testing difficulties and clinical inexperience can delay diagnosis, and that each sufferer is a unique organism that will require a unique treatment protocol, can help assuage the confusion, anger, frustration, anxiety and depression that usually accompanies this disease. This book describes what we know, and how that information can be used to assist the multitude of Lyme Disease sufferers around the world.

Lyme disease is technically an infection with a bacteria called *Borrelia* (*Borreliosis*) but more commonly the term is used to refer to *Borreliosis* plus the cluster of co-infections that often travel together, either from exposure to other infectious agents at the same time as the *Borrelia*, or the opportunistic overgrowth of existing microorganisms due to the suppressed immune system defenses from the initial infections. *Borrelia* and its co-infections together lead to the symptoms (felt) and signs (seen) that affect many systems and functions in the body. The cluster is commonly referred to as *tick-borne infections*, but as transmission to humans can be from other insect hosts of the infective agents, *vector-borne infections* is a more accurate term. Another term, *multi-microbial systemic infectious disease*, accurately describes the scenario, and highlights the difference between this entity and the traditional medical reductionist view of one cause for each disease, and by inference, one pill for each ill.

These different terms that are often used interchangeably, are just the beginning of the sources of confusion and argument in the Lyme Disease world.

That *Borrelia* can cause infection in humans, and that it can become a long-term infection that can be fatal is not argued. But most else to do with the disease is contentious, with different people firmly holding their different views. The different views are all supported by research published in peer-reviewed journals.

The Infectious Disease physicians (led by the Infectious Disease Society of America) believe that a two to four week course of a single antibiotic will cure *Borreliosis*, no matter when in the course of the disease that the antibiotics are commenced, and that any residual or recurring symptoms are due to post-infectious inflammation or auto-immunity (Post-Treatment Lyme Disease Syndrome).

The 'Lyme-literate Medical Doctors' follow the viewpoints of the International Lyme and Associated Diseases Society (ILADS), and believe that four weeks of antibiotics (unless commenced immediately after acquiring the infection) will often not kill *Borrelia* nor many of the co-infections, and that multiple antibiotics for months to years are often necessary.

A third group of doctors and non-medical practitioners believe that any symptomatic infection is the result of an imbalance between the immune system's (and by default, the rest of the body that supports the immune system) ability to control the infectious agent, and the infectious agent's virulence and numbers. Hence optimizing immune function, and reducing infectious agent numbers, is the best possibility for long term health.

It is likely, as with the trillions of other micro-organisms in and on our body with whom we live in balance, that we never fully eliminate *Borrelia* or its co-infections, but that by re-establishing the symbiotic balance, disabling symptoms of dis-ease are resolved, and a long, healthy, happy and productive life can be resumed. However, this goal is more easily described than achieved.

To be sure, an imbalance between *Borrelia* and its co-infections, and the host's defenses, can lead to decades of emotional, physical, financial and spiritual suffering and hardship. There is often years of mis-diagnosis and ineffective treatments because this disease can look like any other disease and the current confirmatory diagnostic tests are unreliable. The diagnosis is often made by the patient's clinical history and physical examination being interpreted by a Lyme aware practitioner, who are unfortunately relatively rare. There is no treatment that works for everyone, and no way to identify in advance the best treatment for an individual. It often takes years of experimenting with different treatments before health and function returns. Life-time attention to health optimization is required to maintain immune health, and sometimes life-time treatments are also necessary to restrict micro-organism overgrowth.

I acknowledge David for this body of work that has significantly contributed to the Lyme Disease literature. The book is extremely well researched and referenced. I strongly recommend this book to people suffering with *multi-microbial systemic infections*, the people who love and care for them, the practitioners who treat them (who sometimes forget the difficulties experienced by the sufferers), and the associations who support the practitioners and the sufferers with information and access to an informed, understanding community.

Dr. John D. Hart
Functional Medicine Practitioner
BMBS, MSptMed, BPE (Ex. Phys.) Honors University Medal, BAppSc, BA
The Hart Clinic
Mosman, NSW, Australia

Prologue

My unwitting and unasked for journey with a *multi-microbial systemic infection* began on November 01, 2012. How do I know that date specifically? That was the date of an air show where I fell extremely ill that very night with a flu-like illness from which I have never fully recovered. The day before is the final time that I was able to log the flight of an aircraft as pilot in command. The man that my wife had known for 18 years figuratively, but could have literally, died that day. The man who woke up at 5 AM to run for two hours, fly airplanes all morning, teach grad students in the afternoons, do an hour of weight lifting before spending time with friends and family, and then writing journal articles into the night, while still finding time to spend with her, renovate the family home, and take extreme adventure holidays, was suddenly bedbound and immobile for two years, couch ridden for two years after that, and only then, able to crawl out of the house a day a week since – if it was a good week.

After falling ill, I sought help from local general practitioners (GPs) who told me *you look really fit and healthy; whatever it is, you'll just fight it off*. Three other GPs, and as many weeks later, I was being told to *just drink more water to flush it out*. It never happened.

Right here, for less than $50, a month- to two-month-long course of antibiotics could have potentially halted my illness. Increased doctor professional development, and public awareness of vector-borne illnesses, would have led to a completely different question-set asked of me as a patient, and I would most likely have made a full recovery and got back to full health relatively quickly. Yet, as I continued to lay immobile, fate had other plans.

Three months later, in northeast Asia, I was sitting in the office of an infectious disease doctor at a major university teaching hospital. I started to hear a familiar phrase – *just drink more water; flush it out.* In the meantime the symptoms saw me passed me off to a lung specialist.

She took a lung x-ray, and determined that all the marks that appeared on my lungs since my last bi-annual work-related health check were obviously from a previous infection, of which I had no history. A lung lavage was then performed to determine if the infection might be tuberculosis. It was not, and it was not a pleasant experience. A lung function test was then ordered, and it showed that my lungs were functioning at the top end of health – no doubt because of the three hours training I had been doing per day over the half-decade prior to falling ill. The other symptoms that I complained about, I was told, were *impossible*. They did, however, suddenly become possible when my wife vouched for their genuine-nature. This shows the very real need, and importance, of having someone advocate for you in any hospital setting. Still, the attending physician denied that my hands and feet were constantly cold, denied that I was unable to get warm, and denied that I was unable to sweat in the middle of summer. This was even though I was in her office, standing in front of her wearing winter clothing, gloves, and a scarf, the day reaching a high of 96.8°F (36°C), my hands freezing, and my fingernails blue and white from being on the cusp of what I considered hypothermia. My tympanic temperature (taken by ear) was 93.56°F (34.2°C) at its lowest. Today it is around the normal range of 97.7°C (36.5°F). I was to later learn that summer was one of the hottest on record, and I had the home heating turned up to 102.2°F (39°C), struggling to get warm. I ended up buying a portable infrared sauna. Regardless, it was all deemed *impossible*.

I was then passed on to a rheumatologist, to see if I had any nerve damage due to the tingling sensations in my fingers and the joint pain in my knuckles. All tests came back normal, with doctors declaring that I was 'fit as a fiddle.'

Next, I was shunted to a neurologist who conducted an MRI (magnetic resonance imaging) of my brain due to the symptoms of brain fog and word finding issues, both of which were something that as a graduate school professor, I had never before experienced. It felt like I had lost half my IQ. I lost the ability to make connections and to think coherently. A familiar pattern began to emerge – the results showed nothing unusual.

Next in line was the ENT (ear, nose and throat) specialist, who performed endoscopies to determine nothing was wrong with my nasal passages, and therefore I should not be constantly dripping wads of mucus out of my nose. That affirmation served in no way to alleviate the problem, and a CT or CAT (computerized axial tomography) scan also came to confirm that everything nasal passage-wise was in order. I was supposedly well – except that I wasn't.

The last straw was the endocrinologist who looked at a print out of all my symptoms, and one by one she began to cross them off saying,

If I remove this one, and that one, and – ha ha ha ha ha – why are you even listing this one? Ha ha ha, ha ha ha! Um, well, now with these symptoms ... Hmm, yes. Ah ha! You have diabetes insipidus! We should check you in immediately for overnight tests, and determine the next steps.

Oddly, the main thing that seemed to confirm this diagnosis for her is the amount of water I was drinking at that time – 7 liters per day. I told her that I was only drinking that amount of water because every time I saw a doctor at that hospital, all they ever said was *drink more water; flush it out*, even though I told them each time that, *I'm drinking 4/5/6 liters of water a day. Should I really be drinking **more** water? It doesn't feel right. It's really hard to do, and it's* *almost becoming physically impossible.** Regardless, each time, the response with a wave of the hand, was, *Yeah, yeah, drink more water. Whatever it is, flush it out!* This endocrinologist just ignored me. In shock, I thought that this has got to be some big joke, and I knew then that I was truly on my own.

Over the course of this period, no pain medication was ever prescribed, and often I would grit my teeth so hard from the aches and pains. The most troublesome pain included hot-poker-like stabbing pains in my calves that were always symmetrical, along with icepick-like pain in the orbs of my eyes where the liquid felt like it was crystalizing and beginning to freeze. It felt like every inch of me was covered with insects that were biting. I was constantly bone-numbingly fatigued to the point of pure exhaustion. I ended up cracking some teeth, and was constantly popping out fillings that needed to be reseated or replaced. Dental problems and problems with dentists then become their own story of permanent teeth pain, caries, and tongue swelling, and there was a six-month period where I could hardly talk or eat due to the size of the tongue. Surgery to cut the tongue was presented as a solution, being told that there would be no side-effects or problems with speaking, but my own research revealed that extensive rehabilitation

---

* I later learned that I probably should not have been drinking that much water at all. Drinking too much water can lead to water toxicity, and even more problems. This taught me a very valuable lesson: always question your doctor.

involving speech therapy would be required. As an assistant professor who lectures graduate students, I did not partake in the surgery. The tongue is still overly large and still causing problems, but along with the other dental issues, it is manageable for the most part, but it will be a life-long problem.

Eventually, the pain became normalized and I got used to it being like a daily companion. I often hear people giving a name to their pain, or their disease, but I never have, although if I had young children around, I would probably tell them that 'insert random name here' is visiting me today – to let them know that I am in pain, or having a bad day. I have since learned that this is called a flare.

On my best day, strong winds have knocked me over on the street. I needed a cane for support, and to get around. There were days when I needed a wheelchair or mobility scooter, but having neither, I just stayed bedbound. I felt more than 80 years old, and the elderly in my community were much sprightlier. Going up stairs, some took two at a time and would be at the top before I was even a quarter of the way. My body felt like it was pulling 5 Gs, and at times, I could not even move or lift my limbs at all.

Every smell was heightened. The scent of laundry detergent on clothing, perfume and cologne, and cleaning agents all caused horrendous itching and discomfort. I could smell the slightest scented beauty products that my wife wore from 16 feet (about 5 meters away) – even those that are supposed to be non-scented, and ones that even she couldn't smell despite wearing them!

The slightest noise was excruciating, and slightly louder than normal noises would trigger an extremely heightened startle response. Fluorescent lights would feel like spotlights trained on me. I was wandering and meandering around hospitals and offices with my eyes squeezed tightly shut. All this, like so many other things with my illness, were strange and new, and things that I had never before experienced.

By this stage, after years of laying immobile, I was beginning to look not so fit, and not so healthy. My hand could now cover the width of my thigh, so I tried shopping to build the muscles back up. I walked with great difficulty, using the cart as support, with eyes shut and ears hurting, while my wife scoured the store. I soon stopped doing that and I have since stopped driving – too weak to hold, guide, or even turn the steering wheel.

Everything caused irritation, and would set off bursts of extreme rage – too much time waiting at a traffic light, someone standing too close to me, someone bumping into me. Anything could set it off. Yet my training from flight school had ensured the need to keep in control in all situations, because in the air if you "panic, you're dead" and you could kill passengers or those on the ground. The spontaneous, unjust, and nonsensical anger could be directed at anyone and anything. At times, my wife turned her back to hide her laughter, which jarred me when I first noticed.

Visual hallucinations became manifest, starting with a scarf that grew a head and limbs, plumped itself up, and started squirming around while I was holding it in my hand. Unsettling, but I knew that it wasn't real.

My experience of time was lost. I felt one week had passed, but it was a year. Eventually, I learned to track the passing of time by my wife's periods. It has made me feel very agrarian.

To this day, I still cannot recall much of those first five years of being ill, the people I met, or the things I said and did. You name it, I tried it: metal fillings removed; quarter-year long parasite cleanses; coffee enemas; latest health pill or powder; photobiomodulation; Rife machines; the use of magnetic, electric, and radio/microwave detectors; alkaline water; salt inhalers; even crystals. The list goes on, and nothing helped.

Many said that they were thinking of me – and praying for me – with some telling me to just think myself better. How many cancer patients or people with AIDS have heard those words? What percentage of those who say them really believe that we could all just think ourselves well? How about polio victims who have been told that their disease is psychogenic (all in their minds), and told that they can really walk if they want to. Did anyone say that to President Roosevelt? Has anyone told Stephen Hawking that he is yet to apply his mind to thinking himself better, and to getting himself out of his wheelchair? If only he applied himself. I wonder if people realize how absurd it sounds to tell the chronically ill to just think themselves better.

A lot of people haven't kept in touch, and I am much better for it. Some that have do not remember how ill I've been, and why should they? Even my wife, together now for nearly a quarter century, forgets how ill I am. Many of the long-term chronically ill don't look sick, and then on top of everything else, end up needing to deal with an 'invisible illness.'

My search far and wide for a medical professional who is able to treat me eventually led to one over 5,000 miles (8,000 kilometers) away on another continent. This doctor supported my mitochondrial function, provided hormonal support, and then ordered the IGeneX test for Lyme. The *Borreliosis* Western blot came back showing some reactivity with two relevant IgG bands visible: 31 kDa, and 41 kDa (58 kDa was also present). There was evidence of co-infection organisms with a low IgG titer for *Babesia duncani* through immunofluorescence assay (IFA), and a borderline positive IgG titer for the *Bartonella henselae* co-infection. It was such a relief to finally get a diagnosis – but then, I found out what this really meant.

After learning more about these afflictions, I think that I have been much luckier than some, although searching for this diagnosis has cost us our life savings, pension, and all of our assets. I'm not the only one.[1,2] Even though my spouse has maintained employment, every cent we have earned from 2012 has been spent on medical care or health-related expenses – and we are massively in debt. Six years later, after two failed crowdfunding attempts, with our plans for children now foregone, I am still in northeast Asia, and this is still ongoing.

It is also important to mention that, like many others, I do not recall ever being bitten by anything, although I did have the tell-tale deep purple striae from the co-infection *Bartonella henselae*. What I do know is that I fell ill with a flu-like illness, almost three weeks to the day of cleaning out a backyard shed full of rat carcasses, fleas, mites, ticks, and their feces. Ironically, after braving many of the most inhospitable, uninhabitable, and desolate places around the world along with the most inhabited and heavily militarized, eating all number of strange and bizarre delicacies, and riding, swimming with, feeding, and coming into contact with all number of animals big and small, it was that little backyard shed that proved to be my undoing, and potentially the most dangerous and treacherous place on the globe that I have ever visited.

References

1. Adrion, E., et al. (2015). Health care costs, utilization and patterns of care following Lyme disease. *PLoS One, 10*(2), e0116767. doi: 10.1371/journal.pone.0116767
2. Buttaccio, J. (2015). A life on pause: When Lyme steals everything, you will spend every last cent trying to get well. *The Lyme Times, 27*(2), 34.

Preface

Ultimately, the result of finding out what it really means to have a multi-microbial systemic infection, a Lyme-like illness, Lyme disease and/or its co-infections, is the reason why this book exists. My wife is a non-native speaker of English, and I was looking for something that could plainly, simply, and easily tell her briefly everything that she needed to know about what was happening to me, what we could do about it, and what others have experienced when going through it. I was also looking for information that was cited, and information that would also answer her initial questions. This was particularly important to me because one statistic or statement I would come across would often prove to be contradictory or to be the exact opposite of another. I could also see others in a similar position, asking in forums for a book that might help their loved ones understand their diagnosis. I could not find a single resource that really did this, and so I decided to write it myself.

    I hope that this book comes to help those who fall ill to understand the fundamentals, acting as a primer to Lyme and its co-infections, and for those who love and care for them to be able to learn what it really means to have a disease or infection like these at this time. For this reason, I have placed the story of my battle in the prologue, rather than weaving it throughout the narrative or main text like many others with Lyme and co-infections have done. That said, I will sometimes need to relate my experience, or the struggles of others, to what is discussed in various chapters, and will also need to use some very complicated scientific language as well.

Who is this Book for?

The book has been designed to be read, in part or in whole, by those who have contracted Lyme, a Lyme-like illness, or a co-infection of Lyme (which are serious infections and diseases in their own right),[1-3] along with those who have been diagnosed with *Debilitating Syndrome Complexes Attributed to Ticks* (DSCATT)[4] or a *Multiple Systemic Infectious Disease Syndrome* (MSIDS).[5] This book can also be read by the families, friends, and caregivers of those who have contracted any of the above conditions.

Layout of the Text

Each chapter highlights a different and common question that patients, their families, friends, and caregivers could ask after diagnosis. The book works from a background of Lyme disease and its co-infections; their transmission; tips for prevention and tick removal; symptoms; testing; potential treatment options; methods of immune support and detox; what to eat and not to eat; and perhaps most importantly, detailing what it can feel like to live with Lyme and/or its co-infections. Also included is a frequently asked questions list, a listing of useful resources, and appendices. The appendices detail the symptoms of *Borreliosis* (Lyme disease); as well as that of *Babesia, Bartonella, Ehrlichia/Anaplasma, Rickettsia,* and *Mycoplasma*; provide a symptoms tracker; detail the bands of the Western blot; and, house an infographic section that details the statistics found in the book in an easy to read graphic-based format. If you wish to make notes while reading there is also a section to do so at the end of the book, following the glossary.

Throughout the book, the small numbers show support for the information written in the text. The main reason to include citations like this, in a book meant for everyday reading, is to provide a means to access further information regarding all of the details presented. It also shows that all possible academic and scholarly attempts have been made to find references that are accurate. However, as protocols change, new research is conducted, and new information comes to light, these sources and citations may become dated or refuted, and it is important to keep this in mind. The journal articles, books, newspapers, newsletters, websites, and online links for these sources are all provided in the relevant references section at the end of each chapter, allowing you to follow up on any points that are of interest.

How to Use this Book

Following the KISS model,[6] of *Keep it simple, stupid*, this book is designed to be as short as possible, and attempts to introduce only the important basics. Why?

1. The basics provide a window on information, of which the most relevant can be followed up or explored elsewhere;
2. People who are ill need easy to read, non-taxing material, split into short chunks; and
3. Family members, spouses, kids, friends, and caregivers may not want to read a long book or, for that matter, any book at all. Short books are more manageable to read between work, school, and/or caring for someone who is ill.

I would also like to suggest that if you intend to give this book to anyone who is not much of a reader, or children who are eager to know about this condition, that you should use a highlighter (perhaps a lime-colored one) to markup the parts of the book you feel are most important for them to read, and if possible, read it together. Also, if your family, friends, or caregivers are not readers, I would instead encourage you to guide them to some of the very well-produced documentaries on Lyme and its co-infections, a select few of which can be found in the resources list.

Finally, I would like to say that if you have a need to read this book then I am truly sorry, especially that your diagnosis, or the diagnosis of someone you love or are close to, has brought you here. Continue the fight – diagnosis is just the beginning!

David Kent, Ed.D.

References

[1] Schaller, J. (2008). Bartonella is becoming the most important issue in treatment of Lyme. *Public Health Alert, 3*(5), 1-2.

[2] Buhner, S. (2013). *Healing Lyme co-infections: Complimentary and holistic treatments for Bartonella and Mycoplasma*. Vermont: Healing Arts Press.

[3] Horowitz, R. (2014). Co-infections presentation, diagnosis, and treatment. *Symposium on tick-borne diseases*. May 17. USA: Maryland. Retrieved from https://www.youtube.com/watch?v=O9a-2Nb2sbk

[4] Department of Health (2017). Australian Government response to the Senate Community Affairs References Committee final report: Inquiry into the growing evidence of an emerging tick-borne disease that causes a Lyme-like illness for many Australian patients. November, 2017. Retrieved from http://www.health.gov.au/internet/main/publishing.nsf/Content/8246306026A29C08CA2581D30010C8E4/$File/Govt-response- Senate-inquiry-final-report-%202017.pdf

[5] Horowitz, R. I. (2013). *Why can't I get better?: Solving the mystery of Lyme and chronic illness*. New York: St. Martin's Press.

[6] Stroop, P. D. (1960, December 04). Project KISS. *Chicago Daily Tribune*, 43.

1. Why This Book?

There are a lot of books about Lyme disease and its co-infections, so why this book? Well, this one is different. It is not just aimed at 'the patient', and/or other 'medical professionals', it is written for those who are ill, their families, their friends, and their caregivers. The focus is on providing important initial information about Lyme and its co-infections along with a perspective of what the person who is ill, the one you may love and care for, is going through in terms of obtaining a diagnosis and then treatment. This book also aims to provide some insight into the experience of battling, living with, and recovering from these infections.

Why Now?

Lyme is an epidemic,[1-3] and some even say a pandemic.[4-6] It is the fastest growing infectious disease in Europe and the USA.[7,8] There are over 30,000 cases reported each year in the United States and estimates are that it actually infects over 300,000[9-11] – a number greater than AIDS, West Nile Virus, and the Avian Flu combined.[12-14]

Unfortunately, the seriousness of Lyme disease, especially that sometimes termed chronic,[15] has long been dismissed, and whimsical language has been associated with it since the 1980s.[16] Despite it and particularly its co-infections like *Bartonella* being widely recognized in the veterinarian world,[17-20] Lyme disease may or may not, depending on where you live, be recognized in humans at all.[21-25] Regrettably, it has long been ignored by the medical community[26] and, particularly in the United States, has been *dismissed as something that's difficult to get, easy to treat, and therefore nothing to really worry about.*[27] Fortunately, as we approach the end of the second decade of the 21st century, some of the old notions surrounding Lyme are beginning to change.

Recently, with celebrities raising awareness after falling ill,[28] Lyme disease is making headlines with articles appearing in magazines like *Rolling Stone*.[29] However, the disease still has much mystery and controversy surrounding it.[30] *Cure Unknown* highlights this well.[31] As more and more people become infected with Lyme and/or its co-infections, awareness needs to increase: about what to do if bitten or infected; about how to prevent infection in the first place; of what having the disease means to those who are ill; and of the importance for a need to increasingly research the disease, particularly in regards to finding an effective means of treatment for those with prolonged symptoms. Volunteer organizations, like CanLyme (The Canadian Lyme Disease Foundation), The Lyme Disease Association of Australia,[32] and others around the world, help to further awareness and are there to help provide support to those who are ill, their families, and friends. If needed, reach out to them.

References

1. Ferrie, H. (2013). *Ending denial: The Lyme disease epidemic a Canadian public health disaster. A call for action from patients, doctors, researchers, and politicians.* Canada: Kos Publishing.
2. Weintraub, P. (2013). *Cure unknown: Inside the Lyme epidemic*, (Revised Ed.). New York: St Martin's Griffin.
3. Newby, K. (2015). Counting cases: The story in charts. *The Lyme Times, 27*(3), 22.
4. Hamilton, D. (1989). Lyme disease. The hidden pandemic. *Postgraduate Medical Journal, 85*(5), 303-308, 313-314.
5. Harvey, W. T., & Salvato, P. (2003). 'Lyme disease': Ancient engine of an unrecognized Borreliosis pandemic? *Medical Hypotheses, 60*(5), 742-759. doi: 10.1016/S0306-9877(03)00060-4
6. Cameron, D. (2016). *Time to designate Lyme disease as a pandemic?* All Things Lyme. Retrieved from: http://daniel cameronmd.com/time-to-designate-lyme-disease-as-a-pandemic
7. McFadzean, N. (2012a). *The beginner's guide to Lyme disease: Diagnosis and treatment made simple.* USA: BioMed Publishing Group.
8. Horowitz, R. I. (2017). *How can I get better?: An action plan for treating resistant Lyme & chronic disease.* New York: St. Martin's Press.
9. CDC. (2015). *How many people get Lyme disease?* Centers for Disease Control and Prevention. Retrieved from https://www.cdc.gov/lyme/stats/humancases.html
10. Keuhn, B. M. (2013). CDC estimates 300,000 US cases of Lyme disease annually. *JAMA, 310*(11), 1110. doi: 10.1001/jama.2013.278331

11. Bransfield, R. (2017). Suicide and Lyme and associated diseases. *Neuropsychiatric Disease and Treatment, 13*, 1575-1587. doi: 10.2147/NDT.S136137
12. AHN-USA. (2011). *Lyme disease: Misdiagnosed, underreported – and epidemic.* Alliance for Natural Health: USA. Retrieved from http://www.anh-usa.org/lymedisease
13. Theodore, Dr. (2012). *Lyme disease.* Bali Advertiser. Retrieved from http://baliadvertiser.biz/lyme-disease
14. FAIM. (2017). *Lyme disease.* Foundation for Alternative and Integrative medicine. Retrieved from http://www.faim.org/lyme-disease
15. Burrascano, J. (2008). *Diagnostic hints and treatment guidelines for Lyme and other tick borne illnesses,* (16th ed). Advanced Topics in Lyme Disease. Retrieved from http://www.lymenet.org/BurrGuide200810.pdf
16. McAllister, M. P., & Kitron, U. (2003). Differences in early print media coverage of AIDS and Lyme disease. In L. K. Fuller. (Ed.), *Media-Mediated Aids* (43-62). New Jersey: Hampton Press.
17. Brewer, J. (2007). Tickborne diseases and co-infections. *The Lyme Times, 48*, 20-27.
18. Kim, Y., et al. (2009). Prevalence of Bartonella henselae and Bartonella clarridgeiae in cats and dogs in Korea. *Journal of Veterinary Science, 10*(1), 85-87. doi: 10.4142/jvs.2009.10.1.85
19. Rippey, M. (2014). *Episode #26: Professor Holly Ahern explains how Borrelia Burgdorferi survive antibiotics and new therapies in the pipeline to kill Lyme bacteria.* Lyme Ninja Radio. Retrieved from https://lymeninjaradio.com/holly_ahern
20. Sherr, V. (2015). The agony of Lyme brain: mainstream medicine misses psychiatric symptoms of neuro-borreliosis. *The Lyme Times, 27*(3), 24.

[21] McFadzean, N. (2012b). *Lyme disease in Australia*. USA: BioMed Publishing Group.

[22] Smith, K. (2013). *Lyme disease: A counter argument to the Australian Government's denial*. Lyme Australia Recognition and Awareness. Retrieved from http://www.lymedisease.org.au/wp-content/uploads/2014/02/attachment_two_lyme_disease_a_counter_argument_of_the_australian_governments_denial.pdf

[23] SBS. (2016). *Episode 38: Tick sick*. Insight. Retrieved from https://www.sbs.com.au/ondemand/video/783633475924/insight-tick-sick

[24] Webb, C. (2016). *What is Lyme disease and does it exist in Australia?* The Conversation. Retrieved from http://theconversation.com/explainer-what-is-lyme-disease-and-does-it-exist-in-australia-57717

[25] Killalea, D. (2017). *Lyme Disease in Australia: 'No one believes me'*. Health. Retrieved from http://www.news.com.au/lifestyle/health/health-problems/lyme-disease-in-australia-no-one-believes-me/news-story/167b759b4 481dc156b0d9557cceeb119

[26] McFadzean, N. (2012a). *Op. cit*.

[27] Rippey, M. (2017). *Episode 123: Jean Monro, MD – UK Lyme expert*. Lyme Ninja Radio. Retrieved from http://lymeninjaradio.com/123-jean-monro-md

[28] Leland, D. (2013). *Touched by Lyme: Recovery is a long, slow, balancing act*. Lymedisease.org: Advocacy, Education, & Research. Retrieved from https://www.lymedisease.org/jen-crystal-lyme-recovery-2

[29] Dimeo-Ediger, W. (2017, June 20). Lyme disease: Inside America's mysterious epidemic. *Rolling Stone*. Retrieved from http://www.rollingstone.com/culture/features/lyme-disease-inside-americas-mysterious-epidemic-w487776

[30] Perrone, C. (2014). Lyme and associated tick-borne diseases: Global challenges in the context of a public health threat. *Frontiers in Cellular and Infection Microbiology, 4*, 74. doi: 10.3389/fcimb.2014.00074

[31] Weintraub. *Op. cit.*

[32] LDAA. (2017). *Tick borne awareness and advocacy*. Lyme Disease Association of Australia. Retrieved from http://www.lymedisease.org.au

2. What Is Lyme?

Lyme disease is caused by a *Borrelia* bacteria that is most easily treated in the early stages of infection, but it becomes more difficult to treat and diagnose if left to the late disseminated stage.[1] The name is often misspelled or mispronounced as Lime or Lymes, but for many, the correct spelling and pronunciation is important.[2,3] Misspelling or mispronunciation may remind those who have been long afflicted with Lyme and/or its co-infections of the shame, the hostility, and the abuse received from many of the trained health professionals that had to be dealt with, argued with, and appeased before and after obtaining a definitive blood test or a clinical diagnosis.[4] That said, alternative spellings and pronunciations of Lyme will no doubt become increasingly acceptable, as more people get sick and mispronounce and mistype the name, just as *amyotrophic lateral sclerosis* (ALS) has become known as Lou Gehrig disease or Lou Gehrig's disease. Perhaps Lyme should actually be called Lymes, with the 's' referring to the many possible co-infections that often accompany the disease. At this stage though, if your healthcare providers are referring to the disease as Lymes, then it might be best to start looking for another physician. Medicine and its practice very often are based on the need for extreme accuracy, and basic errors, such as utilizing the incorrect name for a disease, point toward poor education or professional development in this area.

So already, just in the name, this disease is suddenly complicated and perhaps political, and it only gets more complicated and more political. Who said being ill was ever easy? This book stays away from the politics as much as possible, and focuses on making the complicated easier to understand, especially for those readers with *Lyme brain*.*

Lyme Today

A number of people with Lyme disease will call themselves *Lyme warriors*. The term *Lymie* is also commonly used, and although accepted by many, it is not always favored, with a few considering it to be demeaning.[5] Lyme disease shares a lime colored support ribbon with Lymphoma, and while May is Lyme disease awareness month,[6] July 25 has been designated annual Red Shoe Day.

The first red shoe day was held in 2014, on the anniversary of the death of Australian Lyme patient Theda Myint, in whose memory the day was started.[7] The event is organized by the Global Lyme & Invisible Illness Organization,[8] a non-profit organization that can help to put people in touch

---

* *Lyme brain* includes symptoms such as brain fog, confusion, difficulty retrieving vocabulary, mixing words (word salad), short-term memory loss and word repetition, even anxiety and depression, or rage and irritability.

with others with the same illness, and point to avenues of support worldwide. It is a day to wear red shoes as a way to raise public awareness about the plight of those who are ill with Lyme and/or its co-infections as well as other invisible illnesses like ME/CFS (Myalgic encephalomyelitis/Chronic fatigue syndrome) and fibromyalgia, and about the global need to have these illnesses recognized. It is also a day chosen by the Lyme community to remember the lives that have been lost to Lyme, and the positive impact that those lives have held.[9] This is important because it has been said that we each have three deaths: when our bodily functions cease; when our body is put to rest; and when our name passes someone's lips that one final time.[10] A number of artistic tributes have been made including a poem *I Wear My Red Shoes*[11] which has also been put to music.[12]

Today, medical professionals are often split into one of two camps concerning the treatment of Lyme; one following CDC (Centers for Disease Control and Prevention) or IDSA (Infectious Disease Society of America) guidelines; the other following ILADS (International Lyme and Associated Diseases Society) guidelines. Some of the big names in the field are: Buhner, Cowden, Horowitz, Jones, Klinghardt, Shapiro, and Steere. You will hear and see the names of these people, along with others who are considered to be Lyme literate medical doctors (LLMD). Generally, those who are ill fall into one of four groups:[13] a group which goes back to basics using alternative treatment modalities and diet as part of a plan to get well; two groups following each of the two guidelines for treatment above, perhaps along with some of the basics; and a fourth group generally left to fend for themselves, perhaps due to a lack of financial means as many have lost everything seeking a diagnosis, or the inability to find adequate medical care in their area.

Identifying Lyme – Borreliosis

Lyme disease was first diagnosed in Old Lyme, Connecticut, in the United States of America. Polly Murray, a neighborhood mom who noticed a cluster of symptoms that were not going away – Mrs. Murray's mysterious disease[14] – sounded the original alarm concerning the illness. The disease was named after the town of Lyme in 1975,[15] but it was originally misidentified as juvenile rheumatoid arthritis.[16,17] Lyme disease is actually caused by a *Borrelia* bacteria,[18] such as the bacterium *Borrelia burgdorferi* which was first described by Willy Burgdorfer[19] and named after him. The *Borrelia* species known to cause Lyme disease is actually collectively known as *Borrelia burgdorferi sensu lato*, and is composed of several genospecies such as *Borrelia burgdorferi sensu stricto*, *Borrelia garinii*, and *Borrelia afzelli*.[20] It is sometimes called *Lyme Borreliosis*, and it is an infectious disease.

Lyme Borreliosis

Lyme Borreliosis is caused by a spirochete bacterial pathogen, and it can be transmitted by tick vectors[**] of the genus *Ixodes* (*Ixodes ricinu* in Europe, and *Ixodes scapularis* in the United States).[21] These ticks are commonly found on deer, sheep, cattle, humans, and dogs as an adult, and on rodents and small mammals as nymphs.[22] A spirochete is a flexible spirally twisted bacterium that looks like a miniature spring.[23] It has a cell wall and *flagella* (a whip-like tail) that allows it to move around and propel itself through tissues. The *flagella* is located inside the periplasm, between the inner and outer cell membranes, and traverses the length of the cell body.[24,25] This assists the bacteria in shielding its proteins from the host immune system. The structural form of the spirochete may aid in penetrating tissues and disseminating throughout the body, while the bacteria secretes a protease enzyme that breaks down tissue proteins to enable easier burrowing.[26,27]

The bacteria can also lose its cell wall, changing shape, depending on the nutrients available, and the threat from the environment (e.g., high/low acidity, heat/cold).[28] The cell wall-deficient, cyst, L-form, round body, S-form, or spheroplast[29,30] is the form that sees the spirochete lose its shape, as

---

[**] *Vectors* are organisms, such as a biting insect like a tick, that can transfer diseases or parasites from one animal or plant to another animal or plant.

without a cell wall it cannot hold the spiral. It can then look like a sphere with a thin semi-permeable membrane. In the process of losing the cell wall, proteins that the human immune system recognizes are also shed, so the new form becomes difficult for the immune system to detect. Converting forms from spirochete to cyst uses little metabolic energy.[31] Once in this form the bacteria can continue to survive without expending much energy, with this trait serving to also protect the bacteria against antibiotics that work by inhibiting bacterial energy production. Cystic forms then effectively evade the immune system by locating intracellular or *immune-privileged tissue locations* in order to hide from immune system antibodies, immune cells, and some antibiotics.[32] Persister cells can also form, and are able to survive antibiotics and other stresses.[33] It is estimated that 1 in 5 Lyme spirochetes will take on an extra- or intracellular cyst form and become dormant possibly for long periods of time (10 months to years) – only to reactivate later under more favorable conditions.[34] These dormant forms are hardier, and can still produce toxic products, but with a reduced number of antigenic proteins on their outer membrane, they are able to decrease their visibility to the immune system.

Being one of the most complex of any bacterium,[35] *Borrelia burgdorferi* has many unique protective mechanisms that can assist in its survival and spread. It is a very atypical bacteria,[36] and many of the rules that apply to normal bacterial infections don't apply to it. *Borrelia burgdorferi* "... has motility prowess heretofore unseen in the microbial world. It is built to infiltrate, evade, and persist."[37] Some of its more notable capabilities include the ability to:[38-42]

- Inhibit or kill immune cells (i.e., lymphocytes, B-cells, T-cells, and natural killer cells). For example, the bacteria can enter B-cells and emerge coated in the cell's membrane, and by hiding its own surface proteins in this way it can successfully evade the immune system.
- Effectively use our own cell's enzymes against us in order to travel around the body.
- Proficiently change surface proteins to prevent immune system recognition.
- Rely on chemotactic[***] and niche-seeking traits to evade host immune traffic, taking residence in protective enclaves (e.g., within the central nervous system, intracellular spaces, in ligament/tendon/collagen bundles, in the eyes, or the skin, and in fibroblasts).
- Change forms so it can enter the best state and tissue for optimal survival.
- Maintain a slow growth rate, 12 to 24 hours for replication, meaning antibiotics

---

[***] *Chemotaxis* refers to the movement of an organism in response to a chemical stimulus from within the environment.

that inhibit cell turnover or energy production will then take longer to work.

Also, complicating matters is the formation of biofilms, which are protective environments not unique to *Borrelia*, where bacteria cover themselves with a slime.[43-45] The biofilm environment allows for DNA exchange among bacteria, allows bacteria to hide from immune cells and antibodies, and can help it to resist antibiotic treatment.

Taking all of the above into account, in early disseminated to late disseminated/chronic cases of *Borreliosis*, all forms of the bacteria will need to be treated,[46,47] which is why multiple antibiotic/antimicrobials may be required.

Classification – Types of Lyme

Lyme disease is classified according to where it has spread in the body, the signs and symptoms, how systemic it is, and how long it has been present.[48] Also, Lyme disease can be separated into three stages:[49-51]

1. Primary: early localized (first few days after infection);
2. Secondary: early disseminated (days to months after infection);
3. Tertiary: late disseminated (infection left untreated, ill-treated, or misdiagnosed for months or years).

Clinically however, separating the disease into two stages is more useful:[52,53]

1. acute Lyme (with tick bite, early localized);
2. chronic Lyme (early or late disseminated).

Early localized/Acute Lyme.

Seeking early treatment is important.[54] Horowitz[55] states that 75% to 80% of people can be cured with antibiotics if taken within the first 30 days, whereas others put this figure at 66%.[56] Although 20% of patients may have lingering symptoms (such as fatigue, disrupted sleep, musculoskeletal pains, lack of mental functioning),[57] it is recognized that the earlier the treatment, the greater the success.[58,59] Lyme and co-infections, if left, have led to very prolonged illness,[60] fatal complications,[61,62] and to the onset of other diseases like dementia,[63] heart complications,[64-67] and psychological disorders.[68]

Early disseminated to late disseminated/ Chronic Lyme.

Those that go undiagnosed, or misdiagnosed, for a long period of time will find their recovery process more difficult.[69] Many people who have been ill with Lyme and/or its co-infections for a long while might consider themselves, or explain to others, that they have chronic Lyme disease. However, the term *chronic Lyme disease* is not recognized by the CDC or the IDSA. They use the term *Post Treatment Lyme Disease Syndrome* (PTLDS) to refer to those who, after being treated for Lyme[70] with the recommended antibiotic course,[71] still remain with non-specific relapsing and continuing symptoms like cognitive complaints, fatigue, and musculoskeletal pain. Nonetheless, the term *chronic Lyme disease* is found throughout the medical literature,[72,73] but late Lyme disease might be the preferred term,[74] particularly for those who have never before received treatment and are still presenting with the same symptoms as PTLDS. This aside, healthcare providers who recognize and use the term *chronic Lyme* believe that the disease state is due to an ongoing infection,[75,76] whereas other professionals reject this conclusion outright[77] by describing *chronic Lyme* as a 'medical myth',[78] and as a 'fake medical diagnosis'.[79] In the war of words between these two camps, definitions and terminology suddenly become very important.

A View from the Field – Terminology and Global Lyme

Terminology.

If you do not have the bacterium *Borrelia* then you do not have Lyme. This is because *Lyme Borreliosis*, or Lyme disease, refers to an infection caused by *Borrelia* bacteria, typically *Borrelia burgdorferi*, but also any other strain such as *Borrelia afzelii*, *Borrelia andersonii*, and *Borrelia garnii*.[80,81] For a doctor to diagnose a patient with *Lyme Borreliosis* would require a positive lab test for *Borrelia*,[82] and if you have another type of bacterium that causes similar symptoms, then you may be diagnosed with a Lyme-like illness and/or a number of co-infections which are discussed later. You may also have, what Horowitz[83] has coined, *Multiple Systemic Infectious Disease Syndrome* (MSIDS) which describes a 'symptom complex' that can create a tenaciously persistent illness that is unique to an individual, and is instigated by either Lyme disease, its co-infections, and/or other factors that include parasitic or fungal infections, allergies, environmental toxins, and compromised immune function.[84] Important to note at this juncture is that the Australian government has suggested the total removal of the terms *Lyme disease, Lyme-like illness*, and *chronic Lyme disease* from any diagnostic discussion in the country, proposing instead the use of the term *Debilitating Syndrome Complexes Attributed to Ticks* (DSCATT)[85] to refer to those patients suspected of harboring a tick-borne illness.

It is very important to get the naming right, particularly if you start using these words around medical professionals. Patient experience bears this out well. People have been completely shut down by medical professionals as soon as the word *Lyme* has been mentioned in an area where it is believed not to exist.

> *I asked my doctor to do a blood test for Lyme and he looked at me like I had just slapped his mother* – B.[86]

> *You don't dare say the word 'Lyme' in hospital, they get the psych team on board right away –*
> S.[87]

> *Just saw my new doctor, and mentioned Lyme disease. You would have thought I instantly grew horns. Gosh, these reactions never grow old –* C.[88]

> *Australian medical will always freak at the L word –* L.[89]

Using the wrong language can also make it difficult to get doctors to consider signs and symptoms, or even to test for Lyme and/or its co-infections. I was mostly just fobbed off with, *But you look fit and healthy* – until I didn't. Some patients have been told, *You're a pretty girl, you're just seeking attention*,[90] or *It's all in your head*.[91] This kind of psychogenic misdiagnosis is unfortunate, but it's not a new phenomenon, being arrived at 50% of the time.[92] It is also estimated that between 7% and 17% of hospitalized patients have experienced diagnostic error,[93] and that misdiagnosis in the United States occurs at a rate of between 10% and 20%.[94] Once a misdiagnosis is in place, it can then take a long time to reach the correct one,[95] and between 2.5 to 7 times longer for those with rare diseases.[96]

It will take around 60% of patients with Lyme and/or its co-infections multiple doctors, and two years before they are correctly diagnosed[97] with the delay long recognized as being largely due to physician error.[98] It is for this reason that many people who know that something is wrong with their body end up paying out of pocket for their own tests, and continue to seek out a physician that they can comfortably work with. My eventual diagnosis, took nearly five years, four general practitioners, and nine specialists over two continents.

Taking into account that physicians are human, and that each patient is unique, if you, a family member, or a friend has had Lyme and/or its co-infections for a while, then by now you should know that the path to recovery is going to be different for everyone,[99] and typically a long road to travel.[100] Finding the right doctor is likely going to be not only a necessity but a very important part of the healing process.

Global Lyme.

There are over 300 different strains of *Borrelia* present worldwide, and approximately 100 in the United States,[101-103] but not all strains lead to infection.[104] In 2013, a new species called *Borrelia mayonii* was discovered[105] and later confirmed to be able to infect humans with Lyme disease,[106] and so there are many species of *Borrelia* bacteria to be found worldwide. It is old, even found in *Ötzi* the 5,300-year-old iceman.[107,108] Except for Antarctica, all continents have reported evidence of Lyme infection, from birds carrying infected ticks to positive blood cultures and clinical descriptions.[109] New species of co-infections are also being discovered.[110]

Lyme is not confined to borders; it can be carried internationally by migratory birds, insects, and animals, as well as by people who travel. Lyme has been found across East Asia and into Russia, Turkey, and Nepal,[111] with 6% of the Chinese population thought to be infected.[112] In Europe and Asia, *Borrelia garinii* and *Borrelia afzelii* are the main bacteria responsible,[113,114] with studies indicating the *Borrelia farinii*, *Borrelia lusitaniae*, and *Borrelia burgdorferi sensu stricto* are present in Africa, and spread by the soft tick species *Ornithodorus sonrai* in West Africa.[115-117] There are also reports of *Borrelia burgdorferi* from the Indian sub-continent,[118] the United Kingdom[119] and throughout the rest of the world.[120]

However, the presence of Lyme disease, a Lyme-like illness, or debilitating syndrome complexes attributed to ticks in Australia is still highly debated.[121-125] Although no studies are said to identify *Borrelia burgdorferi* as responsible for locally acquired DSCATT,[126] it still cannot be ruled out,[127] with one study showing that out of 148 Australian patients undergoing specialized lab tests, 70% received a positive result for *Lyme borreliosis*, with 53% of those then testing positive for co-infections.[128] Studies into Lyme and Lyme-like illness from a tick bite are ongoing,[129,130] and genetic evidence of an Australian *Borrelia*, particularly that related to a relapsing fever group,[131,132] is very strong.

References

1. CanLyme. (2017). *Lyme Basics*. Canadian Lyme Disease Foundation. Retrieved from https://canlyme.com/lyme-basics
2. Frino-Harrington, H. (2017). *It isn't Lymes people, it's Lyme*. Lyme Disease Support Group. (September 12). Retrieved from https://www.facebook.com/groups/227910764335351/permalink/337302323396194
3. Langhoff, P. (2007). *"It's all in your head" Patient stories from the front lines: Intimate aspects of chronic and neuropsychiatric Lyme disease*. USA: Allegory Press.
4. Fannin, C. (2017). *The ER visit that made me realize I need to fight the stigma of Lyme disease*. The Mighty. Retrieved from https://themighty.com/2017/08/fighting-stigma-lyme-disease -doctors
5. Keebler. (2012). *Please, do not call me a 'Lymie'*. MdJunction. Retrieved from http://www.mdjunction.com/forums/lyme-disease-support-forums/general- support/3666732-please-do-not-call-me-a-lymie-by-keebler
6. Lymedisease.org. (2017). *Lyme disease awareness month*. Lymedisease.org: Advocacy, Education, & Research. Retrieved from https://www.lymedisease.org/get- involved/take-action/lyme-awareness-month
7. GLIIO. (2017a). *Shining a light on Lyme and invisible illness*. Global Lyme and Invisible Illness Organization. Retrieved from http://www.globallymeinvisible illness.org

8. GLIIO. (2017b). *Red shoe day: A day of remembrance – July 25th*. Global Lyme & Invisible Illness Organization. Retrieved from http://www.globallymeinvisibleillness.org/red-shoe-day.html
9. GLIIO. (2017b). *Ibid*.
10. Eagleman, D. (2009). *Sum: Tales from the afterlives*. USA: Canongate Books.
11. Ally, B. (2004). *I wear my red shoes ...* Red Shoe Day 2014 Artistic Tributes. Global Lyme & Invisible Illness Organization. Retrieved from http://www.globallymeinvisibleillness.org/red-shoe-day-2014-artistic-tributes/red-shoe-day-a-day-of-remembrance-artistic-tribute-i-wear-my-red-shoes-by-ally-b
12. Vitale, L. (2017). *Red shoes*. YouTube. Retrieved from https://www.youtube.com/watch?v=yPljZpyjen0
13. Hilton, L. (2017b). *The reality of Lyme disease, not just two camps anymore*. What is Lyme Disease? Retrieved from http://whatislyme.com/the-reality-of-lyme-disease-not-just-two-camps-anymore
14. Murray, P. (1996). *The widening circle: A Lyme disease pioneer tells her story*. USA: St. Martin's Press.
15. Steere, A., et al. (1983). The spirochetal etiology of Lyme disease. *New England Journal of Medicine, 308*(13), 733-740. doi: 10.1056/NEJM198303313081301
16. Brody, J. E. (1982, November 18). Mystery of Lyme disease is believed solved. *The New York Times*. Retrieved from http://www.nytimes.com/1982/11/18/us mystery-of-lyme-disease-is-believed-solved.html
17. Williams, C. (2007). *Infectious disease epidemiology: Theory and practice*, (2nd ed.). Sudbury, Massachusetts: Jones and Bartlett Publishers.
18. CanLyme. (2017). *Op. cit*.
19. Burgdorfer, W., et al. (1982). Lyme disease – A tick-borne spirochetosis? *Science, 216*(4552), 1317-1319.

20. Dircks, J. H. (ed.). (2012). *Stedman's medical dictionary for the health professions and nursing illustrated*, (7th ed). Wolters Kluwer, Lippincott Williams & Wilkins.
21. Cook, M. J., & Puri, B. K. (2017). Application of Bayesian decision-making to laboratory testing for Lyme disease and comparison testing for HIV. *International Journal of General Medicine, 10*, 113-123. doi: 10.1128/JCM.43.5080 -5084.2005
22. Zeigler, M. (2017). *Ötzi's Lyme disease in context*. Contagions. Retrieved from https://contagions.wordpress.com/2017/02/17/17/otzis-lyme-disease-in-context
23. Brock, T. D., et al. (1994). *Biology of microorganisms*, (7th ed). USA: Prentice Hall.
24. Holligan, D. (2011). Borrelia burgdorferi. Microbe Wiki.
Retrieved from https://microbewiki.kenyon.edu/index.php/Borrelia_burgdorferi
25. Tilly, K., Rosa, P., & Stewart, P. (2008). Biology of infection with Borrelia burgdorferi. *Infectious Disease Clinics of North America, 22*(2), 217-234. doi: 10.1016/j.idc.2007.12. 013
26. Coleman, J., et al. (2013). The HtrA protease of Borrelia burgdorferi degrades outer membrane protein BmpD and chemotaxis phosphatase CheX. *Molecular Microbiology, 88*(3), 619-633. doi: 10.1111/mmi.12213
27. Ullman, A., et al. (2015). Evaluation of Borrelia burgdorferi BbHtrA protease as a vaccine candidate for Lyme Borreliosis in mice. *PLoS One, 10*(16). doi: 10.1371/journal.pone.0128868
28. Horowitz, R. (2017). *How can I get better?: An action plan for treating resistant Lyme & chronic disease*. New York: St. Martin's Press.
29. Miklossy, J., et al. (2008). Persisting atypical and cystic forms of Borrelia burgdorferi and local inflammation

in Lyme Neuroborreliosis. *Journal of Neuroinflammation, 5*, 40. doi: 10.1186/1742-2094-5-40

30. Grier, T. (2017). *Notes and observations on cell wall deficient forms*. LymeNet Europe: Information and Discussion about Lyme Disease. Retrieved from https://www.lymeneteurope.org/info/cell-wall-deficient-bacteria

31. Berndtson, K. (2013). Review of evidence for immune evasion and persistent infection in Lyme disease. *International Journal of General Medicine, 6*, 291-306. doi: 10.2147/IJGM.S44114

32. Berndtson, K. (2013). *Ibid*.

33. Zhang, Y. (2014). Persisters, persistent infections and the yin-yang model. *Emerging Microbes and Infections, 3*(1), e3. doi: 10.1038/emi.2014.3

34. Ahern, H., in Rippey, M. (2014). *Episode #26: Professor Holly Ahern explains how Borrelia burgdorferi survive antibiotics and new therapies in the pipeline to kill Lyme bacteria*. Lyme Ninja Radio. Retrieved from https://lymeninjaradio.com/holly_ahern

35. Brisson, D. et al. (2012). Genetics of Borrelia Burgdorferi. *Annual Review of Genetics, 46*. doi: 10.1146/annurev-genet-011112-112140

36. Anderson, W. (2016). Chapter Two – Wayne Anderson, ND. in C. Strasheim, *New paradigms in Lyme disease treatment: 10 top doctors reveal healing strategies that work*. California, USA: BioMed Publishing Group, LLC.

37. Berndtson, K. (2013). *Op. cit*.

38. Berndtson, K. (2013). *Ibid*.

39. Georgilis, K., Peacocke, M., & Klempner, M. (1992). Fibroblasts protect the Lyme disease spirochete, Borrelia burgdorferi from ceftriaxone

in vitro. *The Journal of Infectious Diseases, 166*, 440-444. doi: 10.1093/infdis/166.2.440

40. Grier, T. (2000). The complexities of Lyme disease (A microbiology tutorial), in *Lyme Disease Survival Manual*. USA: Duluth, MN.

41. Jutras, B., Chenail, A., & Stevenson, B. (2013). Changes in bacterial growth rate govern expression of the Borrelia burgdorferi OspC and Erp infection-associated surface proteins. *Journal of Bacteriology, 154*(4), 757-764. doi: 10.1128/JB.01956-12

42. Todar, K. (2012). Borrelia burgdorferi and Lyme disease. *Todar's Online Textbook of Bacteriology*. Madison, Wisconsin. Retrieved from http://textbookofbacteriology.net/Lyme.html

43. Jefferson, K. (2004). What drives bacteria to form a biofilm? *FEMS Microbiology Letters, 52*(4), 917-924.

44. Sapi, E. (2008). Biofilms: A hideout for Borrelia burgdorferi. *The Lyme Times, 54*, 15-16.

45. Ross, M. (2016). *Biofilms: Lyme disease gated communities*. The Treat Lyme Book. Retrieved from http://www.treatlyme.net/treat-lyme-book/biofilms-lyme-disease-gated-communities

46. Rippey, M. (2015). *Episode 27: Lyme expert – Dr. Nicola McFadzean Ducharme – Author, naturopath*. Lyme Ninja Radio. Retrieved from http://lymeninjaradio.com/nicola_ducharme

47. Ross, M. (2017). A Lyme disease antibiotic guide. *The Treat Lyme Book*. Healing Arts Partnership. Retrieved from http://www.treatlyme.net/treat-lyme-book/lyme-disease-antibiotic-guide

48. McFadzean, N. (2012). *The beginner's guide to Lyme disease: Diagnosis and treatment made simple*. USA: BioMed Publishing Group.

49. Whitmont, R. (2012). *Homeopathy and Lyme disease*. Classical Homeopathic Physician. Retrieved from http://www.homeopathicmd.com/2012/04/homeopathy-and-lyme-disease

50. Merck Manual. (2017). *Lyme disease*. Merck Manual Professional Version. Retrieved from http://www.merckmanuals.com/professional/infectios-diseases/spirochetes/lyme-disease

51. Rawls, W. (2017). *Unlocking Lyme: Myths, truths, & practical solutions for chronic Lyme disease*. USA: FirstDoNoHarm Publishing.

52. LDAA. (2017). *Tick borne awareness and advocacy*. Lyme Disease Association of Australia. Retrieved from http://www.lyme disease.org.au

53. Rawls, W. (2017). *Op. cit.*

54. Elbaum-Garfinkle, S. (2011). Close to home: A history of Yale and Lyme disease. *Yale Journal of Biology and Medicine, 84*(2), 103-108.

55. Horowitz, R., in Manny, D. (2016). *The Lyme disease debate: Can the condition be Chronic?* Fox News Interview.
Retrieved from http://www.foxnews.com/health/2016/05/25/lyme-disease-debate-can-condition-be-chronic.html

56. Rippey, M. (2017). *Episode 123: Jean Monro, MD – UK Lyme expert*. Lyme Ninja Radio. Retrieved from http://lymeninjaradio.com/123-jean-monro-md

Chapter 2: What is Lyme? | 27

57. Melia, M. & Auwaerter, P. (2016). Time for a different approach to Lyme disease and long-term symptoms. *New England Journal of Medicine, 734,* 1277-1278. doi: 1056/NEJMe1502350
58. Maloney, E. (2007). Basic principles of laboratory testing for Lyme disease. *The Lyme Times, 50,* 26-28.
59. McFadzean, N. (2012). *Op. cit.*
60. Weintraub, P. (2013). *Cure Unknown: Inside the Lyme epidemic,* (Revised Ed.). New York: St Martin's Griffin.
61. Schaller, J. (2007). *Ignore Bartonella and die: Trivializing Bartonella is like ignoring TNT.* Public Health Alert: Investigating Lyme and Chronic Illness. Retrieved from http://www.publichealthalert.org/ignore-bartonella-an d-die-trivializing-bartonella-is-like-ignoring-tnt.html
62. Bushak, L. (2013). *3 People die suddenly from Lyme disease, CDC investigates.* Medical Daily. Retrieved from http://www.medicaldaily.com/3-people-die-suddenly-lyme-disease-cdc-investigates-264991
63. Yoon, E., et al. (2015). Lyme disease: A case report of a17-year-old male with fatal Lyme carditis. *Journal of Cardiovascular Pathology, 24*(5), 317-321. doi: 10.1916/j.carpath.2015.03.003
64. Blanc, F., et al. (2014). Lyme neuroborreliosis and dementia. *Journal of Alzheimer's Disease, 41*(4), 1087-1093. doi: 10.3233/JAD-130446
65. Afari, M., et al. (2016). Lyme carditis: An interesting trip to third-degree heart block and back. *Case Reports in Cardiology, 2016.* Article ID 5454160. doi: 10.1155/2016/5454160

66. Parish, D. (2016). Lyme: The infectious disease equivalent of cancer, says top Duke oncologist. Huffington Post. Retrieved from http://www.huffingtonpost.com/dana-parish/lyme-the-infectious-disea_b_92 43460.html
67. Kostic, T., et al. (2017). Manifestations of Lyme carditis. *International Journal of Cardiology, 232,* 24-32. doi: 10.1016/j.ijcard.2016.12.169
68. Singleton, K. (2008). *The Lyme disease solution.* USA: BookSurge Publishing.
69. Rawls, W. (2017). *Op. cit.*
70. Marques, A. (2008). Chronic Lyme disease: An appraisal. *Infectious Disease Clinics of North America, 22*(2), 341-60. doi: 10.1016/j.idc.2007.12.011
71. Rawls, W. (2017). *Op. cit.*
72. Logigian, E., Kaplan, R., & Steere, A. (1990). Chronic neurologic manifestations of Lyme disease. *New England Journal of Medicine, 323,* 1438-1444.
73. Berghoff, W. (2012). Chronic Lyme disease and co-Infections: Differential diagnosis. *The Open Neurology Journal, 6,* 158-178. doi: 10.2174/1874205X01206010158
74. Feder, H., et al. (2007). A critical appraisal of 'chronic Lyme disease'. *New England Journal of Medicine, 357,* 1422-1430. doi: 10.1056/NEJMra072023
75. Burrascano, J. (2008). *Diagnostic hints and treatment guidelines for Lyme and other tick borne illnesses* (16th ed.). Advanced Topics in Lyme Disease. Retrieved from http://www.lymenet.org/ BurrGuide200810.pdf
76. Rippey, M. (2014). *Op. Cit.*
77. Lantos, P. M. (2015). Chronic Lyme disease. *Infectious disease clinics of North America, 29*(2), 325-40. doi: 10.1016/j.idc.2015.0 2.006
78. Rosner, B. (2008). *Lyme disease annual report.* USA: BioMed Publishing Group.

79. Orac. (2017). *Deaths and complications due to treating the fake disease known as 'chronic Lyme disease'*. Respectful Insolence. Retrieved from http://scienceblogs.com/insolence/2017/06/21/deaths-and-complications-due-to-treating-the-fake-disease-known-as-chronic-lyme-disease
80. McFadzean, N. (2012). *Lyme disease in Australia*. USA: BioMed Publishing Group.
81. Leydet, B., & Liang, F. (2014), Detection of Lyme Borrelia in questing Ixodes scapularis (Acari: Ixodidae) and small mammals in Louisiana. *Journal of Medical Entomology, 51*(1), 278-282.
82. Rawls, W. (2017). *Op. cit.*
83. Horowitz, R. (2013). *Why can't I get better?: Solving the mystery of Lyme and chronic illness*. New York: St. Martin's Press.
84. Horowitz, R. (2013). *Ibid*.
85. Department of Health (2017). Australian Government response to the Senate Community Affairs References Committee final report: Inquiry into the growing evidence of an emerging tick-borne disease that causes a Lyme-like illness for many Australian patients. November, 2017. Retrieved from http://www.health.gov.au/internet/main/publishing.nsf/Content/8246306026 A29C08CA2581D30010C8E4/$File/Govt-response-Senate-inquiry-final-report-%202017.pdf
86. B., in Jackie. (2015). *Quotes from the warriors ...* The Lessons of Lyme: Finding the Silver Lining. Retrieved from https://thelessonsoflyme.wordpress.com/2015/05/21/quotes-from-the-warriors

87. S., in King, S. (2017). I can't help thinking about the Merry Go Round we are on. Lyme Australia & Friends. (August 08). Retrieved from https://www.facebook.com/groups/LymeAustraliaandFriends/permalink/1602211616478253
88. C., in Gavish, A. (2017). *Finish the Sentence – You now you have a chronic invisible illness when …* Lyme Disease Group. (September 07). Retrieved from https://www.facebook.com/groups/227910764335351/permalink/335350296924730
89. L., in King. (2017). *Op. cit.*
90. Wilson, A. (2008). *Under our skin.* United States: Open Eye Pictures.
91. Hinton, L. (2017). *Institutionalized gaslighting; or, When the experts are part of the problem.* https://www.facebook.com/notes/lucy-hinton/institutionalised-gaslighting-or-when-the-experts-are-part-of-the-problem/10158957508
92. O'Leary, D. (2016). *'All in your head'. The problem of psychogenic diagnosis for Ehlers-Danlos patients.* EDS Awareness 'Educational Series'. Webinar. Retrieved from http://www.chronicpainpartners.com/webinar/free-webinar-head-problem-psychogenic-diagnosis-ehlers-danlos-patients
93. Murphy, J. (2016). A correct diagnosis is of increasing importance. *Irish Medical Journal, 109*(1), 324. Retrieved from http://imj.ie/a-correct-diagnosis-is-of-increasing-importance-2

94. Booman, S. (2013). *Doctors' diagnostic errors are often not mentioned but can take a serious toll*. Kaiser Health News. Retrieved from http://khn.org/news/doctor-errors-misdiagnosis-more-common-than-known-serious-impact
95. O'Rourke, M., (2014). *Doctors tell all – and it's bad*. The Atlantic. Retrieved from https://www.theatlantic.com/magazine/archive/2014/11/doctors-tell-all-and-its-bad/380785/?utm_source= atlfb
96. O'Leary. (2017). *Op. cit.*
97. Editor. (2017). Do you have Lyme? *The Lyme Times Special Issue: Patient's Issue.* Retrieved from https://www.lymedisease.org/members/lyme-times/special-issues/patient-issue/do-you-have-lyme-disease
98. Maloney, E. (2007). Basic principles of laboratory testing for Lyme disease. *The Lyme Times, 50,* 26-28.
99. Burrascano, J. (2008). *Op. cit.*
100. Leland, D. (2013). *Touched by Lyme: Recovery is a long, slow, balancing act.* Lymedisease.org: Advocacy, Education, & Research. Retrieved from https://www.lymedisease.org/jen-crystal-lyme-recovery-2
101. Horowitz, R. (2014). Co-infections presentation, diagnosis, and treatment. *Symposium on Tick-borne Diseases.* May 17. USA: Maryland. Retrieved from https://www.youtube.com/watch?v=O9a-2Nb2sbk
102. Horowitz, R., in Manny, D. (2016). *Op. cit.*
103. Horowitz, R. (2017). *Op. cit.*
104. Khatchikian, C., et al. (2015). Public health impact of strain specific immunity to Borrelia burgdorferi. *BMC Infectious Diseases, 15,* 472. doi: 10.1186/s12879-015-1190-7

105. CDC. (2015). *Borrelia mayonii*. Diseases transmitted by ticks. Centers for Disease Control and Prevention. Retrieved fromhttps://www.cdc.gov/ticks/mayonii.html
106. CDC. (2016b). *New Lyme-disease-causing bacteria discovered – Press Release*. Centers for Disease Control and Prevention. Retrieved from https://www.cdc.gov/media/releases/2016/p0208-lyme-disease.html
107. Keller, A., et al. (2012). *New insights into the Tyrolean Iceman's origin and phenotype as inferred by whole-genome sequencing*. Nature Communications, 3, 698. doi: 10.1038/ncomms1701
108. Parry, W. (2012). *Iceman mummy may hold earliest evidence of Lyme disease*. LiveScience. Retrieved from https://www.livescience.com/18704-oldest-case-lyme-disease-spotted-iceman-mummy.html
109. Yannielli, L. (2004). *Deadly diseases and epidemics: Lyme disease*. New York: Chelsea House. Vayssier-Taussat, M., et al. (2016). Identification of novel zoonotic activity of Bartonella spp., France. *Emerging Infectious Diseases*, 22(3), 457-462. doi: 10.3201/eid2203.150269
110. Vayssier-Taussat, M., et al. (2016). Identification of novel zoonotic activity of Bartonella spp., France. *Emerging Infectious Diseases*, 22(3), 457-462. doi: 10.3201/eid2203. 150269
111. Masuzawa. T. (2004). Terrestrial distribution of the Lyme borreliosis agent Borrelia burgdorferi sensu lato in East Asia. *Japanese Journal of Infectious Diseases, 57*, 229–235.
112. Horowitz, R., in Manny, D. (2016). *Op. cit.*
113. Strle, F., et al. (2006). Comparison of findings for patients with Borrelia garinii and Borrelia afzelii isolated from cerebrospinal fluid. *Clinical Infectious Diseases*, 43(6), 704-710.

114. Theel, E. (2016). *Lyme Disease part 1: The common culprits worldwide – Borrelia burgdorferi, Borrelia garinii, Borrelia afzelii.* Mayo Clinic: MML Education. Retrieved from https://news.mayomedicallaboratories.com/2016/05/02/lyme-disease-part-1-the-common-culprits-worldwide-borrelia-burgdorferi-borrelia-garinii-borrelia-afzelii-hot-topic
115. Kaf-Ngoune, S. (2006). *Lyme Disease: The forgotten scourge of West Africa.* IRIN: The Inside Story on Emergencies. Retrieved from http://www.irinnews.org/news/2006/08/ 23
116. Mediannikov, O., et al. (2014). Identification of *Bartonellae* in the soft tick species *Ornithodoros sonrai* in Senegal. *Vector Borne and Zoonotic Diseases, 14*(1), 26-32.
117. Jairath, V., et al. (2014). Lyme disease in Haryana, India. *Indian Journal of Dermatology, Venereology and Leprology, 80*(4), 320-323.
118. Cook, M. J., & Puri, B. K. (2017). *Op. cit.*
119. Rosner, B. (2008). *Op. cit.*
120. McFadzean, N. (2012). *Op. cit.*
121. Smith, K. (2013). *Lyme disease: A counter argument to the Australian government's denial.* Lyme Australia Recognition and Awareness. Retrieved from http://www.lymedisease.org.au/wp-content/uploads/2014/02/attachment_two_lyme_disease_a_counter_argument_of_the_australian_governments_denial.pdf
122. SBS. (2016). *Episode 38: Tick sick.* Insight. Retrieved from https://www.sbs.com.au/ondemand/video/783633475924/insight-tick-sick

123. Webb, C. (2016). *What is Lyme disease and does it exist in Australia?* The Conversation. Retrieved from http://theconversation.com/explainer-what-is-lyme-disease-and-does-it-exist-in-australia-57717
124. Killalea, D. (2017). *Lyme disease in Australia: 'No one believes me'*. Health. news.com.au. Retrieved from http://www.news.com.au/lifestyle/health/health-problems/lyme-disease-in-australia-no-one-believes-me/news-story/167b759 4b481dc156b0d9557cceeb119
125. Chalada, M. J., Stenos, J., & Bradbury, R. S. (2016). Is there a Lyme-like disease in Australia? Summary of the findings to date. *One Health, 2*, 42-54. doi: 10.1016/j.one hlt.2016.03.003
126. NSW Health. (2016). *Lyme disease fact sheet*. Communicable Diseases. Retrieved from http://www.health.nsw.gov.au/Infectious/factsheets/Factsheets/Lyme-disease.pdf
127. McFadzean. (2012). *Op. cit.*
128. Russell, R., et al. (1994). Lyme disease: A search for a causative agent in ticks in south-eastern Australia. *Epidemiology & Infection, 112*(2), 375-384. doi: 10.1017/S0 950268800057782
129. Gofton, A. et al., (2015). Inhibition of the Endosymbiont 'Candidatus Midichloria mitochondrii' during 16s rRNA gene profiling reveals potential pathogens in Ixodes ticks from Australia. *Parasites & Vectors, 8*, 345. doi: 10.1186/s13071-015-0958-3
130. Murdoch. (2017). *Pilot study*. Research Group: Vector and Waterborne Pathogens. Retrieved from: http://www.murdoch.edu.au/Research-capabilities/Vec tor-and-Waterborne-Pathogens-Group/Pilot-Study
131. Gofton. (2015). *Op.cit.*

[132.] Loh, S., et al. (2016). Novel Borrelia species detected in Echidna ticks, Bothriocroton Concolor, in Australia. *Parasites and Vectors, 9*, 339. doi: 10.1186/s13071-016-1627-x

3. What Are The Co-infections That Can Come with Lyme?

Lyme usually comes with friends, and just like people have friends and a family, Lyme doesn't like to be lonely either. Sometimes the friends of Lyme, the co-infections, can be worse than the Lyme bacterium itself.[1,2] These friends also have long, tongue twisting names, and they might lead to other opportunistic infections such as *Candida* overgrowth.[3]

Common Co-infections
The following common co-infections,[4] and some brief information about each of them, are introduced here:[5-11]
- *Babesia*
- *Bartonella*
- *Ehrlichia, Anaplasma, Rickettsia*
- *Mycoplasma*

Babesia.
This is a malaria-like parasite that infects red blood cells.[12] The severity of infection can vary, with two species causing the majority of human disease: *Babeisa duncani* and *Babesia microti*.[13]

Bartonella.

This is a genus of bacteria that has a double cell wall (gram negative), and primarily infects and lives inside endothelial cells that comprise the wall of blood vessels and the lymphatic system. *Bartonella* is also known to infect red blood cells, along with the liver and spleen, as well as every other organ of the body including the heart where it can deposit fat that in turn disrupts the heartbeat. It has been described as more serious than Lyme,[14] and the most intense tick-borne infection.[15] Three species tend to cause the majority of human disease:[16] *Bartonella henselae* (cat scratch disease), *Bartonella quitana* (trench fever), and *Bartonella bacilliformis* (Oroya fever/verruga peruana).

Ehrlichia, Anaplasma, Rickettsia.

Ehrlichiosis and *Anaplasmosis* are two disease conditions that are caused by two different organisms in the same bacterial family, and they are in the same family as the bacterium *Rickettsia rickettsii* (Rocky Mountain spotted fever).[17,18] The spotted fever group (SFG) is large, with many of these pathogens able to cause febrile illnesses, severe damage to organ systems, septic shock, and potentially death. *Rickettsia rickettsii* is the most virulent[19] and it infects cells that line the blood vessels (endothelial cells).[20] *Ehrlichia chaffeenis* is typically the primary cause of *Ehrlichiosis*, while *Anaplasma phagocytophilum* (formerly *Ehrlichia phagocytophila*) is the cause of *Anaplasmosis* (formerly HGE or Human Granulocytic Ehrlichiosis, now HGA or Human Granulocytic Anaplasmosis), and presents similarly to *Ehrlichiosis*.[21] Both of these are infections that kill white blood cells.[22]

Mycoplasma.

This is the smallest bacteria, commonly infecting white blood cells and favoring myelin covered nerves and collagen-rich areas of the body such as the brain, joints, and skin.[23] About 4,000 *Mycoplasma* could fit into a red blood cell, whereas only 12 *Bartonella* bacteria could do so.[24] About seven species of *Mycoplasma* cause the most disease in humans: *Mycoplasma pnuemoniae*, *Mycoplasma genitalium*, *Mycoplasma hominis*, *Mycoplasma fermentans*, *Ureaplasma urealyticum*, *Ureaplasma parvum*, and *Mycoplasma penetrans*.[25] Nicholson[26] has found *Mycoplasma fermentans* to be the one most common in people with Lyme, with *Mycoplasma* infections similar in symptoms to *Borreliosis* and linked to a number of neurodegenerative diseases, chronic illnesses, and potentially responsible for triggering numerous autoimmune responses.

A View from the Field – Co-infections

Co-infections are considered to be common with Lyme rather than being exceptions, and they are distinct pathogenic microbes carried by the same route.[27] This is potentially one reason why many people don't get better, because they contract multiple viruses and bacteria from a single bite, which then overwhelm the immune system.[28] Co-infections can consist of many species and many strains, and over 60% of Lyme patients have them.[29] In one study[30] it was shown that 23.5% of those with Lyme were infected with a single co-infection, while 29.8% were infected with two or more co-infections. Statistics from this study see co-infections present at the rate of: 32.3% for *Babesia*, 28.3% for *Bartonella*, 14.5% for *Ehrlichia*, 15.1% for *Mycoplasma*, 5.6% for *Rickettsia*, 4.8% for *Anaplasma*, but only 0.8% for *Tularemia*.

References

[1.] Schaller, J. (2007). *Ignore Bartonella and die: Trivializing Bartonella is like ignoring TNT*. Public Health Alert: Investigating Lyme and Chronic Illness. Retrieved from
http://www.publichealthalert.org/ignore-bartonella- and-die-trivializing-bartonella-is-like-ignoring-tnt.html

[2.] Buhner, S. (2013). *Healing Lyme co-infections: Complimentary and holistic treatments for Bartonella and mycoplasma*. Vermont: Healing Arts Press.

[3.] McFadzean, N. (2012). *The beginner's guide to Lyme disease: Diagnosis and treatment made simple*. USA: BioMed Publishing Group.

[4.] Fearn, D. (2017). Co-infections: Answers to the most commonly-asked questions. *The Lyme Times Special*

Issue: Patients Issue. Retrieved from https://www.lymedisease.org/members/lyme-times/special-issues/patient-issue/lyme-disease-co-infections

5. McFadzean, N. (2012). *Op. cit.*
6. Horowitz, R. (2014). Co-infections presentation, diagnosis, and treatment. *Symposium on Tick-borne Diseases.* May 17. USA: Maryland. Retrieved from https://www.youtube.com/watch?v=O9a-2Nb2sbk
7. Horowitz, R. (2017). *How can I get better?: An action plan for treating resistant Lyme & chronic disease.* New York: St. Martin's Press.
8. Buhner, S. (2013). *Op. cit.*
9. Buhner, S. (2015a). *Healing Lyme: Natural healing of Lyme Borreliosis and the co-infections Chlamydia and Spotted Fever Rickettsioses.* New Mexico: Raven Press.
10. Buhner, S. (2015b). *Natural treatments for Lyme co-infections: Anaplasma, Babesia, and Ehrlichia.* Vermont: Healing Arts Press.
11. Rawls, W. (2017). *Unlocking Lyme: Myths, truths, & practical solutions for chronic Lyme disease.* USA: FirstDoNoHarm Publishing.
12. Brewer, J. (2007). Tickborne diseases and co-infections. *The Lyme Times, 48,* 20-27.
13. Cameron, D. (2017). *The role of co-infections.* All Things Lyme. Retrieved from http://danielcameronmd.com/co-infections
14. Schaller, J. (2008). Bartonella is becoming the most important issue in treatment of Lyme. *Public Health Alert, 3*(5), 1-2.
15. Buhner, S. (2013). *Op. cit.*
16. Wenzel, R. (2017). *Bartonella syndromes.* The Journal of Family Practice. Frontline Medical Communications. Retrieved from http://www.mdedge.com/jfponline/dssm/961/infectious-diseases/bartonella-syndromes

17. Singleton, K. (2008). *The Lyme disease solution*. USA: BookSurge Publishing.
18. Rawls, W. (2017). *Op. cit.*
19. Buhner, S. (2015a). *Op. cit.*
20. Rawls, W. (2017). *Op. cit.*
21. Holman, M., et al. (2004). Anaplasma phagocytophilum, Babesia microti, and Borrelia burgdorferi in Ixodes scapularis, southern coastal Maine. *Emerging Infectious Diseases, 10*(4). 744-746. doi: 10.3201/eid1004.030566
22. Cameron, D. (2017). *Op. cit.*
23. Rawls, W. (2017). *Op. cit.*
24. Buhner, S. (2013). *Op. cit.*
25. Buhner, S. (2013). *Ibid.*
26. Forsgren, S. (2009). *Mycoplasma – often overlooked in chronic Lyme disease*. Public Health Alert. Retrieved from http://www.publichealthalert.org/mycoplasma---often-overlooked-in-chronic-lyme-disease.html
27. Jaller, D. (2017). *Lyme primer*. LymeMD. Retrieved from http://lymemd.blogspot.com
28. Horowtiz, R., in Manny, D. (2016). *The Lyme disease debate: Can the condition be chronic?* Fox News Interview. Retrieved from http://www.foxnews.com/health/2016/05/25/lyme-disease-debate-can-condition-be-chronic.html
29. Horowitz, R. (2014). *Op. cit.*
30. Johnson, L., et al. (2014). Severity of chronic Lyme disease compared to other chronic conditions: A quality of life survey. *PeerJ, 2*, e322. doi: 10.7717/peerj.322

4. How Do You Get Lyme And/Or Its Co-infections?

Although not all ticks carry Lyme disease,[1] and most tick bites are generally harmless,[2] a single bite has the potential to transmit a range of pathogens.[3,4] Some of these diseases might be stealth pathogens that can live inside the human body undetected for many years, and others might make you very ill very quickly.[5-7] It has been found that over 50% of patients with early to late Lyme disease have shown to be infected with at least one co-infection, 30% having two or more co-infections.[8] Co-infections can be passed on the same way as Lyme, but they can also be obtained via other means, and tend to vary from region to region.[9]

Transmission
Lyme Borreliosis.
According to the Centers for Disease Control and Prevention (CDC),[10] Lyme is transmitted as a result of a bite from a blacklegged tick. However, Lyme can reside in creatures other than ticks,[11] and there is also the belief that Lyme can be spread by other means including bites from mosquitos, spiders, fleas, and mites.[12] Indeed, Lyme has been found in mosquitos,[13,14] but there has been research to show that other creatures including flies,[15] while being carriers of the disease, are unable to transmit it to

humans. Dogs, cats, and other pets can get Lyme, and although they cannot pass it on to you, they might be harboring a tick that could infect you.[16]

Other methods of transmission, although controversial, have also been studied. For example, the transmission of the disease among horses[17] and rodent populations[18] by urine. Unfortunately, like almost everything else associated with Lyme and its co-infections, there is still much debate about whether or not they can be passed onto family members, sexual partners, and in utero (see chapter 14).

Co-infections.

Babesia. This malaria-like parasite can be transmitted by a tick bite,[19] has been seen to pass from mother to child in utero,[20-22] and has been acquired through contaminated blood during a transfusion.[23,24]

Bartonella. This bacteria has been found in fleas in Australia, and in multiple marsupial hosts[25] including feral cats, bush rats, rabbits, and foxes. Predominantly, cat scratch fever, *Bartonella henselae*, can be transmitted by the bite or scratch of a cat or bites from fleas[26] or from exposure to flea feces. Trench fever, *Bartonella Quintana*, is transmitted by human lice.[27] Carrion's disease, *Bartonella bacilliformis*, can be transmitted by fleas, sandflies, and ticks. Bartonella can also be passed from mother to fetus,[28,29] and possibly between partners.[30]

Ehrlichia, Anaplasma, and Rickettsia. These disease conditions are primarily transmitted by ticks. *Ehrlichiosis*, a term describing several bacterial diseases, one of which is *Anaplasmosis*, can be transmitted by the *Ixodes* tick in the United States, while others can be transmitted by the lone star tick. The spotted fever group (SPG) *rickettsiosis* is a group of diseases caused by closely related bacteria. There are many, and they are found worldwide. In the United States this includes: *Rickettsia rickettsii* which is often transmitted by American or brown dog ticks, or Rocky Mountain wood ticks, and it is the causative agent behind Rocky Mountain spotted fever, *Rickettsia parkeri rickettsiosis* which is transmitted by Gulf Coast ticks,[31] Pacific Coast tick fever, caused by *Rickettsia philipii*, and Rickettsialpox transmitted by mouse mites, caused by *Rickettsia akari*.[32] Others, for example, such as *Rickettsia australis*, found in three *Ixodes* tick species, is pretty much limited to Australia, while *Rickettsia africae* "has been found in thirteen different tick species in three different genera and causing African tick bite fever in Sub-Saharan Africa, Asia, North and Central America, the Caribbean, and the Pacific islands", with *Rickettsia japonica* found in seven ticks in three genera causing Oriental or Japanese spotted fever in Asia (primarily Japan and South Korea).[33] Human granulocytic anaplasmosis

(HGA) has been found to be transmissible in utero[34] and through blood transfusion.[35] Risks of obtaining *Ehrlichia* from organ transplants or from blood transfusions are also probable,[36,37] as is *Rickettsia*.[38]

Mycoplasma. This bacteria can be spread in a variety of ways including bites from ticks, mosquitos, fleas, and biting flies. Depending on the strain, it can also be obtained from sexual contact, contaminated food, and airborne droplets.[39]

A View from the Field – What Makes a Tick, Tick?

Vector-borne diseases are of a rising global concern,[40] with ticks considered the main culprit behind the spread of Lyme (*Borrelia*), *Babesia*, *Bartonella*, *Ehrlichia*, *Anaplasma*, *Rickettsia*, along with countless other illnesses.[41,42] Yet, most people may not even know what a tick really is, or perhaps will vaguely recall learning something about it in high school biology.

Ticks are arthropods,* and they can be classified into two groups: the hard (*Ixodes*) tick which undergoes three molts during its lifecycle, and the soft (*Argasidae*) tick which undergoes seven molts during its lifecycle.[43] The ticks carrying Lyme disease, and those capable of passing it on, are hard ticks, which means that throughout their four-stage

---

* *Arthropods* are invertebrate animals with an exoskeleton, a segmented body, and paired jointed appendages.

lifecycle, with each cycle perhaps taking six months, they will feed on three different mammals.[44]

As the tick hatches from its egg (first stage) as a larva with six legs (second-stage), it seeks out a blood meal (typically on smaller animals such as birds, mice, and rabbits). After fully feeding, the larva will drop off that first host and molt into a nymph (third stage) and acquire two additional legs. The nymph will then seek out a blood meal (typically on the same type of smaller animals as the larva). The nymph, when full, will drop off the second host animal and molt into an adult tick (fourth stage), and then seek out a blood meal (typically on larger animals like deer, cattle, sheep, horses, or humans). After dropping off the third host when full, the female will then lay its eggs. The life cycle, which can take up to two years to complete[45] will then repeat.[46]

In the above model, the way that Lyme and co-infections get passed on are through the tick as a vector.** The tick initially feeds on a reservoir host,*** and then feeds on a second, then a third host, picking up, and passing on, any infection(s) along the way.

Ticks are typically active spring through fall/autumn.[47] They do not jump like fleas, and they

---

** *Vectors* are organisms, such as a biting insect like a tick that can transfer diseases or parasites from one animal or plant to another animal or plant.
*** *Reservoir hosts* are the long-term host of a pathogen, and typically do not get the disease or present as asymptomatic.

do not fly like mosquitos. Ticks usually rely on questing behavior to ambush hosts, as they will climb a tall blade of grass or plant stem, extending their front legs ready to grab onto a passing creature once they sense one in the vicinity.[48] The front legs contain sensory organs, Haller's organ, that respond to host stimuli (e.g., odors of sweat, exhaled carbon-dioxide, temperature changes, and movement).[49] Some hunter ticks will make a run for you when they sense you nearby. Regardless of the type of tick, once on you it will crawl up your body looking for a place to attach, usually in sheltered and warm places like in the hair, in or behind the ears, armpits, the belly button, or the groin.[50] The anesthetic property within the tick saliva usually means that you will not feel the feeding tube that allows the tick to suck blood being cut into the skin.[51] In recent years, rising temperatures have started to lead to longer and warmer seasonal temperatures, seeing a growth in tick populations and activity in more places,[52,53] sometimes year-round.[54] Urban sprawl into those places, along with better weather conditions, are seeing more people engage in outdoor activities for longer periods of time, and making it increasingly difficult to avoid being bitten.[55]

References
[1.] Shapiro, E. (2011). Lyme disease in children. In J. Halperin (Ed.). *Lyme Disease: An Evidence-based Approach* (221-231). USA: CABI.

2. Pietro, M. (2016). *Should I worry about a tick bite?* Medical News Today. Retrieved from http://www.medicalnewstoday.com/articles/313733.php
3. Liu, X., & Bonnet, S. (2014). Hard tick factors implicated in pathogen transmission. *PLoS Neglected Tropical Diseases, 8*(1), e2566. doi: 10.1371/journal.pntd.0002566
4. Yu, Z., et al. (2015). Tick-borne pathogens and the vector potential of ticks in China. *Parasites and Vectors, 8*(24). doi: 10.1186/s13071-014-0628-x
5. Embers, E., Ramamoorthy, R., & Philipp, M. (2004). Survival strategies of Borrelia burgdorferi, the etiologic agent of Lyme disease. *Research in Immunology, 6*(3), 312-318.
6. Stricker, R., & Johnson, L. (2011). Lyme disease: The next decade. *Infection and Drug Resistance, 4*, 1-9. doi: 10.2147/IDR.S15653
7. Peake, T. (2013). *Bartonellosis: Diagnosing a stealth pathogen.* NC State News. Retrieved from https://news.ncsu.edu/2013/04/tpbartonellosis-diagnosis
8. Johnson, L., et al. (2014). Severity of chronic Lyme disease compared to other chronic conditions: A quality of life survey. *PeerJ, 2*, e322. doi: 10.7717/peerj.322
9. Swanson, S., et al. (2006). Co-infections acquired from Ixodes Ticks. *Clinical Microbiology Reviews, 19*(4), 708-727. doi: 10.1128/CMR.00011-06
10. CDC. (2015). *Transmission.* Centers for Disease Control and Prevention. Retrieved from https://www.cdc.gov/lyme/transmission/index.html
11. Netsuil, J., et al. (1005). Presence of Borrelia burgdorferi sensu lato in mites parasitizing small rodents. *Vector-Borne Zoonotic Diseases, 5*(3), 227-232.

12. Klinghardt, D., in Scutti, S. (2013). *What is Lyme disease?: Signs and symptoms of the invisible illness*. Medical Daily: Healthy Living. Retrieved from http://www.medicaldaily.com/what-lyme-disease-signs-and-symptoms-invisible-illness-247742
13. Hard, S. (1966). Erythema chronicum migrans (Afzelii) associated with mosquito bite. *Acta Dermato-Venereologica, 46*(6), 473-476.
14. Melaun, C., et al. (2016). Occurrence of *Borrelia burgdorferi s.l.* in different genera of mosquitoes (Culcidae) in Central Europe. *Ticks and Tick-borne Diseases, 7*(2), 256-263.
15. Magnarelli, L., Anderson, A., & Barbour, A. (1986). The etiologic agent of Lyme disease in deer flies, horse flies, and mosquitoes. *The Journal of Infectious Diseases, 154*(2), 355-358. doi: 10.1093/infdis/154.2.355
16. CDC. (2015). *Op. cit*.
17. Manion, T., et al. (1998). Viable Borrelia burgdorferi in the urine of two clinically normal horses. *Journal of Veterinary Diagnostic Investigation, 10*(196-199). doi: 10.1177/104063879801000219
18. Bosler, E., & Schulze, T. (1986). The Prevalence and significance of Borrelia burgdorferi in the urine of feral reservoir hosts. *Zentralbblatt fur Bakteriologie, Mikrobiologie, und Hygiene. Series A, Medical Microbiology, Infectious Diseases, Virology, Parasitology, 263*(1-2), 40-44.
19. Kjemtrup, A., & Conrad, P. (2000), Human Babesiosis: An emerging tick-borne disease. *International Journal of Parasitology, 30*(12-13), 1323-1337.
20. Sethi, S., et al. (2009). Probable congenital Babesiosis in infant, New Jersey, USA. *Emerging Infectious Diseases, 15*(5), 788-791. doi: 10.3201/eid1505.070808

21. CDC. (2017a). *Tickborne diseases of the United States: A reference manual for health care providers*, (4th ed). U.S. Department of Health and Human Services. Centers for Disease Control and Prevention.
22. Trivino, C. (2017). *Thompson mom passed rare tick borne illness to newborn*. NBC Connecticut. Retrieved from http://www.nbcconnecticut.com/news/local/Thompson-Mom-Passed-Rare-Tick-Borne-Illness-to-Newborn-44 2057583
23. Horowitz, R. (2014). Co-infections presentation, diagnosis, and treatment. *Symposium on Tick-borne Diseases*. May 17. USA: Maryland. Retrieved from https://www.youtube.com/watch?v=O9a-2Nb2sbk
24. LeBel, D., et al. (2017). Cases of transfusion-transmitted Babesiosis occurring in nonendemic areas: A diagnostic dilemma. *Transfusion*. doi: 10.1111/trf.1426
25. Kaewmongkol, G., et al. (2011). Genetic characterization of flea-derived Bartonella species from native animals in Australia suggests host-parasite co-evolution. *Infection Genetics and Evolution*, 11(8), 1868-1872.
26. Singleton, K. (2008). *The Lyme disease solution*. USA: BookSurge Publishing.
27. Fearn, D. (2017). Co-infections: Answers to the most commonly-asked questions. *The Lyme Times Special Issue: Patients Issue*. Retrieved from https://www.lymedisease.org/members/lyme-times/special-issues/patient-issue/lyme-disease-co-infections
28. Breitschwerdt, E., et al. (2010). Molecular evidence of perinatal transmission of Bartonella vinsonii susbsp. Berkhoffii and Bartonella henselae to a Child. *Journal of Clinical Microbiology*, 48(6), 2289-2293. doi: 10.1128/JCM. 00326-10

29. Horowitz, R. (2017). *How can I get better?: An action plan for treating resistant Lyme & chronic disease*. New York: St. Martin's Press.
30. Hirsch, E. (2017). Co-infection Bartonella treatment. *Chronic Lyme Disease Summit 2*, June 21. Health Talks Online. Retrieved from http://chroniclymediseasesummit2.com/expert/evan-h-hirsch
31. CDC. (2017a). *Op. cit.*
32. CDC. (2017b). Other spotted fever group rickettsioses. Centers for Disease Control and Prevention. Retrieved from https://www.cdc.gov/otherspottedfever
33. Buhner, S. (2015). *Healing Lyme: Natural healing of Lyme Borreliosis and the co-infections Chlamydia and Spotted Fever Rickettsioses*. New Mexico: Raven Press.
34. Dhand, A., et al. (2007). Human Granulocytic Anaplasmosis during pregnancy: Case series and literature review. *Clinical Infectious Diseases, 45*(5), 589-593. doi: 10.1086/520659
35. Jereb, M., et al. (2012). Severe Human Granulocytic Anaplasmosis transmitted by blood transfusion. *Emerging Infectious Diseases, 18*(8), 1354-1357. doi: 10.320 1/eid1808.120180
36. Rowan, K. (2013). *Ehrlichiosis, rare tick infection, spread to 9-year-old boy via blood transfusion*. Huffington Post. Retrieved from http://www.huffingtonpost.com/2013/0 4/03/ehrlichiosis-blood-transfusion-tick-infection-9-year-old-boy_n_3009093.html
37. CDC. (2016). *Preventing ticks in the yard – Create a tick-safe zone through landscaping*. Centers for Disease Control and Prevention. Retrieved from https://www.cdc.gov/lyme/prev/in_the_yard.html

38. Nicholson, W., & Paddock, C. (2017). Rickettsia (spotted & typhus fevers) & related infections, including Anaplasmosis & Ehrlichiosis. In G. Brunette (Ed.). *CDC Yellow Book 2018: Health Information for International Travel*. USA: Oxford University Press.
39. Rawls, B. (2016). *Understanding Mycoplasma: Mycoplasma, the most common Lyme co-infection*. RawlsMD. Retrieved from https://rawlsmd.com/health -articles/mycoplasma-the-most-common-lyme-co-infec tion
40. Institute of Medicine. (2011). *Critical needs and gaps in understanding prevention, amelioration, and resolution of Lyme and other tick-borne diseases: The short-term and long-term outcomes: Workshop report*. Washington, DC: The National Academies Press. doi: 10.17226/13134
41. Berghoff, W. (2012). Chronic Lyme disease and co-infections: Differential diagnosis. *The Open Neurology Journal*, 6, 158-178. doi: 10.2174/1874205X01206010158
42. De la Fuente, J., Kocan, K., & Contreras, M. (2017). Tick-pathogen interactions and vector competence: identification of molecular drivers for tick-borne diseases. *Frontiers in Cellular and Infection Microbiology*, 7, 114. doi: 10.3389/fcimb.2017.00114
43. Institute of Medicine. (2011). *Op. cit*.
44. Vredevoe, L. (2017). Background information on the biology of ticks. Tick Biology. University of California: UC Davis Department of Entomyology and Nematology. Retrieved from http://entomology.ucda vis.edu/Faculty/Robert_B_Kimsey/Kimsey_Research/Tick_Biology

45. Theel, E. (2016). *Lyme Disease part 1: The common culprits worldwide – Borrelia burgdorferi, Borrelia garinii, Borrelia afzelii*. Mayo Clinic: MML Education. Retrieved from https://news.mayomedicallaboratories.com/2016/05/02/lyme-disease-part-1-the-common-culprits-worldwide-borrelia-burgdorferi-borrelia-garinii-borrelia-afzelii-hot-topic
46. CDC. (2017c). Life cycle of hard ticks that spread disease – How ticks survive. Centers for Disease Control and Prevention. Retrieved from https://www.cdc.gov/ticks/life_cycle_and_hosts.html
47. Stafford, K. (2004). *Tick management handbook*. The Connecticut Agricultural Experiment Station.
48. Simpson, S., & Casas, J. (Eds.). (2009). Advances in insect physiology. Volume 37. UK: Academic Press.
49. Mitchell, R., et al. (2017). Infrared light detection by the haller's organ of adult American dog ticks, Dermacentor variabilis (Ixodida: Ixodidae). *Ticks and tick-borne diseases, 8*(5), 764-771. doi: 10.1016/j.ttbdis.2017.06.001
50. CDC. (2017a). *Op. cit.*
51. CDC. (2017c). *Op. cit.*
52. Jaenson, T., et al. (2012). Why is tick-borne encephalitis increasing? A review of the key factors causing the increasing incidence of human TBE in Sweden. *Parasites and Vectors, 5*, 184. doi: 10.1186/1756-3305-5-184
53. De la Fuente, J., Kocan, K., & Contreras, M. (2017). *Op. cit.*

[54] Salkeld, D., et al. (2014). Seasonal activity patterns of the Western black-legged tick, Ixodes pacificus, in relation to onset of human Lyme disease in northwestern California. *Ticks and Tick-Borne Diseases, 5*(6), 790-796.

[55] ESA. (2015). *ESA position statement on tick-borne diseases*. Entomological Society of America. Retrieved from http://www.entsoc.org/PDF/2015/ESA-PolicyStatement-TickBorneDiseases.pdf

5. How Can You Prevent Getting Bitten By A Tick?

The best way to prevent any disease is to avoid catching it in the first place, and in the case of Lyme and co-infections, that generally means avoiding a tick bite. If you are in an area where ticks or other biting insects are prevalent, it is likely best to take the following precautions in order to prevent any bites, particularly when outside near bush or grassy areas.

Prevention
For prevention of a tick bite, consider the following tips regarding clothing, hiking, checking, repelling, and landscaping.[1-3] Information on vaccinating, and obtaining a preventative, is also touched upon.

Clothing.
Dress defensively. Wear light colored clothing so it is easier to see a tick, wear long sleeved shirts and pants, and tuck the pants into your socks or boots so you have less skin exposed, and wear close-toe shoes. Also, make sure to apply repellant.

Hiking.
When hiking, stay in the middle of trails, and try to avoid tall grass and other areas where ticks might

be hiding like leaf litter, grassy areas, and fallen logs. Carry a specialist tick removal tool with your gear.

Checking.

Periodically check for ticks when outside. If you find a tick on your clothing, use tweezers to pick them off and dispose of them in the garbage or place them in a container for later testing. Once home, remove your hiking clothes before entering the house. As heat can kill ticks, a recommendation is to place clothes directly into a dryer for a minimum of six minutes on high heat, or if washing clothes first, do so in water that is greater than or equal to 130°F (54°C).[4] Then, take a shower and look yourself over. Feel for any embedded bumps that could be a tick. Pay particular attention to where ticks like to hide on the body including the armpits, belly button, groin, and scalp. Remember to check your kids, your pets, and all your hiking gear as well.

Repelling.

Spray clothing with a repellent that contains an active ingredient like DEET[5] (N,N-Diethyl-meta-toluamide) or lemon eucalyptus oil.[6,7]

Landscaping.

At home, a 3 foot (90cm) or more barrier of gravel, mulch, or wood chips around the borders of a yard may prevent ticks from entering the yard.[8] The removal of leaf litter reduces the abundance of nymphs* by nearly 75-77%, whereas the use of chemical or natural treatments on yards varies between products, and it generally lasts for only a short period of time.[9]

Vaccinating/Preventative.

Currently, there is no known vaccine for Lyme and its co-infections. The LymeRix vaccine that was available from 1998 to 2002,[10] like almost everything associated with Lyme, is surrounded by controversy, politics, and an air of conspiracy. However, Valneva has been working on a vaccine, and it has recently been approved for clinical trials in America and Europe.[11] The Lyme pre-exposer prophylaxis (Lyme PReP)[12] is an injectable preventative that would provide protection from Lyme over a spring to fall time-frame, and is currently showing promising results with mice. Herbal alternatives used as a preventative are currently available.[13]

A View from the Field – Rash, What Rash? Bite?

I am one of the people who do not recall ever having a tick on me, or being bitten. I was also never examined by a doctor for *erythema migrans*, the EM

---

* The *nymph* is the third stage in a four-stage tick life cycle – egg, larvae (seed tick), nymph, adult

rash associated with a tick bite and an early sign of disease, and if there was one, it was not visible to me when showering or looking in the mirror. This is not unusual. Only 50% of people ever recall seeing a rash,[14] and as ticks numb the skin before attaching,[15] less than 50% of the people that do find *erythema migrans* on themselves ever recall being bitten.[16,17] It is also important to know that the rash may not always look like a 'bull's eye', especially with co-infections.[18] As for children, only 50% ever recall a tick attachment, and less than 10% present with *erythema migrans*.[19,20] This is the main reason why you can't always wait for a rash to appear if you know that you have been bitten.

If you do start to experience any symptoms, then aim to present these to a physician for evaluation, but this can be problematic. If only there was increased physician awareness of the possibility of contracting Lyme, or a *Lyme-like illness* and/or its co-infections where I was living at the time that I contracted my illness, as well as increased public awareness of the possibility of exposure, then I would have pushed for treatment or a blood test. Instead, I was simply told to *just drink more water, flush it out, and come back in a week if you still feel fluish*. After one month of being ill, and one month of visiting a GP every week, I was also constantly told that *there is no need for antibiotics or tests*, that I *look fit and healthy*, and that I'll *just fight it off*. Today, I'm still struggling to fight it off. Early treatment and a correct diagnosis are important.[21,22]

So is the quick removal of a tick if seen on you, your family, your friends, or your pets.[23]

References

1. CDC. (2016). *Preventing ticks in the yard – Create a tick-safe zone through landscaping*. Centers for Disease Control and Prevention. Retrieved from https://www.cdc.gov/lyme/prev/in_the_yard.html
2. LDAA. (2017). *Prevention*. Lyme Disease Association of
Australia. Retrieved from http://www.lymedisease.org.au/about-lyme-disease/prevention
3. WebMD. (2017). *Ticks: How to avoid and remove ticks – Overview*. First Aid & Emergencies. Retrieved from http://www.webmd.com/first-aid/tc/how-to-remove-a-tickoverview#1
4. Nelson, C., et al. (2016). The heat is on: Killing blacklegged ticks in residential washers and dryers to prevent tick borne diseases. *Ticks and Tick-Borne Diseases, 7*(5), 958-963. doi: 10.1016/j.ttbdis.2016.04.016
5. Alperm, J., et al. (2016). Personal protection measures against mosquitoes, ticks, and other arthropods. *Medical Clinics, 100*(2), 303-316. doi: 10.1016/j.mcna.2-15.08.019
6. Gandulf, A., Wohlfart, I., & Gustafson, R. (2004). A prospective cross-over field trial shows protection of lemon Eucalyptus extract against tick bites. *Journal of Medical Entomology,* 41(6), 1064-1067. doi: 10.1603/0022-2585-41.6. 1064
7. Diaz, J. (2016). Chemical and plant-based insect repellents: Efficacy, safety, and toxicity. *Wilderness & Environmental Medicine, 27*(1), 153-163. doi: 10.1016/j.wem.2015.11.007

8. Stafford, K. (2004). *Tick Management Handbook*. The Connecticut Agricultural Experiment Station.
9. Eisen, L., & Dolan, M. (2016). Evidence for personal protective measures to reduce human contact with blacklegged ticks and for environmentally based control methods to suppress host-seeking blacklegged ticks and reduce infection with Lyme disease spirochetes in tick vectors and rodent reservoirs. *Journal of Medical Entomology, 53*(5), 1063-1092. doi: 10.1093/jme /tjw103
10. Mosher, D. (2016). *A new Lyme disease vaccine will soon be tested on Americans and Europeans*. Business Insider. Retrieved from http://www.businessinsider.com/lyme-disease-vaccine-valneva-clinical-trial-2016-12
11. Valneva. (2016). *Valneva Receives FDA and European Approvals to Start Clinical Testing of Lyme Disease Vaccine Candidate*. Investor Meeting and Live Webcast on Lyme Disease. Global Newswire. Retrieved from http://www.Einnews.com/pr_news/357341934/valneva-valneva-received-fda-and-european-approvals-to-start-clinical-testing-of-lyme-disease-vaccine-candidate
12. Ward, B., & Leslie, J. (2017). Local doctor explains a new shot that could protect you from Lyme disease. WesternMass News. Retrieved from http://www.westernmassnews.com/story/35852852/local-doctor-explains-a-new-shot-that-could-protect-you-from-lyme-disease

13. Buhner, S. (2017). *Q & A. Stephen Harrod Buhner answers questions about his herbal protocols for Lyme disease and co-infections.* Buhner Healing Lyme: Planet Thrive Inc. Retrieved from http://buhnerhealinglyme.com
14. Singleton, K. (2008). *The Lyme disease solution.* USA: BookSurge Publishing.
15. McFadzean, N. (2012). *The beginner's guide to Lyme disease: Diagnosis and treatment made simple.* USA: BioMed Publishing Group.
16. Mercola, J. (2012). *Under our skin: The untold story of Lyme disease.* Mercola: Take Control of Your Health. Retrieved from http://articles.mercola.com/sites/ /articles/archive/2012/10/13/under-our-skin-documentary.asp x
17. LDAA. (2017). *Op. cit.*
18. Horowitz, R., in Manny, D. (2016). *The Lyme disease debate: Can the condition be chronic?* Fox News Interview. Retrieved from http://www.foxnews.com/health/2016/05/25/lyme-disease-debate-can-condition-be-chronic.html
19. Lymedisease.org. (2017). *Children with Lyme disease.* Lymedisease.org: Advocacy, Education, & Research. Retrieved from https://www.lymedisease.org/lyme-basics/lyme-disease/children
20. Jones, C. (2017). *50 Frequently asked questions & answers.* Dr. Jones Kids. Retrieved from https://sites.google.com/site/drjoneskids/faq-answers
21. Manny, D. (2016). *The Lyme disease debate: Can the condition be chronic?* Fox News Interview. Retrieved from http://www.foxnews.com/health/2016/05/25/lyme-diseas e-debate-can-condition-be-chronic.html

22. Rippey, M. (2017). *Episode 123: Jean Monro, MD – UK Lyme expert*. Lyme Ninja Radio. Retrieved from http://lymeninjaradio.com/ 123-jean-monro-md
23. Cook, M. (2015). Lyme Borreliosis: A review of data on transmission time After tick attachment. *International Journal of General Medicine, 8*, 1-8. doi: 10.2147/IJGM.S 73791

6. How Do You Remove A Tick?

If you notice a tick on you, on your friends and family including pets, or on clothing, you'll need to know some of the best ways to remove it, and also take into account any allergies or toxic effects that may result from a bite. Not all ticks carry Lyme and/or its co-infections,[1] but you should still keep a watch for any symptoms in yourself or any children that have been bitten, and if a pet has been bitten, then a vet visit would be wise. Once removed, the tick could be sent for testing to determine if there is a need for any treatment, and as an alternative to relying on herbals,[2] you could seek conventional medical advice.

Tick Removal

You might decide to remove the tick yourself or you could seek medical help for removal. However, it is recommended to remove the tick as soon as possible.[3] Possible ways to remove a tick include: use of a special tool, fine-tipped-pointed tweezers, cotton thread, or by freezing. If you do decide to remove the tick yourself and are having any trouble seek medical assistance from a clinic, hospital, or emergency department to safely remove it.

Specialist Tool.

A special tick removal tool is designed to grip the head of the tick itself and not to squash its body. Follow the manufacturer instructions carefully.

Fine-Tipped, Pointed, Tweezers.

Using fine-tipped pointed tweezers, grasp the tick as close to the skin as you can, then pull the tick out without twisting.[4] However, it might be difficult to use tweezers without separating the head of the tick from the body.

Cotton Thread.

If you do not have access to the special tool or the fine-tipped pointed tweezers, then you might be able to use a cotton thread.[5] Tie a single loop around the mouth of the tick, as close to the skin as you can, then pull up and out without twisting.

Freezing.

Ticks can prove very difficult to remove and freezing is another option for removal. One that may prevent live contents from the tick midgut being injected into the blood stream if the body of the tick is squashed in an attempt to remove it. You could use an over-the-counter product such as Aerostart (a spray containing benzene used to start car engines that is not registered for use on humans) or ether-containing sprays like those that are used to freeze off warts.[6] Doctors or other medical professionals would likely use liquid nitrogen. Killing the tick by freezing prior to removal is the method recommended by the Australasian Society of Clinical Immunology and Allergy (ASCIA), as this method can potentially reduce the risk of developing tick sensitization while also preventing it from injecting more allergen-containing saliva into the body.[7]

After Removal.

Once the tick is removed, disinfect the bite area and the removal tool, fine-tipped pointed tweezers, or cotton thread with rubbing alcohol, store the tick in a container and consider sending it for testing, and then wash your hands. After tick removal, keep an eye out for the emergence of a rash (*erythema migrans*) or other symptoms of illness. Seek medical advice where necessary, telling the doctor about the recent tick bite, when it occurred, and where it occurred.[8]

Things to Avoid.

Avoid crushing the tick with your fingers, burning the tick, or painting the tick with any substance, such as methylated spirits. Avoid squeezing the body of the tick. Squeezing the tick while it is attached to you could release toxic contents into your blood stream.[9] Toxins from tick saliva can cause tick paralysis, leading to unsteadiness, lethargy, visual disturbances, breathing difficulties, and weakness of arms, face, or legs, and these would require immediate medical attention.[10]

Allergic Reaction.

Allergic reaction to a tick bite could be mild or severe. Mild reactions can cause itching and swelling, can be treated with cold compresses and moisturizes and if persistent will need medical attention.[11] Severe reactions may lead to anaphylactic shock, and would need immediate medical attention as these can be life-threatening. If you are allergic to a tick bite, seek medical assistance from a clinic, hospital, or emergency department to safely remove the tick. There are also recommendations for those with allergies to kill the tick with a product that will rapidly freeze it prior to removal.[12]

A View from the Field – Time to Lyme Infection

Ticks that carry Lyme disease are now spread across almost half of all counties in the United States, and are particularly increasing in the northeastern and northcentral states while southern states remain stable.[13] To date, regular tick checks and the quick removal of them, if seen, are the best methods of preventing the transmission of Lyme disease, along with controlling tick populations and the animal populations that ticks feed upon.[14] It has been found that nymphs, as opposed to larval and adult ticks, are the most common source of transmission for Lyme,[15] with infection greatest in late spring and during summer.[16] Recent animal studies show low risk of infection from a single nymph to a mouse in the first 48 hours. After 72 hours, 31% of mice were infected, 57% after 4 to 5 days,[17] but with two ticks attached, transmission did result after 48 hours. Still, no minimum transmission time has been confirmed across the literature, and it could vary upon the type of vector, the *Borrelia* species, or other pathogens involved.[18] It is deemed likely that infection could occur in humans shortly after a tick attachment. Experimental data indicates that Lyme disease spirochete transmission can occur in less than 16 hours and frequently in less than 24 hours.[19] However, studies also suggest that 11% of nymphal ticks have systemic infection,[20] and in cases where spirochetes are present in the tick mouth parts and salivary glands transmission can potentially be instant upon attachment to a host.[21] With *Ixodus scapularis* (the black-legged tick, or deer tick) it has been found that 14 times more spirochetes are required in midgut extracts to infect compared to salivary gland extracts, with the median infective dose being 18 spirochetes within salivary gland extract compared to that of 251 with midgut extract.[22]

References

[1] Shapiro, E. (2011). Lyme disease in children. In J. Halperin (Ed.). *Lyme Disease: An Evidence-based Approach* (221-231). USA: CABI.

[2] Buhner, S. (2017). *Q & A. Stephen Harrod Buhner answers questions about his herbal protocols for Lyme disease and co-infections*. Buhner Healing Lyme: Planet Thrive Inc. Retrieved from http://buhnerhealinglyme.com

[3] CDC. (2017). *Tick removal and testing*. Centers for Disease Control and Prevention. Retrieved from https://www.cdc.gov/lyme/removal/index.html

[4] CDC. (2015). *Tick Removal*. Centers for Disease Control and Prevention. Retrieved from https://www.cdc.gov/ticks/removing_a_tick.html

[5] LDAUK. (2017). *Tick removal. How do I remove a tick?* Lyme Disease Association of the United Kingdom. Retrieved from http://www.lymediseaseaction.org.uk/about-ticks/tick-removal

[6] Ryan, C., & Hales, L. (2016). *Tick removal: What's the best way to get them out?* Health News. Retrieved from http://www.abc.net.au/news/health/2016-11-02/the-tick-debate:-how-should-you-pull-them-out/7541358

[7] ASCIA. (2016). *Tick allergy*. Australasian Society of Clinical Immunology and Allergy. Retrieved from https://www.allergy.org.au/patients/insect-allergy-bites-and-stings/tick-allergy

[8] CDC. (2015). *Op. cit*.

[9] LDAA. (2017). *Personal protection*. Lyme Disease Association of Australia. Retrieved from http://www.lymedisease.org.au/about-lyme-disease/prevention

[10] NSW Health. (2016). *Tick alert*. Ticks. Retrieved from http://www.health.nsw.gov.au/environment/pests/parasites/Pages/ticks.aspx

11. NSW Health. (2016). *Ibid*.
12. Ryan, C., & Hales, L. (2016). Tick removal: What's the best way to get them out? ABC News. Retrieved from http://www.abc.net.au/news/health/2016-11-02/the-tick-debate:-how-should-you-pull-them-out/7541358
13. Eisen, R., Eisen, L., & Beard, C. (2016). County-scale distribution of Ixodes scapularis and Ixodes pacificus (Acari: Ixodidae) in the continental United States. *Journal of Medical Entomology, 53*(2), 349-386. doi: 10.1093/jme/tjv237
14. Eisen, L., & Dolan, M. (2016). Evidence for personal protective measures to reduce human contact with blacklegged ticks and for environmentally based control methods to suppress host-seeking blacklegged ticks and reduce infection with Lyme disease spirochetes in tick vectors and rodent reservoirs. *Journal of Medical Entomology, 53*(5), 1063-1092. doi: 10.1093/jme/ tjw103
15. Dolan, M., et al. (2017). Transmission of the Lyme disease spirochete Borrelia mayonii in relation to duration of attachment by Nymphal Ixodes scapularis (Acari: Ixodidae). *Journal of Medical Entomology, tjx089*, 1-5. doi: 10.1093/jme/tjx089
16. CDC. (2017). Life cycle of hard ticks that spread disease – How ticks survive. Centers for Disease Control and Prevention. Retrieved fromhttps://www.cdc.gov/ticks/life_cycle_and_hosts.html
17. Dolan, M., et al. (2017). *Op. cit.*
18. Richards, S., et al. (2017). Do Tick Attachment Times Vary between Different Tick-Pathogen Systems? *Environments, 4*(37), 1-14. doi: 10.3390/environments4020037

[19] Cook, M. (2015). Lyme Borreliosis: A review of data on transmission time After tick attachment. *International Journal of General medicine, 8,* 1-8. doi: 10.2147/IJGM.S73791

[20] Lebet, N. & Gern, L. (1994). Histological examination of *Borrelia burgdorferi* infections in unfed *Ixodes ricinus* nymphs. *Experimental and Applied Acarology, 18*(3), 177-183. doi: 10.1007/BF02353685

[21] Cook, M. (2015). *Op. cit.*

[22] Lima, C. et al. (2005). Differential infectivity of the Lyme disease spirochete Borrelia burgdorferi derived from Ixodes scapularis salivary glands and midgut. *Journal of Medical Entomology, 42*(3), 506-510. doi: 10.1603/0022-2585(2005)042[0506:DIOTLD]2.0.CO;2

7. What Are The Symptoms Of Lyme And Its Common Co-infections?

The signs and symptoms lists in this chapter aim to present those that are most commonly seen in people with the infections. It is important to understand that not all people will develop all of the symptoms on each list, and the number and the combination of symptoms will also vary from one person to another.[1] This is one of the reasons why Lyme and/or its co-infections are so difficult to diagnose, and because the signs and symptoms can present like a number of other diseases, people can go misdiagnosed for many years.[2,3]

Indicators of Lyme and its Co-infections

The section below will look at some of the diseases that Lyme likes to mimic, along with the symptoms associated with the disease in various stages. This includes taking into account how it can present differently in children and what might need to be taken into account for those who are aged. An overview of symptoms associated with a number of the co-infections that people may acquire will also be presented, while more comprehensive lists (covering *Borrelia* as well as *Babesia*, *Bartonella*, *Ehrlichia/ Anaplasma*, *Rickettsia*, and *Mycoplasma*), can be found in the appendices.

The Great Imitator.

Lyme is a spirochete like syphilis, and like syphilis, it is called a *stealth pathogen*[4,5] and *the great imitator*.[6,7] Symptoms are widely variable because the microbe affects each person differently,[8] working its way into every possible body system.[9] It is often misdiagnosed because it can mimic over 250 other diseases.[10,11] A short list of these include:[12-16]

- Alzheimer's disease
- Amyotrophic lateral sclerosis (ALS – Lou Gehrig's disease)
- Attention deficit disorder (ADD)
- Autism
- Bipolar disorder
- Chronic fatigue syndrome (CFS)
- Crohn's disease
- Encephalitis
- Fibromyalgia
- Interstitial cystitis
- Irritable bowel syndrome (IBS)
- Juvenile rheumatoid arthritis
- Lupus
- Meningitis
- Motor neuron disease
- Multiple sclerosis (MS)
- Neuralgia

Chapter 7: Signs & Symptoms | 73

- Obsessive compulsive disorder (OCD)
- Parkinson's disease
- Raynaud's syndrome
- Rheumatoid arthritis
- Scleroderma
- Sjorgen's syndrome
- Thyroiditis
- Vaculitis ... ... The list goes on.

Lyme Borreliosis Symptoms.

Symptoms of Lyme disease can be vague, non-specific, changeable, and not all present at the same time. However, it is important to be aware of what *might* be associated with the disease[17] in both the acute and early to late phases, and when looking for symptoms in children.

Early Localized/Acute Lyme Symptoms –

The Rash & the Flu. The best indications of an initial infection with Lyme disease are:[18]

- The emergence of *erythema migrans*, or a 'bull's eye rash'
- A rash appearing between 3 and 32 days after a tick bite

Other early symptoms include:[19,20]

- A flu-like illness
- Muscle/joint pain
- Stiff neck
- Tender glands
- Sensitivity to light

- Sound sensitivity
- Temperature sensitivity
- Unexplained fatigue

Early Disseminated to Late Disseminated Lyme Symptoms. The following list provides possible indicators of Lyme at the early and the late disseminated stages.[21,22] However, a much more comprehensive list of symptoms for Lyme disease (*Borreliosis*) can be found in Appendix A, and this has been provided courtesy of the Lyme Disease Association of Australia.[23] Lyme disease has a multitude of symptoms,[24] and not all will be present simultaneously. They may come and go, and be subtle or pronounced.[25]

Early disseminated (1 to 4 months of infection).
- Fainting spells
- Fatigue, extreme tiredness
- Headaches, severe/recurring
- Heart palpitations
- Irritability
- Memory and concentration problems
- Mood disorders
- Migrating pains
- Panic attacks
- Rashes
- Twitching muscles
- Vibration/buzzing feeling
- Vision problems
- Weakness/numbness in arms/legs

Late disseminated (4+ months of infection).

- Abdominal pains, nausea
- Back pain
- Blurred vision and eye pain
- Change in bowel functions, diarrhea
- Chest pain and heart palpitations
- Depression
- Disturbed sleep – too much, too little, early awakening
- Dizziness
- Facial paralysis, numbness, pain, tingling, palsy
- Fatigue, tiredness, low stamina
- Fever, low grade (hot flashes/chills)
- Headaches
- Irritability and mood swings
- Jaw pain
- Lightheadedness, wooziness
- Migrating joint pain, stiffness and, less commonly, frank arthritis
- Muscle pain
- Night sweats
- Poor concentration and memory loss, difficulty in thinking
- Sore throat
- Stiff neck
- Swollen glands
- Testicular/pelvic pain
- Tinnitus
- Vertigo

Symptoms in Children. It can be difficult for parents to know if children are sick with Lyme[26] because they may not always be able to describe their symptoms as effectively as adults. While the signs and symptoms of Lyme in children are similar to adults, there are some differences,[27,28] particularly:

- Being overwhelmed by schoolwork
- Confusion
- Difficulty making decisions
- Difficulty thinking and expressing thoughts
- Difficulty with reading and writing
- Dizziness
- Fatigue (can be severe, unrelieved by rest)
- Fevers/chills
- Headaches
- Impaired concentration
- Inability to sustain attention
- Insomnia
- Joint pain
- Nausea, abdominal pain
- Noise and light sensitivity
- Outbursts and mood swings
- Poor short-term memory
- Uncharacteristic behavior

The Aged. As we age, the decline in our overall physical fitness and of our bodily functions is often seen as normal or expected,[29] as are the symptoms of dementia and Alzheimer's.[30] It may be difficult to determine if or how Lyme and its co-infections might impact a geriatric patient.[31] If you have an older loved one in a nursing home or at home, then there may be a need to advocate for them if they have been infected. Even if not infected, they will likely still need to be monitored for a potential infection as they age and become more dependent on others, particularly if they live in an endemic area, and especially if they are unable to express symptoms that could indicate Lyme or a co-infection.

Symptoms of Common Co-infections

All symptoms of Lyme tend to be worse with co-infections,[32] and over 60% of Lyme patients have one or more,[33] and they are some of the main reasons that many people with Lyme do not get better. Appendix B provides a comprehensive symptoms list for *Babesia, Bartonella, Ehrlichia/Anaplasma, Rickettsia,* and *Mycoplasma*, while a very brief overview of the symptoms for each is presented below.

Babesia[34-36]
- Anemia
- Perspiration – day/night sweats
- Fatigue
- Fever
- Jaundice
- Shortness of breath
- Weakness

Bartonella[37-40]

- Cognitive dysfunction
- Fatigue
- Headache
- Mood swings
- Muscle weakness
- Seizures
- Swollen lymph nodes
- Symptoms that may come and go
- Vision and eye problems

Ehrlichia/Anaplasma[41-44]

- Bloodshot eyes
- Chills
- Confusion
- Fever
- Gastrointestinal symptoms (anorexia, diarrhea, nausea, vomiting)
- Headaches
- Malaise
- Muscle Pain
- Rashes (more common in children)

Rickettsia[45-47]

- Digestive problems
- Fever
- Headache
- Nausea/vomiting
- Muscle pain
- Rash

Mycoplasma[48]
- Anxiety
- Confusion
- Decreased attention
- Fatigue
- Fever
- Insomnia
- Joint pain, occasional swelling
- Memory problems
- Mood changes
- Muscle pain

A View from the Field – Symptoms Surveys, Questionnaires, and Checklists

If you, your loved one, or someone who you are caring for is being treated for Lyme disease, and/or its co-infections, then symptoms need to be tracked. If health is improving, then a physician might advise weaning off medication. If things are on a plateau, a physician could advise a need to adjust medication or supplements. If things are going backwards, a physician may then advise the need for more medication or a change in the ones being taken.

A paper-based diary can be used to track levels of fatigue and symptoms, and along with medication reminders, food trackers, and note taking, there are a number of smart-phone or computer-based diary applications available as well (see the resources list). You might also decide to create your own survey, questionnaire, or checklist once you are well enough, and such a symptoms tracker is included in Appendix C. Additionally, there are a number of symptom surveys, questionnaires, and checklists available from a number of different sources including online. Several that assess for Lyme disease or a co-infection are presented below.

- The Lymedisease.org website has a useful online survey to check if your symptoms are that of Lyme disease.[49]
- Jenner[50] has also compiled a comprehensive symptom list regarding Lyme co-infections.
- In his latest book, Horowitz[51] presents The *Horowitz Lyme-MSIDS Questionnaire,* and it can help in determining the likelihood of having Lyme and/or an associated tick-borne disorder. It is also available from the book's website.[52]

References

[1] Burrascano, J. (2008). *Diagnostic hints and treatment guidelines for Lyme and other tick borne illnesses 16th ed.* Advanced Topics in Lyme Disease. Retrieved from http://www.lymenet.org/BurrGuide200810.pdf

[2] Maloney, E. (2007). Basic principles of laboratory testing for Lyme disease. *The Lyme Times, 50,* 26-28.

3. Editor. (2017). Do you have Lyme? *The Lyme Times Special Issue: Patient's Issue*. Retrieved from https://www.lymedisease.org/members/lyme-times/sp ecial-issues/patient-issue/do-you-have-lyme-disease
4. Stricker, R., & Johnson, L. (2011). Lyme disease: The next decade. *Infection and Drug Resistance, 4*, 1-9. doi: 10.2147/IDR.S 15653
5. Radolf, J., et al. (2016). Treponema pallidum, the Syphilis spirochete: Making a living as a stealth pathogen. *Nature Reviews Microbiology, 14*(12), 744-759. doi: 10.1038/nrmicro.2016.141
6. Hamilton, D. (1989). Lyme disease. The hidden pandemic. *Postgraduate Medical Journal, 85*(5), 303-308, 313-314.
7. Margulis, L., et al. (2009). Lyme disease & AIDS: Resurgence of the 'great imitator'. *Symbiosis, 47*, 51-58.
8. Rawls, W. (2017). *Unlocking Lyme: Myths, truths, & practical solutions for chronic Lyme disease*. USA: FirstDoNoHarm Publishing.
9. McFadzean, N. (2012). *The beginner's guide to Lyme disease: Diagnosis and treatment made simple*. USA: BioMed Publishing Group.
10. UMMC. (2005). *Conditions with similar symptoms as: Lyme disease*. University of Maryland Medical Center. Retrieved from http://www.umm.edu/health/medical / altmed/condition-symptom-links/conditions-with-similar-symptoms-as-lyme-disease
11. Jenner, L. (2013). *Lyme is often misdiagnosed as other diseases and disorders*. Lyme-Symptoms. Retrieved from http://www.lyme-symptoms.com/Lyme Mimics.html

12. Klinghardt, D. (2005). Lyme disease: A look beyond antibiotics. *Explore Magazine, 14*(2). Retrieved from http://www.psychostrategy.net/article-lyme-disease-a-look-beyond-antibiotics-dietrich-k-klinghardt-md-phd-67183654.html
13. UMMC. (2005). *Op. cit.*
14. Singleton, K. (2008). *The Lyme disease solution.* USA: BookSurge Publishing.
15. McFadzean, N. (2012). *Op. cit.*
16. Jenner, L. (2013). *Op. cit.*
17. Vanderhoof-Forschner, K. (2004). *Everything you need to know about Lyme disease and other tick-borne disorders.* USA: John Wiley & Sons.
18. Merck Manual. (2017). *Lyme disease.* Merck Manual Professional Version. Retrieved from http://www.merckmanuals.com/professional/infectious-diseases/spirochetes/lyme-disease
19. McFadzean, N. (2012). *Op. cit.*
20. Stanek, G., Wormser, G., & Strle, F. (2012). Lyme Borreliosis. *Lancet, 379*(9814), 461-473. doi: 10.1016/S014 0-6736(11)60103-7
21. Bean, C., & Fein, L. (2008). *Beating Lyme: Understanding and treating this complex and often misdiagnosed disease.* USA: AMACOM.
22. ILADS. (2004). *The International Lyme and Associated Diseases Society: Evidence-based guidelines for the management of Lyme disease.* The ILADS Working Group: Future Drugs Ltd.
23. LDAA. (2017). *About Lyme disease.* Lyme Disease Association of Australia. Retrieved from http://www.lymedisease.org.au/about-lyme-disease-2
24. Global Lyme Alliance. (2017b). *The diagnosis dilemma.* Global Lyme Alliance. Retrieved from https://globallyme alliance.org/about-lyme/diagnosis

25. Singleton, K. (2008). *Op. cit.*
26. Lymedisease.org. (2017). *Children with Lyme disease*. Lymedisease.org: Advocacy, Education, & Research. Retrieved from https://www.lymedisease.org/lyme-basics/lyme-disease/children
27. Vanderhoof-Forschner, K. (2004). *Op. cit.*
28. Jones, C. (2017). *Lab test info*. Children with Lyme & TickBorne Diseases. Dr. Jones Kids. Retrieved from https://sites.google.com/site/drjoneskids/lab-tests
29. Milanovic, Z., et al. (2013). Age-related decrease in physical activity and functional fitness among elderly men and women. *Clinical Interventions in Aging, 8,* 549-556. doi: 10.2147/CIA.S44112
30. Harada, C., Love, M., & Triebel, 2016). Normal cognitive aging. *Clinics in Geriatric Medicine, 29*(4), 737-752. doi: 10.1016/j.cger.2013.07.002
31. Langhoff, P. (2007). *"It's all in your head" Patient stories from the front lines: Intimate aspects of chronic and neuropsychiatric Lyme disease*. USA: Allegory Press.
32. Horowitz, R. (2017). *How can I get better?: An action plan for treating resistant Lyme & chronic disease*. New York: St. Martin's Press.
33. Horowitz, R. (2014). Co-infections presentation, diagnosis, and treatment. *Symposium on Tick-borne Diseases*. May 17. USA: Maryland. Retrieved from https://www.youtube.com/watch?v=O9a-2Nb2sbk
34. Anderson, W. (2010). *Babesia like organisms (BABLO): Consideration, signs, and symptoms*. Gordon Medical. Retrieved from http://www.gordonmedical.com/unravelling-complex-chronic-illness/babesia-like-organisms-bablo-consideration-signs-and-symptoms

35. Schaller, J., & Mountjoy, K. (2015, July). Advanced 2015 Babesia care: Profound testing defects and preventing disability and death. *Townsend Letter: The Examiner of Alternative Medicine*. Retrieved from http://www.townsendletter.com/July2015/babesia0715.html
36. Fearn, D. (2017). Co-infections: Answers to the most commonly-asked questions. *The Lyme Times Special Issue: Patients Issue*. Retrieved from https://www.lymedisease.org/members/lyme-times/special- issues/patient-issue/lyme-disease-co-infections
37. Schaller, J. (2007). *Ignore Bartonella and die: Trivializing Bartonella is like ignoring TNT*. Public Health Alert: Investigating Lyme and Chronic Illness. Retrieved from http://www.publichealthalert.org/ignore-bartonella-and-die-trivializing-bartonella-is-like-ignoring-tnt.html
38. Singleton, K. (2008). *Op. cit.*
39. Forsgren, S. (2015, July). Unravelling the mystery of Bartonellosis. *Townsend letter: The Examiner of Alternative Medicine*. Retrieved from http://www.townsendletter.com/July2015/bartonellosis0715.html
40. Fearn, D. (2017). *Op. cit.*
41. Buhner, S. (2015). *Natural treatments for Lyme co-infections: Anaplasma, Babesia, and Ehrlichia*. Vermont: Healing Arts Press.
42. McFadzean, N. (2012). *Op. cit.*
43. Cameron, D. (2017). *The role of co-infections*. All Things Lyme. Retrieved from http://danielcameronmd.com/co-infections

44. CDC. (2017). *Tickborne diseases of the United States: A reference manual for health care providers*, (4th ed). U.S. Department of Health and Human Services. Centers for Disease Control and Prevention.
45. Buhner, S. (2015a). *Healing Lyme: Natural healing of Lyme Borreliosis and the co-infections Chlamydia and Spotted Fever Rickettsioses*. New Mexico: Raven Press.
46. Cox, R. (2016). *Rocky Mountain Spotted Fever symptoms in pictures*. OnHealth. Retrieved from http://www.onhealth.com/content/1/rocky_mountain_spotted_fever
47. CDC. (2017). *Rocky Mountain Spotted Fever (RMSF)*. Centers for Disease Control and Prevention. Retrieved from https://www.cdc.gov/rmsf/symptoms/index.html
48. Brewer, J. (2007). Tickborne diseases and co-infections. *The Lyme Times, 48*, 20-27.
49. Lymedisease.org (2017). Do you have Lyme disease? Lymedisease.org: Advocacy, Education, & Research. Retrieved from http://www.lymedisease.org/lyme-disease-symptom-checklist
50. Jenner, L. (2016). *Comparison chart of Lyme disease and co-infections symptoms*. Lyme-Symptoms. Retrieved from http://www.lyme-symptoms.com/LymeCo-infectionChart.html
51. Horowitz, R. (2017b). The Horowitz Lyme – MSIDS Questionnaire. How Can I get Better? Retrieved from http://www.cangetbetter.com/symptom-list
52. Horowitz, R. (2017). *Op. cit.*
53. Mackey, R. (2018). *Symptom Tracker*. Lyme Ninjas Radio. Retrieved from http://lymeninjaradio.com/tracker

8. What Can Tests Tell You If You Have Lyme And/Or Its Co-infections?

When you are ill, finding out what disease you are fighting means everything. If it is Lyme and/or a co-infection that has been misdiagnosed or left undiagnosed for a long period of time, then it is like an onion – it needs peeling and it has many layers – and now it's a long haul. Lyme may come with any number of co-infections which themselves might come with other co-infections and even without Lyme.[1] Regardless, each infection diagnosed will likely need to be treated.

Typically, doctors follow a linear pattern, and end up treating the worst thing first, since these are the symptoms you will complain about the most. Their training "since the time of Koch and Pasteur" sees them focus on the "defect, or dysfunction, within the patient ... [and] on the physical and biological aspects of specific diseases and conditions" as they manifest.[2] Doctors are trained to categorize the signs and symptoms of illness that are presented by the patient into a meaningful disease grouping. So when tests for Lyme and its co-infections fail, or present as a false negative, doctors such as LLMD (Lyme literate medical doctors) are able to provide a clinical diagnosis.[3] Unfortunately, due to the politics and controversy surrounding Lyme disease, the type of tests you might be offered and how the physician interprets the results will vary. That is, if you are lucky enough to actually get tested. You may need to demand the test as, contrary to recommended practice, only about 75% of health care providers in the United States will order a test when a patient presents with tell-tale signs of infection, such as an EM (*erythema migrans*) rash.[4]

Available Tests

Diagnosing Lyme can be a very real challenge, even for the best physicians, due to lack of a gold standard test.[5] Nonetheless, there are several kinds of tests available to assist a clinician in looking for Lyme which include:

- Antigen detection
- Culture testing
- PCR – polymerase chain reaction
- ELISA – enzyme linked immunosorbent assay
- Western blot

Accuracy of Tests

Unfortunately, Lyme tests are highly inaccurate.[6] Using two-tiered testing in early stages sees false-negatives of up to 36%,[7] but with a specificity of 99%, it sees few false positives.[8] For those "patients with relapsing or persistent symptoms, screening tests such as ELISA are usually negative, but Western blots often show antibody reactions to highly specific proteins."[9] As the process misses 44 out of every 100 patients,[10] Horowitz[11] considers the test a "coin flip",[12] as does Johnson,[13] as it lacks sensitivity to the "100 types of Lyme in the United States and 300 worldwide".[14] Cook and Puri[15] indicate the probability of a false negative test for early-stage Lyme disease is as high as 66.8%, and higher for two-tier testing at 74.9%, generating 60 times as many false negatives compared to similar testing for HIV. For late stage Lyme disease, 16.7% false negatives were found compared to 0.095% for HIV, leading to 500 times more false negative results than two-stage HIV testing.[16] That said, doctors and scientists are continually looking for ways to improve testing, and to accurately identify Lyme and its co-infections in patients[17] such as identifying biomarkers for diagnosis.[18,19] For now though, let's look at some of the tests available.

Testing for Lyme
Antigen Detection, Culture Testing, and PCR (polymerase chain reaction).

Antigen detection, culture testing, and PCR are known as 'direct' tests because these kinds of tests seek to detect the actual bacteria, and not just an immune response to their presence. Antigen tests examine fluids like blood and urine for the presence of proteins only found on the bacteria. Culture tests also take samples of fluid and, using a special medium, attempt to grow Lyme spirochetes. On the other hand, PCR tests attempt to multiply and identify unique portions of DNA from the bacteria. It can be highly accurate when Lyme is detected, but it can produce many false negatives because the Lyme bacteria may not be present in any of the samples provided for testing.[20]

Two-Tier Testing.

The two tests that have most commonly been employed when checking for Lyme disease are the ELISA followed by the Western blot. Both are 'indirect' tests because they look for an antibody response, or an immune response, to the bacteria instead of looking for the actual bacteria. This is done by examining two different antibodies:
- IgM (Immunoglobulin M) which is the first antibody that is made by the body to fight an infection, although it might take several weeks to appear and is mainly found in blood and lymph fluid. IgM usually declines over a few months, but it can remain elevated for years if the immune system is dysregulated.
- IgG (Immunoglobulin G) which is the most abundant type of antibody, and it is found in all body fluids and protects against bacterial and viral infections. IgG usually appears a couple of months after the onset of the infection, and remains for years. But it may

disappear earlier, or never appear, if the immune system is suppressed.

Although the two-tier testing system is useful for surveillance,[21] it should not be used as the sole criterion for a diagnosis, as a clinical diagnosis for Lyme and co-infections is actually considered essential.[22,23] Such a diagnosis is often necessary, particularly since serology is often negative for recent infections and in the presence of primary *erythema migrans*.[24,25]

EIA (enzyme-linked immunoassay)/ ELISA (enzyme-linked immunosorbent assay), and IFA (indirect immuno- fluorescence assay).

The EIA/ELISA test, along with the IFA, are the initial screening tests recommended by the Centers for Disease Control and Prevention (CDC),[26] which can be followed up by an immunoblot test, such as Western blot, if positive. The CDC[27] suggests that physicians consider history of exposure to vectors along with signs and symptoms before ordering blood tests. Unfortunately, the EIA/ELISA as a diagnostic test is problematic for several reasons, but mainly because it does not fit the CDC criteria for two-tier testing in terms of sensitivity, and it is "one of the least useful" tests, missing between "30-35% of confirmed Lyme cases."[28] If you have been ill for a while, this test will likely be negative, even if you do have Lyme.[29] However, the IFA test can be useful when run in conjunction with other tests, with McMcFadzean[30] believing the test to show "good specificity and sensitivity", especially when run through a specialist Lyme testing lab. Specificity means the accuracy of a test in measuring what it is looking for, and sensitivity means the likeliness of a test to find an infection. Keeping this in mind, if a physician actually suspects Lyme disease, and has decided to perform a blood test, then it would make much more sense to skip the ELISA because a negative test is of no use, and a positive ELISA test would require the undertaking of a Western blot anyway.[31]

Western Blot.

The Western blot test evaluates IgM and IgG antibodies separately, and provides results as numbers or 'bands' which can be positive, negative, or indeterminate, with the numbers used along with them referring to the molecular weight in kilodaltons (kDa) of the proteins being measured. For example, *flagellin* (a component of bacterial *flagellum*, or the tail of a spirochete) weighs 41 kDa, so if any of these are detected in your samples, then band 41 would be present in your results. Appendix D provides a breakdown of the Western blot bands, and a detailed explanation for each.

The protein bands 23, 31, 34, 39, and 83/93,[32] are referred to by Horowitz[33] as "Lyme bingo", because he believes that "you have been exposed to the

Lyme bacteria"[34,35] if these appear in your test results, as "Borrelia-specific bands reflect outer surface proteins (Osp) on the surface of the organism that are seen more often in Lyme disease than in other infections."[36] Meanwhile, the CDC criteria for a positive Lyme result would be to record two of either of the three bands 23-25, 39, 41 kDa on an IgM Western blot, or five out of the ten bands 18, 23-25, 28, 30, 39, 41, 45, 58, 66, 83-93 kDa on an IgG Western blot, along with a positive EIA/ELISA or IFA test.[37] For this reason, Horowitz,[38] and others[39,40] rely on exposure, history, signs and symptoms in order to make a clinical diagnosis rather than believing that a diagnosis should be based solely upon the detection of antibodies.

The potential for false negatives will see between 20-30% of culture-positive Lyme disease patients testing negative on a Western blot.[41] Bransfield,[42] along with Grier[43] and Kaplan,[44] outline a range of reasons why a false negative on a direct Lyme disease blood test, or a seronegative (blood antibody negative) test result might come about. These include:

- A lack of standardized control with most controls using only a few strains as a reference point, but there is genetic heterogeneity of *Borrelia* with over 300 strains worldwide and approximately 100 in the United States.

- The laboratory is unable to detect the antibodies against *Borrelia burgdorferi* that are present.
- Antibacterial effects of antibiotics can reduce the body's production of antibodies, meaning that antibodies against *Borrelia burgdorferi* may not be present at a detectable level.
- Anti-inflammatory steroidal drugs can reduce or prevent an antibody response as they can suppress a person's immune system, in turn reducing the detectable levels of antibodies against *Borrelia burgdorferi*.
- Antibodies may become bound with the bacteria, with not enough free antibodies available for testing at a detectable level as there is "too much bacteria for the immune system to handle."
- Immunosuppression for any number of reasons can mean that the immune system is not reacting to the bacteria, and antibodies may then not be present at a detectable level (e.g., concomitant infection with *Babesia* may cause immunosuppression).
- The bacteria are encapsulated in a clear gel-like coating of glyco-proteins (a slime or 'S-layer') which impairs recognition, and can bind to IgM.
- The bacteria may have changed the antigenic proteins on its surface (antigenic shift), limiting recognition by the immune system.

- Surface antigens change with temperature, antibodies are in immune complexes, or spirochetes are encapsulated by host tissue (i.e., lymphocytic cell walls).
- Spirochetes are in a dormant phase (cyst, L-form, round body, S-form, or spheroplast), or are deep in host tissue, or there are too few present in body fluids on the day of the test.
- Blebs in body fluid, no whole organisms for a polymerase chain reaction test.
- The "utilization of host protease instead of microbial protease."
- "There may be possible down regulation of the immune system by cytokines."
- The immune system may not have been stimulated in a way to produce antibodies (e.g., a blood test is taken too soon after infection)
- The laboratory has raised its antibody detection cutoff, has poor technical capability for detection, has no standardization for late stage disease detection, or tests are labeled 'for investigational use only'.
- Reactions to the 'right' bands are not occurring, with CDC criteria epidemiological not diagnostic.

Testing for Co-infections

Testing for the co-infections along with Lyme is also important, as some can be worse than Lyme

itself.[45,46] Several tests are available for this purpose including:
- Antibody tests – IgM and IgG
- FISH – fluorescent in-situ hybridization
- PCR – polymerase chain reaction

Antibody Tests.

In the case of IGeneX,[47] co-infections that are tested for using antibodies include: *Babesia* (*duncani, microti*), *Bartonella* (*henselae, quintana*), *Ehrlichia chaffeensis* (HME), *Anaplasma phagocytophilium* (HGA), and *Rickettsia* (*rickettsia, felis/typhi*). Typical results would show titer values which indicate how many antibodies are present. For example:

IgM	
<20	Negative
20-160	May/may not indicate active infection
>160	Active infection

IgG	
<40	Negative
40-160	May/may not indicate active infection
>160	Active infection

FISH Tests.

The fluorescent in-situ hybridization (FISH) test, like the PCR test, is a direct test where a sample is examined as a thin smear with the intent to identify and mark ribosomal ribonucleic acid (rRNA). If an active infection is present, then the bacteria, or parasites, can be visually detected under a microscope as they will glow in the dark. FISH tests have few false positives.[48]

PCR Tests.

The PCR test for co-infections is similar to that for Lyme. As it is a direct test, blood samples need to be evaluated for DNA.

A View from the Field – Reading Example Test Results and Preparing for Tests

Reading Example Test Results.

Getting test results for the first time can be daunting, and reading them can be difficult. The results below are an example from an IGeneX test. The tests use blood (serum) tests that look for both the IgM, and IgG antibodies, and include a Western blot for Borreliosis (Lyme), an IFA test for Babesia, and an IFA test for Bartonella. A summary of the example test results is then provided.

Borreliosis – Western blot.

Western blot IgM serum	Negative 0 bands present
Western blot IgG serum	Indeterminate 3 bands present (31kDa, 41kDa, 58kDa)

These results show that IgM antibodies are not present, indicating no recent infection. However, IgG antibodies are present and reactive across 3 bands. As band 31 is reactive, this means at some point there has probably been exposure to the Lyme bacteria. This is supported by band 41, indicating the presence of *flagellin*, but this could be in response to other *Borrelia* or other bacteria as well. Band 58 indicates the presence of a heat shock protein, but it is unclear what role this protein plays at this time. This result is also marked indeterminate, meaning bands are present and reactive with a level of intensity below that of a 'low reading'. Some clinicians could interpret this as a weak positive when taking appropriate symptoms into account. See Appendix D for a further explanation regarding the scale of intensity, and for a detailed breakdown of all the Western blot bands.

Babesia – IFA.

B. duncani IFA – IgM   <20 titer
serum
Reference ranges:
- <20   Negative
- =20   May or may not indicate active infection
- ≥40   Indicates active infection

B. duncani IFA – IgG   80 titer
serum
Reference ranges:
- <40   Negative
- <160   May or may not indicate active infection
- ≥160   Indicates active infection

The *Babesia* results show that IgM antibodies are below a titer of 20, meaning negative. However, the IgG antibodies have a titer rate of 80 which is above negative but still falls below the possibility of perhaps having an active infection. Therefore, indeterminate.

Bartonella – IFA.

B. henselae IFA – IgM   <20 titer
serum
Reference ranges:
- <20   Negative
- =20   May or may not indicate active infection
- ≥40   Indicates active infection

B. duncani IFA – IgG   160 titer
serum
Reference ranges:
- <40   Negative
- <160   May or may not indicate active infection
- ≥160   Indicates active infection

The *Bartonella* results above show that IgM antibodies are below a titer of 20, meaning negative, for *Bartonella henselae*. For IgG antibodies, however, the titer rate is 160, which is spot on the measure indicating the possibility of infection. This result indicates a borderline positive for the *Bartonella* co-infection.

Summary of Example Test Results.

The *Borreliosis* Western blot shows some reactivity with two relevant IgG bands visible (31kDa, 41kDa). There is evidence of co-infection organisms. There is a low IgG titer (showing as indeterminate) for *Babesia duncani* through immunofluorescence assay (IFA). There is also a borderline positive IgG titer for a *Bartonella* co-infection.

Preparing for Tests.

Preparing for blood and urine tests may be daunting for many people, but they are important for a variety of reasons.[49] They can initially be used to help pinpoint infections for treatment, and during treatment, they can then be used in an ongoing manner to track infections and the rate of progress being made in fighting disease. If you are on medication, follow your physician's advice, including advice about fasting before any tests deemed necessary.

Blood tests being ordered for Lyme and its co-infections will likely be both time sensitive and require the blood to be taken at a specialist laboratory or collection center. The colored caps, or stoppers, on top of the blood draw tubes (vacutainers) will tell the laboratory the order of draw, as the needle which pierces the tubes can carry additives from one vacutainer into the next, as well as how to handle and prepare the sample after the draw.[50] For example, stoppers with a gold top, red with a gold ring on top, or a marbled red and grey top refer to an SST or serum separating tube which are used in tests requiring blood serum. This tube will contain a gel that separates blood cells from the serum as well as particles that cause the blood to clot quickly, and centrifuging the sample will allow the clear serum to be removed for testing.[51] Green top tubes are usually used for plasma determinations, and purple or lavender top tubes for complete blood counts (CBC) when whole blood is required for analysis.[52]

As for urine collection, this may be required over several days, and at several points during the day. It may also include a clean catch first thing in the morning, another at midday, and one prior to sleep. It is important to follow your physician's instructions regarding collection days and times, as this can vary depending on the tests required. Instructions on how to go about collecting the urine samples will be provided with the test kit, and it is important to follow these correctly, and to ask your physician if you do not understand any aspect of the procedure. Samples may or may not require refrigeration.

When undertaking a direct test for Lyme and its co-infections, it may be beneficial to 'challenge' the bacteria prior to collection.[53] Irritating the bacteria one to two hours before taking blood and urine samples for a direct test can potentially trigger the bacteria to leave hiding places (within the central nervous system, eyes, ligaments, tendons, or collagen bundles, for example), enter bodily fluids, and go looking for a more comfortable location. While it is in transit, it may be located in the blood or urine. Challenge techniques may include the use of herbals, ultrasound, deep tissue massage, intense exercise, or sauna. Klinghardt[54] has particularly found that one-hour rolfing sessions, focusing on symptomatic areas prior to urine collection, lead to great success with PCR tests.

A final note is that in most cases, all blood and urine samples will need to be taken for shipment to occur on a Monday in order to reach the appropriate testing lab in time. If you are posting the samples yourself, make sure that they are shipped as soon as possible after collection, and this may involve taking them to a courier or post office in person.

References

[1] Shapiro, E. (2011). Lyme disease in children. In J. Halperin (Ed.). *Lyme Disease: An Evidence-based Approach* (221-231). USA: CABI.

[2] O'Brian, C. (2013). *Mosby's dictionary of medicine, nursing & health Professions*, (9th ed.). Missouri: Elsevier.

[3] Cameron, D., et al. (2014). Evidence assessments and guideline recommendations in Lyme disease: The clinical management of known tick bites, erythema migrans rashes and persistent disease. *Expert Review of Anti-infect Therapy, 9*(12), 1103-1135. doi: 10.1586/1478 7210.2014. 940900

4. Aguero-Rosenfeld, M., & Wormser, G. (2015). Lyme disease: Diagnostic issues and controversies. *Expert Review of Molecular Diagnostics, 15*(1), 1-4. doi: 10.1586/14737159.2015.989837
5. Perrone, C. (2014). Lyme and associated tick-borne diseases: Global challenges in the context of a public health threat. *Frontiers in Cellular and Infection Microbiology, 4*, 74. doi: 10.3389/fcimb.2014.00074
6. Coulter, P., et al. (2005). Two-year evaluation of Borrelia burgdorferi culture and supplemental tests for definitive diagnosis of Lyme disease. *Journal of Clinical Microbiology, 45*(1), 277.
7. Steere, et al. (2008). Prospective study of serologic tests for Lyme disease. *Clinical Infectious Diseases, 47*(2). doi: 10.1086/589242
8. Stricker, R. (2007). Let's tackle the testing. *BMJ, 335*(7628), 1008. doi: 10.1136/bmj.39394.676227.BE
9. Donta, S. (2012). Issues in the diagnosis and treatment of Lyme. *Open Neurology Journal 6*, 140-145.
10. Johnson, L. (2015). FDA proposal threatens Lyme labs: Restricting independent labs impedes development of critical diagnostic tools. *The Lyme Times, 27*(2), 28.
11. Manny, D. (2016). *The Lyme disease debate: Can the condition be chronic?* Fox News Interview. Retrieved from http://www.foxnews.com/health/2016/05/25/lyme-disease-debate-can-condition-be-chronic.html
12. Rippey, M. (2014). *Episode #26: Professor Holly Ahern explains how Borrelia burgdorferi survive antibiotics and new therapies in the pipeline to kill Lyme bacteria*. Lyme Ninja Radio. Retrieved from https://lymeninjaradio.com/holly_ahern

13. Johnson, L. (2014). Lyme policy wonk: Two-tiered lab testing for Lyme disease – No better than a coin toss. Time for change? Lymedisease.org: Advocacy, Education, & Research. Retrieved from https://www.lymedisease.org/lymepolicywonk-two-tiered-lab-testing-for-lyme-disease-no-better-than-a-coin-toss-time-for-change-2
14. Horowitz, R. (2014). Co-infections presentation, diagnosis, and treatment. *Symposium on Tick-borne Diseases*. May 17. USA: Maryland. Retrieved from https://www.youtube.com/watch?v=O9a-2Nb2sbk
15. Cook, M. J., & Puri, B. K. (2017). Application of Bayesian decision-making to laboratory testing for Lyme disease and comparison testing for HIV. *International Journal of General Medicine, 10*, 113-123. doi: 10.1128/JCM.43.5080-5084.2005
16. Cook, M. J., & Puri, B. K. (2017). *Ibid*.
17. Caruso, C. (2017). Tests for Lyme disease miss many early cases – But a new approach could help. *STAT*. Retrieved from https://www.statnews.com/2017/06/28/early-lyme-tests
18. Wu, Q., et al. (2015). RNA-Seq-based analysis of changes in Borrelia burgdorferi gene expression linked to pathogenicity. *Parasites and Vectors, 8*, 155. doi: 10.1186/s13071-014-0623-2
19. Bouquet, J., et al. (2016). Longitudinal transcriptome analysis reveals a sustained differential gene expression signature in patients treated for acute Lyme disease. *mBio, 7*(1), e00100-16. doi: 10.1128/mBio.00100-16

20. Kaplan, M. (2003). *Reasons for false negative (seronegative) test results in Lyme disease*. Lyme Disease: Part of the Anapsid.org Chronic Neuroimmune Diseases Information Resources for CFS, FM, MCS, Lyme Disease, Thyroid, and more. Retrieved from http://www.anapsid.org/lyme/lymeseroneg.html
21. NNDSS. (2017). *Lyme disease (Borrelia burgdorferi) 2017 case definition. CSTE position statement(s)*. National Notifiable Disease Surveillance System. Retrieved from https://wwwn.cdc.gov/nndss/conditions/lyme-disease/ca se-definition/2017
22. Bransfield, R. (2017). Suicide and Lyme and associated diseases. *Neuropsychiatric Disease and Treatment, 13*, 1575-1587. doi: 10.2147/NDT.S136137
23. CDC. (2017). *Diagnosis and testing*. Centers for Disease Control and Prevention. Retrieved from https://www.cdc.gov/lyme/diagnosistesting/index.html
24. Wormser, G., et al. (2007). The clinical assessment, treatment, and prevention of Lyme disease, Human Granulocytic Anaplasmosis, and Babesiosis: Clinical practice guidelines by the Infectious Diseases Society of America. *Clinical Infectious Diseases, 43*(9), 1089-1134. doi: 10.1086/508667
25. Peronne, C. (2014). *Op. cit.*
26. CDC. (2017). *Op. cit.*
27. CDC. (2017). *Ibid.*
28. McFadzean, N. (2012). *The beginner's guide to Lyme disease: Diagnosis and treatment made simple*. USA: BioMed Publishing Group.
29. McFadzean, N. (2012). *Ibid.*
30. Maloney, E. (2007). Basic principles of laboratory testing for Lyme disease. *The Lyme Times, 50*, 26-28.

31. Schaller, J. (2007). [Lyme] *Western blots made easy*. Public Health Alert: Investigating Lyme and chronic illness. Retrieved from http://www.publichealthalert.org/lyme-western-blots-made-easy.html
32. Horowitz, R., in Manny, D. (2016). *Op. cit.*
33. Horowitz, R. (2014). *Op. cit.*
34. Horowitz, R., in Manny, D. (2016). *Op. cit.*
35. Horowitz, R. (2017). *How can I get better?: An action plan for treating resistant Lyme & chronic disease*. New York: St. Martin's Press.
36. Horowitz, R. (2017). *Ibid.*
37. McFadzean, N. (2012). *Op. cit.*
38. Horowitz, R., in Manny, D. (2016). *Op. cit.*
39. Kaplan, M. (2003). *Op. cit.*
40. McFadzean, N. (2012). *Op. cit.*
41. McFadzean, N. (2012). *Ibid.*
42. Bransfield, R. (2017). *Seronegative Lyme disease*. Mental Health and Illness. Retrieved from http://www.mentalhealthandillness.com/seronegativelymedisease.html
43. Grier, T. (2003). *Reasons for false negative (Seronegative) test results in Lyme disease*. Lyme disease: Part of the Anapsid.org Chronic Neuroimmune Diseases Information Resources for CFS, FM, MCS, Lyme Disease, Thyroid, and More. Retrieved from http://www.anapsid.org/lyme/lymeseroneg.html
44. Kaplan, M. (2003). *Op. cit.*
45. Schaller, J. (2008). Bartonella is becoming the most important issue in treatment of Lyme. *Public Health Alert, 3*(5), 1-2.
46. Buhner, S. (2013). *Healing Lyme co-infections: Complimentary and holistic treatments for Bartonella and mycoplasma*. Vermont: Healing Arts Press.

47. IGeneX. (2017). *Test interpretations*. IGeneX Inc. Retrieved from http://www.igenex.com/testing/interpretations
48. Institute of Medicine. (2011). *Critical needs and gaps in understanding prevention, amelioration, and resolution of Lyme and other tick-borne diseases: The short-term and long-term outcomes: Workshop report*. Washington, DC: The National Academies Press. doi: 10.17226/13134
49. McFadzean, N. (2012). *Op. cit.*
50. NIH. (2017). *Blood tests*. National Heart, Lung, and Blood Institute. Retrieved from https://www.nhlbi.nih.gov/health-topics/blood-tests
51. Phlebotomy. (2017). *Blood collection: Routine venipuncture and specimen handling*. University of Utah. Retrieved from https://library.med.utah.edu/WebPath/TUTORIAL/PHLEB/PHLEB.html
52. Mitchell, B., Neary, M., & Kelly, G. (2003). *Blood sampling in sheep*. Purdue University of Animal Sciences. Purdue University. Retrieved from https://www.extension.purdue.edu/extmedia/as/as-557-w.pdf
53. BD. (2017). *BD Vacutainer Tube Guide*. Becton Dickinson. Retrieved from https://iti.stanford.edu/content/dam/sm/iti/documents/himc/immunoassays/BDVacutainerTubeGuide.pdf
54. Strasheim, C. (2016). *Tests for Lyme disease that truly work*. ProHealth. Retrieved from http://www.prohealth.com/library/showarticle.cfm?libid=29281
55. Klinghardt, D. (2016). Chapter Two – Dietrich Kinghardt, MD, PHD. in C. Strasheim, *New paradigms in Lyme disease treatment: 10 top doctors reveal healing strategies that work*. California, USA: BioMed Publishing Group, LLC.

9. How Can You Approach The Treatment Of Lyme And/Or Its Co-infections?

If you have recently been bitten, show signs of a rash, or have a number of symptoms, then you should consult with a physician. On the other hand, if you have been ill for a very long time, you could treat yourself, and financially you may be at a point where you very well have to. In either case, seeking professional medical advice and obtaining confirmation through a blood test or via a clinical diagnosis of what is making you ill is important. You need to know what you are fighting because that can impact treatment.

Treatment Options

For Lyme and its co-infections, treatment will be for either a recent known bite/exposure, a recent rash, or for prolonged symptoms. Individual physicians will likely have their own recommended protocols, favored antibiotics, and detoxification methods, and taking their medical advice, suggestions, and guidance into account would likely be important for the success of any treatment. That said, the main avenue of treatment options, which can perhaps be grouped into three, are discussed below along with how each might be applied to early localized or

acute Lyme, early disseminated, and late disseminated or chronic Lyme and its co-infections. The treatment options are:
- an allopathic (prescription-based) approach
- a holistic (herbal/supplement-based) approach
- a combined allopathic/holistic approach

No matter the treatment path chosen, keep in mind that it may take years for antibodies to decline, and as there are no tests to prove that the Lyme bacteria has been removed completely from all body compartments, treatment will usually need to continue for two to three months after symptom resolution. It can then be tapered off slowly, but if symptoms reoccur, treatment would need to be restarted or modified.

Allopathic Approach – Prescription-Based.

There is no universal antibiotic available for the treatment of Lyme and its co-infections, and medication choice and dosage will need to vary across individuals.[1] Factors considered in regard to dosage might include: either the use of oral or IV antibiotics; medicating at a pulsed (on/off) or continual (daily) rate; length of treatment; as well as detoxification and probiotic use to manage side effects and Jarisch-Herxheimer reactions.[2-4] Antibiotic use, particularly in late stage Lyme, should also address all forms of *Borrelia*.[5,6] There is evidence to support the relapse and progression of

Lyme if antibiotic therapy is stopped before symptoms are resolved,[7,8] and unfortunately, treatment failure rates, particularly those following the Infectious Diseases Society of America (IDSA) guidelines, are high – up to 40% for early Lyme, and over 65% for late Lyme.[9]

Early Localized/Acute Lyme. Evidence for the use of antibiotics as a successful treatment for Lyme is still very thin, contradictory, and developing.[10] Yet, it is recognized that early treatment can lead to success,[11-13] with most guidelines[14-16] recommending a two- to four-week or more initial treatment period.[17,18]

Early Disseminated to Late Disseminated/ Chronic Lyme. For those who are not diagnosed early, there is no real evidence that long-term antibiotic use,[19,20] or a very prolonged course of antibiotic therapy will provide any benefit.[21] However, four- to six- month courses have been recommended, with the very ill also requiring ongoing maintenance for years.[22] In other words, responses to treatment can be highly variable.[23]

If prescribed, any long-term antibiotics would also depend upon the co-infections present, with the delivery method up to the physician of choice, and likely coming with a range of potential side effects.[24,26] Antibiotics can be taken orally, through intramuscular injections (IM), or intravenously (IV). Those undergoing very long-term IV antibiotic therapy, or other treatments like nutritional therapy or chemotherapy, are likely to use a PICC (peripherally inserted central catheter) line, with the tip inserted into a large vein that carries blood into the heart. Long-term PICC use can be harmful,[27] and the benefit of it for Lyme is not supported by any studies.[28]

Holistic Approach – Herbals/Supplements.

There are a number of herbal protocols that exist for the prevention and treatment of early localized or acute Lyme, and for fighting early disseminated Lyme, and late disseminated or chronic Lyme.

Preventative. For those living in Lyme endemic areas, Buhner[29] suggests a preventative dosage of herbs. As the herbs and dosages suggested may change, it would be best to consult the information directly from the herbalists' books.

Early Localized/Acute Lyme. A number of herbal protocols are available for those freshly bitten, or exhibiting signs of early localized or acute Lyme. Once again, Buhner[30] provides suggestive herbals and dosages, but as these may be updated, it is best to consult the herbalists' books directly.

Early Disseminated to Late Disseminated/ Chronic Lyme. Two herbal-based protocols used to fight early disseminated to late disseminated or chronic Lyme and its co-infections are those of Buhner[31-34] and Cowden.[35] Other protocols are also available like the Byron White Formulas[36] or the Zhang protocol based on a Chinese medicine approach.[37] However, the Buhner and Cowden protocols are the ones discussed here as their products are readily available for purchase, whereas those of other protocols may not be as easily accessible globally. For example, the Byron-White product line can only be purchased by certified practitioners or office managers at this time.

The Buhner Protocol. This protocol was developed by Stephen Buhner, ND[38] and utilizes a range of commonly available herbals and supplements to treat Lyme and its co-infections. It has an overall self-reported success rate of around 75%,[39] and aside from the core protocol for Lyme, there are protocols for co-infections such as *Babesia, Bartonella, Chlamydia, Ehrlichia/Anaplasma, Mycoplasma,* and *Rickettsioses.* Basic elements of each protocol are outlined on a website,[40] with an extensive question and answer section. However, the full protocols are only available from a series of books.[41-43]

The Cowden Protocol. This protocol, developed by William Lee Cowden, MD[44] utilizes 14 different Nutramedix products taken on rotation.[45] The duration of the program is nine months, with recommendation to repeat months 7, 8, and 9 as needed. The Cowden Support Program[46] has been known to provide symptomatic improvement for 80% of patients, assessed by a self-questionnaire, and 90% of patients confirmed by blood work.[47] The program includes natural anti-inflammatories, and is broad-spectrum, aimed at bacteria, fungi, parasites, and viruses. Cowden has a series of videos on YouTube where he outlines the program and each of the products used in it.[48]

Allopathic/Holistic Approach.

For early disseminated to late disseminated or chronic Lyme, a combined antibiotic/herbal/supplement approach might involve the use of antibiotics, at a recommended physician dosage, along with the use of various herbals and supplements, combined with a range of other modalities.

Early Localized/Acute Lyme. Treating early localized or acute Lyme with a basic allopathic/holistic centered approach includes taking antibiotics prescribed at physician dosage and recommended method, along with reliance on a herbal protocol of choice (like Buhner or Cowden) until advised to stop treatment after symptoms clear.

Early Disseminated to Late Disseminated/ Chronic Lyme. Two combined allopathic/holistic approaches to treating early to late disseminated or chronic Lyme are that of the Lyme ABC approach, developed by Klinghardt,[49] and the Ross approach, developed by Ross.[50] Other protocols are also available.

The Lyme ABC Approach. This method provides an allopathic/holistic approach to treatment where a mixture of methods including herbals, supplements, antiparasitics, antibiotics, bee venom, and pulsed electromagnetic fields are applied.[51] It focuses upon, in order:

- Deworming
- Antiparasitics
- Treating strep infections
- Tackling Babesia
- Beginning a herbal antiviral treatment
- Addressing fungal/yeast issues, while taking dietary considerations into account
- Addressing Mycoplasma
- Treating spirochetes and any co-infections last, along with a regime of specific supplements and antibiotics used at particular doses

The Ross Approach. This approach involves a 'treatment recipe'[52] focusing on the following:
- Sleep
- Diet
- Cytokine control
- The use of adaptogens
- Hormone balancing
- Yeast control and Lyme treatment with prescription-based medicine, herbals, and supplements
- Detoxification
- Co-infection treatment
- Additional management of symptoms and problems with natural medicine
- Exercise
- Any unique/special considerations for each individual

A View from the Field – Alternative Treatment Approaches for Late Disseminated or Chronic Lyme

In a search to get well, many people often turn to alternative treatment approaches, and can end up spending every last cent in an attempt to save their life and their health.[53] Anecdotal reports of people getting well from any approach should be interpreted based on the results of placebo studies, some of which see placebo and treatment having similar effect sizes[54] up to 50%.[55] As such, alternative approaches are not recommended without full physician support, but when people are left with limited options, are extremely ill, and are desperate to get better, they are willing to try almost anything to heal.[56] Some of the more radical approaches that are being widely discussed in online support forums include bee venom therapy (BVT), hyperbaric oxygen therapy (HBOT), ozone treatment, as well as whole-body hyperthermia treatment (WBHT), and a variety of other anecdotal alternatives.

Bee Venom Therapy (BVT).

This therapy has been used to relieve pain,[57] with the melittin peptide in bee venom found to inhibit Lyme.[58] BVT has a long history, traced to use in ancient Egypt and ancient Greece, and dating back 5,000 years in China.[59] Bee venom contains 18 pharmacologically active components, and it has been used to treat a number of diseases including arthritis, multiple sclerosis (MS), lupus, and sciatica.[60] Although bee venom creams and oils are available for purchase, and a number of people elect to use live bees to self-sting at home, the treatment is not without the potential for adverse risk, ranging from skin reactions to anaphylaxis.[61]

Hyperbaric Oxygen Therapy (HBOT).

This therapy has been used in a range of medical and surgical conditions, including burn and wound treatment,[62] and it can stimulate the immune system.[63] Inside a HBOT chamber, air pressure is built up to 2-3 times normal, possibly with increased oxygen concentration, and this increased pressure allows the uptake of oxygen into the lungs and throughout the body to stimulate the release of growth factors and stem cells to assist in the healing process.[64] Although HBOT has been in use since the 1990s,[65] studies showing the efficacy of the treatment for late disseminated or chronic Lyme are limited.[66]

Ozone Treatment.

This treatment can be administered in several ways which includes: intravenously; via gaseous insufflation (rectally or vaginally); by infusing the blood with ozone after withdrawal, and then feeding it back into the body (autohemotherapy); by drinking ozone infused water, or by topically applying ozone infused oils.[67] Treatment with ozone is believed to stimulate a pro-inflammatory response, and result in stimulating the immune system to promote healing.[68,69]

Whole-Body Hyperthermia Treatment (WBHT).

This treatment is also known as thermal therapy or thermotherapy, and it has been used as an approach to treat metastatic cancer,[70] and when used for cancer, it is in combination with radiation or chemotherapy.[71-73] It is an expensive and risky treatment modality, but when used in combination with antibiotics, it has seen reported success for people with late disseminated or chronic Lyme.[74] WBHT for use with Lyme patients involves the use of an incubation chamber and warming the patient up to a temperature of 107°F (41.6°C) over two hours, maintaining that temperature for two more hours, then cooling them down over an additional two hours. This has seen 60% of patients using the modality able to return to a normal life, 30% requiring additional treatment, and 10% not experiencing any improvement.[75]

Anecdotal Alternatives.

Several other alternative techniques that have anecdotal support, and are also currently being widely discussed across online forums, include use of the following during treatment:

- Borax
- Chlorine dioxide
- Dimethyl sulfoxide (DMSO)
- High dose iodine
- High dose niacin
- Hydrogen peroxide
- Methylsulfonylmethane (MSM)
- Rifing
- Salt and vitamin C
- Water fasting

References

[1] Burrascano, J. (2008). *Diagnostic hints and treatment guidelines for Lyme and other tick borne illnesses*, (16th ed). Advanced Topics in Lyme Disease. Retrieved from http://www.lymenet.org/ BurrGuide200810.pdf

[2] Nicolson, G. (2007). Diagnosis and therapy of chronic systemic co-infections in Lyme disease and other tick-borne infectious diseases. *Townsend Letter: The Examiner of Alternative Medicine, 285*, 93-98.

[3] Burrascano, J. (2008). *Op. cit.*

[4] Ross, M. (2017). A Lyme disease antibiotic guide. *The Treat Lyme Book*. Healing Arts Partnership. Retrieved from http://www.treatlyme.net/treat-lyme-book/lyme-disease-antibiotic-guide

5. Stricker, R., & Johnson, L. (2011). Lyme disease: The next decade. *Infection and Drug Resistance, 4*, 1-9. doi: 10.2147/IDR.S15653
6. Rippey, M. (2015). *Episode 27: Lyme expert – Dr. Nicola McFadzean Ducharme – Author, naturopath.* Lyme Ninja Radio. Retrieved from http://lymeninjaradio.com/nicola_ducharme
7. Preac-Mursic, V., et al. (1989). Survival of Borrelia burgdorferi in antibiotically treated patients with Lyme Borreliosis. *Infection, 17*, 335-339.
8. Logigian, E., Kaplan, R., & Steere, A. (1990). Chronic neurologic manifestations of Lyme disease. *New England Journal of Medicine, 323*, 1438-1444.
9. Johnson, L. (2015). Guidelines process remains flawed: Despite the antitrust investigation, IDSA priorities remain unchanged: Revenues, reputation and reduced liability. *The Lyme Times, 27*(2), 10-11.
10. Cameron, D., et al. (2014). Evidence assessments and guideline recommendations in Lyme disease: The clinical management of known tick bites, erythema migrans rashes and persistent disease. *Expert Review of Anti-infect Therapy, 9*(12), 1103-1135. doi: 10.1586/14787210.2014.940900
11. Elbaum-Garfinkle, S. (2011). Close to home: A history of Yale and Lyme disease. *Yale Journal of Biology and Medicine, 84*(2), 103-108.
12. McFadzean, N. (2012). *The beginner's guide to Lyme disease: Diagnosis and treatment made simple.* USA: BioMed Publishing Group.

13. Horowitz, R., in Manny, D. (2016). *The Lyme disease debate: Can the condition be chronic?* Fox News Interview. Retrieved from http://www.foxnews.com/health/2016/05/25/lyme-disease-debate-can-condition-be-chronic.html

14. Wormser, G., et al. (2007). The clinical assessment, treatment, and prevention of Lyme disease, Human Granulocytic Anaplasmosis, and Babesiosis: Clinical practice guidelines by the Infectious Diseases Society of America. *Clinical Infectious Diseases, 43*(9), 1089-1134. doi: 10.1086/508667

15. Mygland, A., et al. (2010). EFNS guidelines on the diagnosis and management of European Lyme Neuroborreliosis. *European Journal of Neurology, 17*, 8-16. doi: 10.1111/j.1468-1331.2009.02862.x

16. Berende, A., et al. (2016). Randomized trial of longer-term therapy for symptoms attributed to Lyme disease. *The New England Journal of Medicine, 374*, 1209-1220. doi: 10.1056/NEJMOA1505425

17. Stricker, R. (2007). Counterpoint: Long-term antibiotic therapy improves persistent symptoms associated with Lyme disease. *Clinical Infectious Diseases, 45*(2), 149-157.

18. Cameron, D., et al. (2014). *Op. cit.*

19. Berende, A., et al. (2016) . *Op. cit.*

20. Melia, M. & Auwaerter, P. (2016). Time for a different approach to Lyme disease and long-term symptoms. *New England Journal of Medicine, 734*, 1277-1278. doi: 1056/NEJMe1502350

21. Rawls, W. (2017). *Unlocking Lyme: Myths, truths, & practical solutions for chronic Lyme disease*. USA: FirstDoNoHarm Publishing.

22. Burrascano, J. (2008). *Op. cit.*

23. Johnson, L. (2008). Medical necessity letter template – IV Rocephin. *The Lyme Times, 51*, 46-51.
24. Burrascano, J. (2008). *Op. cit.*
25. Abeles, S., et al. (2015). Effects of long term antibiotic therapy on human oral and fecal viromes. *PLoS One, 10*(8), e0134941. doi: 10.1371/journal.pone.0134941
26. Langdon, A., Cook, N., & Dantas, G. (2016). The effects of antibiotics on the microbiome throughout development and alternative approaches for therapeutic modulation. *Genome Medicine, 8*, 39. doi: 10.1186/s13073-016-0294-z
27. Wormser, G., et al. (2007). *Op. cit.*
28. Marzec, N., et al. (2017). Serious bacterial infections acquired during treatment of patients given a diagnostic of chronic Lyme disease. *Weekly, 66*(23), 607-609.
29. Buhner, S. (2017). *Q & A. Stephen Harrod Buhner answers questions about his herbal protocols for Lyme disease and co-infections.* Buhner Healing Lyme: Planet Thrive Inc. Retrieved from http://buhnerhealinglyme.com
30. Buhner, S. (2017). *Ibid.*
31. Buhner, S. (2013). *Healing Lyme co-infections: Complimentary and holistic treatments for bartonella and mycoplasma.* Vermont: Healing Arts Press.
32. Buhner, S. (2015a). *Healing Lyme: Natural healing of Lyme Borreliosis and the co-infections Chlamydia and Spotted Fever Rickettsioses.* New Mexico: Raven Press.
33. Buhner, S. (2015b). *Natural treatments for Lyme co-infections: Anaplasma, Babesia, and Ehrlichia.* Vermont: Healing Arts Press.
34. Buhner, S. (2017). *Op. cit.*

35. Cowden, L. (2012). *The Cowden support program*. Austria ILADS Lyme Conference, May 18-19. Klagenfurt: University of Klagenfurt. Retrieved from https://www.youtube.com/watch?v=c9t43NbIR2A
36. White, B. (2017). *Immune support formulas*. Byron White Formulas Inc. Retrieved from http://www.byronwhiteformulas.com
37. Zhang, Q., & Zhang, Y. (2007). Treating Lyme disease with modern Chinese medicine. *The Lyme Times: Alternative Medicine 49*, 21-23.
38. Buhner, S. (2007). Herbal approaches to Lyme disease. *The Lyme Times: Alternative Medicine 49*, 24-25.
39. Buhner, S. (2017). *What is the success rate of the healing Lyme protocol? FAQs*. Buhner Healing Lyme: Planet Thrive, Inc. Retrieved from http://buhnerhealinglyme.com/faqs
40. Buhner, S. (2017). *Op. cit.*
41. Buhner, S. (2013). *Op. cit.*
42. Buhner, S. (2015a). *Op. cit.*
43. Buhner, S. (2015b). *Op. cit.*
44. Cowden, W. (2007). Herbal treatment for Lyme disease: An integrated approach. *The Lyme Times: Alternative Medicine, 49*, 19-20.
45. Nutramedix. (2017). *Cowden support program*. Nutramedix. Retrieved from https://www.nutramedix.com/products/cowden-support-program
46. Cowden, L. (2012). *Op. cit.*
47. Nicolaus, C. (2012). Use of naturopathic medicine in Treatment of Tick-borne Diseases. *Austria ILADS Lyme Conference*, May 18-19. Klagenfurt: University of Klagenfurt.

48. Pepeicaza. (2017). *Pepeicaza channel*. YouTube. Retrieved from https://www.youtube.com/user/pepeicaza/videos
49. Klinghardt, K. (2005). Lyme disease: A look beyond antibiotics. *Explore Magazine, 14*(2). Retrieved from http://www.psychostrategy.net/article-lyme-disease-a-look-beyond-antibiotics-dietrich-k-klinghardt-md-phd-67183654.html
50. Ross, M. (2017). Brain fog in Lyme disease. You can fix it. *The Treat Lyme Book.* Healing Arts partnership. Retrieved from http://www.treatlyme.net/treat-lyme-book/brain-fo g-lyme-disease
51. Klinghardt, K. (2005). *Op. cit.*
52. Ross, M. (2017). *Op. cit.*
53. Buttaccio, J. (2015). A life on pause: When Lyme steals everything, you will spend every last cent trying to get well. *The Lyme Times, 27*(2), 34.
54. Howick, J., et al. (2013). Are treatments more effective than placebos? A systematic review and meta-analysis.
PLoS One, 8(5), e62599. doi: 10.137/journal.pone.0062599
55. Kam-Hansen, S., et al. (2014). Altered placebo and drug labeling changes the outcome of episodic migraine attacks. *Science Translational Medicine, 6*(218), 218ra5. doi: 10.1126/scitranslmed.3006175
56. Lantos, P., et al. (2015). Unorthodox alternative therapies marketed to treat Lyme disease. *Clinical Infectious Diseases, 60*(12), 1776-1782. doi: 10.1093/cid/civ186
57. Klinghardt, D. (1990). Bee venom therapy for chronic pain. *Journal of Neurological and Orthopedic Medicine and Surgery, 11*(9), 195-197.

58. Lubke, L., & Garon, J. (1997). Bee stings as Lyme inhibitor. *Clinical Infectious Diseases 25*(1), 48-51. doi: 10.1086/516165
59. Rose, A. (1994). *Bee in balance: A guide to healing the whole person with honeybees, oriental medicine and commonsense*. Maryland: Starpoint Enterprises Ltd.
60. Ali, M. (2012). Studies on bee venom and its medical uses. *International Journal of Advancements in Research & Technology, 1*(2). Retrieved from http://www.ijoart.org/ docs/Studies-on-Bee-Venom-and-Its-Medical-Uses.pdf
61. Park, J. et al. (2015). Risk associated with bee venom therapy: A systematic review and meta-analysis. *PLoS One, 10*(5), e0126971. doi: 10.1371/journal.pone.0126971
62. Gill, A., & Bell, C. (2004). Hyperbaric oxygen: Its uses, mechanisms of action and outcomes. *Quarterly Journal of Medicine*, 97(7), 385-395.
63. Kinderlehrer, D. (2007). Please pass the oxygen. *The Lyme Times: Alternative Medicine 49*, 26-27.
64. Mayo Clinic. (2017). *Hyperbaric oxygen therapy*. Tests and Procedures. Retrieved from http://www.mayoclini c.org/tests-procedures/hyperbaric-oxygen-therapy/basics/definition/prc-20019167
65. Huang, C., et al. (2014). Hyperbaric oxygen therapy as an effective adjunctive treatment for chronic Lyme disease. *Journal of the Chinese Medicine Association, 77*(5), 269-271.
66. Burkland, G. (2007). Hyperbaric Oxygen Therapy (HBOT) for patients diagnosed with Lyme disease. *The Lyme Times: Alternative Medicine, 49*, 34.
67. Lantos, P. M. (2015). Chronic Lyme disease. *Infectious disease clinics of North America, 29*(2), 325-40. doi: 10.10 16/j.idc.2015.02.006

68. Gracer, R., & Bocci, V. (2005). Can the combination of localized 'proliferative therapy' with 'minor ozonated autohemotherapy' restore the natural healing process? *Medical Hypotheses, 65*(4), 752-759. doi: 10.1016/j.mehy.2005.04.021

69. Smith, A., et al. (2015). Ozone therapy: A critical physiological and diverse clinical evaluation with regard to immune modulation, anti-infectious properties, anti-cancer potential, and impact on anti-oxidant enzymes. *Open Journal of Molecular and Integrative Physiology, 5*, 37-48. doi: 10.4236/ojmop.2015.53004

70. NIH. (2011). *Hyperthermia in cancer treatment*. National Cancer Institute, at the National Institutes of Health. Retrieved from https://www.cancer.gov/about-cancer/treatment/types/surgery/hyperthermia-fact-sheet

71. Wust, P., et al. (2002). Hyperthermia in combined treatment of cancer. *The Lancet Oncology, 3*(8), 487-497.

72. Van der Zee, J. (2002). Heating the patient: A promising approach? *Annals of Oncology, 13*(8), 1173-1184.

73. Moen, I., & Stuhr, L. (2012). Hyperbaric oxygen therapy and cancer – A review. *Targeted Oncology, 7*(4), 233-242.

74. McKeon, M. (2014). *Whole-body hyperthermia treatment*. Public Health Alert: Investigating Lyme and Chronic Illness. Retrieved from http://www.publichealthalert.org/-whole-body-hyperthermia-treatment.html

75. Douwes, F. (2016). How I discovered hyperthermia for Lyme disease and why it works. In C. Strasheim, *New paradigms in Lyme disease treatment: 10 top doctors reveal healing strategies that work.* 265-288. California, USA: BioMed Publishing Group.

10. How Can You Support Your Health When Fighting Lyme And/Or Its Co-infections?

At the best of times, living a healthy lifestyle is important, and it is just one way of enabling all of the body systems from the digestive system to the immune system to function more effectively.[1] Also at the best of times, the body will require decent rest, exercise, and a variety of vitamins and minerals from good foods in order to help the immune system fight off any invading pathogens.[2] These factors become even more important after being ill for a long period of time, and when attempting to subdue or eradicate any infection. For those chronically ill, other steps may also be required in order to provide long-term health support to an ailing or overburdened immune system, particularly since "the three I's of Lyme – infection, inflammation, and immune dysfunction – are the biological triad responsible for many commonly observed symptoms."[3]

Methods of Immune Support

The immune system can be thought of as a kind of guardian that protects the body from any harmful influences originating from the environment,[4] and there are a number of methods available for providing support to this system so that it can assist with micro-organism control or eradication. Some methods are tried and true, while others are more unconventional, or are relatively new responses to more recent changes in the environment and technology. Taking this into account, the benefits of a handful of methods for boosting general health and for providing immune support, particularly for those with Lyme and its co-infections, will be explored. These include earthing, ensuring some sun exposure, and considering the importance of brain, gut, and dental health. The impact of the environment is also taken into account with the need to identify and remove any buildup of toxic metals from the body, treat any mold toxicity or exposure, and to minimize contact with man-made electromagnetic fields (EMF) and radio frequency (RF) radiation.

Earthing.

Wearing shoes with insulated soles, and living in apartments and houses isolated from the earth have today disconnected most people from ever being in contact with it. Grounding, or earthing, involves connecting the body directly with the earth and its energy by walking upon it barefoot or lying down on the ground in order to reestablish this connection.[5] Earthing can also be achieved when

Chapter 10: Immune Support | 129

working, sitting, or sleeping indoors while being connected to conductive systems.[6]

The beneficial effects of grounding stem from being in direct contact with the planet which, as a result of the Earth's electromagnetohydrodynamic potential,[7] enables diurnal electrical rhythms and free electrons to flow from the earth into the body[8] to regulate bioelectrical and bioenergetical processes. Diurnal rhythms set the biological clocks for hormones that regulate sleep and activity, and free electrons neutralize positively charged free radicals that cause chronic inflammation. This is important because the higher the amount of negative charge that your body has, the better all of your cells are able to function.[9]

Oxidation causes cells in the body to lose their negative charge, and this is why antioxidants are important.[10] In the grounding process, the transfer of mobile electrons from the earth are considered to be beneficial in helping to resolve chronic inflammation by acting as natural antioxidants, particularly since inflammation and oxidative stress are recognized as being behind many chronic illnesses.[11] Grounding then, comes to serve as a kind of 'electric nutrition.'[12]

Grounding is also reported to improve sleep, normalize cortisol, reduce pain and stress;[13] reduce blood viscosity and clumping by increasing the surface charge of red blood cells,[14] and reduce exercise-induced inflammation[15] along with delayed onset muscle damage.[16] An hour spent being grounded was also reported to provide an improvement in mood more than that of simple relaxation.[17] It also influences human physiological processes to promote proper functioning of the body's systems,[18] calms the nervous system,[19] and promotes self-regulating and self-healing mechanisms throughout the body.[20,21]

A number of companies make grounding products that can be safely plugged into the earth wire of the electrical system of most homes. These include accessories such as grounding mats, throws, sheets, and pillow cases. These accessories can also be connected to a ground rod that is directly inserted into the earth. However, there is some contention over the benefit of grounding via the electrical system of an apartment or house due to 'dirty electricity'. This aside, to get the benefits of earthing is as simple as walking barefoot outside for a few minutes to an hour each day, and like sun exposure, it is free.

Sun exposure.

'Sun eating' or sun gazing has been practiced by many ancient civilizations such as the Aztecs, Egyptians, Greeks, and Mayans.[22] However, it is a practice that advocates looking directly at the sun, which is extremely hazardous and can cause long-lasting and damaging effects that include solar retinopathy and blindness.[23] Certainly this is not advocated, but some sensible sun exposure and spending time outdoors at particular times of the day can be beneficial for many reasons,[24] some of which will be discussed below, and it is one of the easiest ways of applying heliotherapy for health purposes.

Circadian rhythm. Spending time in the sun can help to reset the circadian rhythm,[25] as light stimulates protein synthesis in the brain that leads to phosphorylation.* This is important because if the circadian rhythm is off, then this may cause a disruption in biological clocks.[26] This can change hormone production in the body which leads to sleeplessness, mood disturbances, and obesity as these processes all operate based on a daily rhythm.[27] Other body systems also follow a daily cycle, with chemicals involved in the functioning of the immune system seeing compounds that encourage an inflammatory response generally rise at night, and be inhibited during the day.[28] The circadian cycle is therefore responsible for more than just promoting wakefulness and sleep, and keeping it well-synced is now recognized as being beneficial for the overall maintenance of health.

Light, Inflammation, and Structured Water. Spending time in the sun will expose you to natural electromagnetic energy known as the solar spectrum, consisting of ultraviolet (UV), visible,

---

* *Phosphorylation*, along with *dephosphorylation*, are critical for many cellular processes.

and infrared light.[29] Exposure to UV light can increase beta-endorphin production[30] which can make you feel happier and, particularly for fibromyalgia patients, also reduce pain.[31] Serotonin is also boosted when exposed to UV light, with UV and blue light therapy a long time treatment for seasonal affective disorder (SAD).[32]

Today, the use of light therapy to relieve pain or to heal wounds is becoming increasing popular, and it is known as photobiomodulation.[**] Light therapy uses a range of wavelengths to support healing and health, such as the near- and far-infrared wavelengths that are also used in a number of saunas.[33] This light is believed to affect the body by altering protein structures, mediated by nanostructured water.[34] Pollack refers to this as EZ (exclusion zone) water – water with a negative charge, higher refractive index, and density.[35] It is created by exposure to light, and it is said that this type of water is able to hold energy and to deliver energy to the cells of the body. It is perhaps also one of the reasons that hyperbaric treatment assists in healing, as normal water put under pressure can help build EZ water in the body.[36] Further, if the cells of the body do not contain enough EZ water, then they are not as negatively charged as they

---

[**] *Photobiomodulation* refers to using photons (light) to modulate biological processes. Typically, it refers to therapeutic techniques that utilize low-level laser light therapy (LLLT) or light emitting diodes (LED) to relieve pain or to heal wounds.

could be, and in the brain, this can mean that neurons will not be able to communicate optimally which can potentially lead to cognitive issues, depression, or other mood disorders.[37] EZ water was also found to help blood and lymphatic fluid to flow through narrow capillaries more quickly, something that can help lessen chronic inflammation, and something that the microtubules in the mitochondria[***] can also benefit from.[38] In line with this, hemoglobin molecules when exposed to sunlight have been found to release carbon monoxide which, in small amounts, can cause vasodilation and help to reduce blood pressure while also acting as a neurotransmitter causing relaxation and anti-inflammatory activity in the nervous system.[39]

So too, the blue light in the sun's rays, which is part of the visible light spectrum and balanced by near-infrared radiation, can along with UVA be beneficial as it can directly activate immune cells (i.e., T lymphocytes) by increasing their motility and their antioxidant capacity.[40] Blue light also helps to keep us alert, support memory and cognitive function, and elevate mood.[41] However, blue light exposure by itself, such as that from LED (light emitting diode) lighting, televisions, and monitors, may actually be quite harmful,

---

[***] *Mitochondria* are organelles in the cells responsible for converting oxygen, along with the sugars, fats, and proteins from food, to usable energy (ATP, or *adenosine triphosphate*).

particularly to the eye,[42] and be a risk factor for age-related macular degeneration (AMD),[43] and too much exposure at night can reduce the production of melatonin potentially causing insomnia.[44] Putting this information into practice may see you need to change some of the lighting sources in your home, and a number of companies produce lighting products in a range of colors, lux, and kelvin temperatures that may be more suitable. For example: warm white and Edison bulbs; incandescent or low-voltage halogens. There are also computer programs that can be installed to adjust the color temperature of displays to assist in reducing eye-strain and to aid in reducing any patterns of sleep disruption.

Ultraviolet Radiation and Vitamin D. UV rays have been found to kill bacteria, with application particularly in hospital settings.[45] While UVA rays promote photoaging of the skin,[46] nitric oxide is also produced in skin in response to UVA light,[47] and this helps to dilate blood vessels and reduce blood pressure, thereby lessening the chances for a heart attack or stroke.[48] Nitric oxide can also induce melanin production (a natural sunscreen),[49] alter immune function,[50] and enhance wound healing.[51] UVB rays, on the other hand, when hitting unexposed skin, can cause burning in as little as 15 minutes, but these are the ones that promote vitamin D production.[52] Knowing the optimal time of day to obtain UVB rays from the sun while also minimizing burn time and UVA exposure can be difficult, particularly since UVB rays can cause sunburn and damage the DNA (deoxyribonucleic acid) of melanocytes and potentially lead to cancer. However, several applications are available that can track the optimal time to be in the sun for vitamin D synthesis, the level of Vitamin D you will be able to produce specific to your location and Fitzpatrick skin phototype, and track the time before you will burn. This is important, as obtaining a blood serum vitamin D level of ≥40 ng/ml can actually reduce the risk of developing cancer by 67%, compared to having a level of 20 ng/ml or lower.[53]

Of note, Vitamin D, actually a fat-soluble prohormone, gets converted into a steroid hormone responsible for regulating more than 1,000 different physiological processes in the body.[54] It also has bactericidal and immune-boosting effects,[55] and has been found to increase fertility[56] with a lack of it reducing libido.[57] There is also evidence to support that improvement in vitamin D levels during early life may reduce the risk for many autoimmune diseases.[58] If adequate levels are received early on in life, it may also reduce the onset of myopia (short-sightedness) by causing the retina to release more dopamine which can inhibit the axial elongation of the eyeball associated with the condition.[59] So it is important to maintain a good level of vitamin D from food sources like mushrooms and fatty fish,[60] and also to synthesize it from adequate sun exposure with 20-30 minutes every few days likely enough to generate the minimum daily requirements.[61] Although not as effective as some sunscreens, which may contain chemical compounds that can become carcinogenic when exposed to UV light,[62] certain foods can help protect you from sensitivity to UV light, like those containing carotenoids that are typically found in orange-yellow vegetables, lycopene from tomatoes, as well as omega-3s and green tea.[63]

Ultimately, avoiding the sun at the right time, like avoiding man-made electromagnetic frequencies, can be beneficial. However, some sun exposure is important just like gastrointestinal, brain, and dental health, particularly if you tend to always wear sunscreen, hats, sunglasses, long sleeves, and long pants when outdoors, and are spending most of your time indoors under artificial lighting or in the dark.

The Importance of Gastrointestinal, Brain, and Dental Health.

Gastrointestinal Health.

Hippocrates is often quoted as saying 'all diseases begin in the gut,' and indeed Lyme and its co-infections can cause immune dysregulation that may affect gut health[64] and potentially lead to diseases not normally considered to be related to problems in the gastrointestinal tract.[65] Gastrointestinal health and any food sensitivities and intolerances, as well as nutritional deficiencies or gut issues such as *Candida* overgrowth, increased intestinal permeability (*leaky gut*), a *Helicobactor pylori* infection, irritable bowel syndrome (IBS), or small intestinal bacterial overgrowth (SIBO), will then likely need to be addressed during any treatment of Lyme and its co-infections as these may disrupt the immune system making it more difficult to fight off disease.[66] Lowering the toxic burden in the gastrointestinal (GI) tract while providing essential nutrients is also important,[67] as is restoring beneficial gut flora particularly if on antibiotics.

There is an increasing link between the brain and the gut and the role that the gut microbiota plays in this,[68] with antibiotic use seen to decrease cognitive function and neurogenesis. However, looking after the gut with probiotics and exercise can rescue this decline.[69] Supplementation with prebiotics (with *fructooligosaccharides*, FOS), eating fermented vegetables, and taking probiotics can all help to increase the healthy bacteria in the gut.[70] Probiotics have also been found to stimulate a protective response from intestinal epithelial cells, promote epithelial cell survival, enhance intestinal barrier function, enhance immunity, and modulate pathogen-induced inflammation, with *Lactobacillus*, *Bifidobacterium*, and *Saccharomyces* extensively studied.[71,72]

Horowitz[73] points out that *Lactobacillus rhamnosus* can help prevent antibiotic-associated diarrhea (AAD), that certain Bifidobacterium strains can help with constipation and in speeding up transit time of waste removal, reduce bloating and discomfort for those with functional bowel disorders, enhance immunity and decrease allergic reactions, and that *Saccaromyces boulardii* (a healthy yeast) can create a temporary barrier which can potentially help to prevent infection of the colon by the bacterium *Clostridium difficile*. He then recommends daily supplementation with probiotics containing *Lactobacillus acidophilus* at a high rate of 200 billion colony-forming units (CFU), and suggests keeping up fluid and fiber intake to support intestinal health, as this can help cleanse the bowel of toxins by increasing the frequency of bowel movements. Strasheim[74] also suggests drinking filtered water, consuming fiber and eating real foods (mostly organic as they may have a lower toxicity level), implementing detoxification methods (such as taking toxin binders 2 hours before or after meals, medication, and supplements), supplementing with gut-soothing substances for inflammation (such as aloe vera, marshmallow root, or slippery elm), taking enzymes and supplements to help with nutrient absorption and in breaking down foods for digestion (for example, hydrochloric acid, HCL, or apple-cider vinegar), and to test for parasites (such as pinworms, roundworms, and tapeworms).

If required, your clinician will be able to work with you to support your gastrointestinal health, and tests such as the comprehensive digestive stool analysis (CDSA)[75] can be employed to evaluate the gut microbiome and determine if any bacteria, *Candida*, or parasite infections are present. As there is a mind-gut connection, healing the gut might also help to heal the brain.[76]

Brain Health.

Lyme and its co-infections (such as *Babesia* and *Bartonella*) can all cause cognitive impairment, behavioral and psychiatric changes,[77] and come to impact almost all areas of the brain and nervous system[78-80] which can lead to a host of problems[81] that include balance, concentration and cognitive issues, depression, insomnia, irritability, and rage, through to long-term issues such as Alzheimer's disease.[82-84] In one study,[85] *Borrelia burgdorferi* was found in 25.3% of Alzheimer's cases, with others reliably linking cerebral vasculitis, chronic debilitating encephalomyelitis, and focal myositis to *Borrelia* infections,[86] and showing that 40% of those with Lyme experience neurological involvement of the central or peripheral nervous system,[87] with such issues manifesting in children as behavioral and emotional disturbances.[88]

These neurological manifestations for Lyme can be attributed in part to *Borrelia burgdorferi* penetration of the blood-brain barrier (BBB) and invasion of the central nervous system (CNS),[89] as well to the toxins released by the bacteria themselves (including those from co-infections).[90] The toxins released from these infections all cause inflammation in the brain and nervous system that end up causing similar symptoms and compromising the body in similar ways,[91] and include exotoxins released as waste material, and endotoxins which are released when the cell wall of the bacteria is damaged by antibiotics or the immune system. *Candida* and other fungal infections can also release toxins that can be a major cause of symptoms that reflect those of Lyme (such as allergy and sinus issues, brain fog, digestive problems, joint pain, and fatigue).[92] All of these toxins can then accumulate in the brain and body, with their presence stimulating the immune system to release cytokines that lead to inflammation and the exacerbation of symptoms.

One toxin often high with those that have Lyme and its co-infections is ammonia, and high levels of it are toxic and inflammatory.[93] An accumulation of it in the brain can have a damaging effect, altering the permeability of the BBB, leading to what Jergin calls a *leaky brain*, which can then potentially be the cause of chemical sensitivities, cognitive dysfunction, and other chronic conditions.[94] High ammonia levels can also lead to a reduction in the production of usable energy (ATP, or adenosine triphosphate) and to symptoms such as fatigue, muscle weakness, nausea, back pain, mood disturbances, the inability to concentrate, and insomnia.[95] A lack of sleep can in turn lower the immune system, inhibiting the body's ability to recover from infections, and lower libido, fertility, cognitive ability, and life-expectancy, while also increasing the risk of having an accident, or developing chronic diseases.[96] It is for these reasons that both detoxification and the reduction of inflammation through various means including diet, supplementation, getting regular exercise, engaging in stress reduction activities, and getting an adequate amount of sleep can be important for keeping up immunity, optimizing neurological function, and for supporting long-term health.[97] Putting this into practice may mean eating more healthy fats such as omega-3s to help reduce inflammation and saturated fats to repair cell membranes, taking antioxidants like glutathione to reduce oxidative stress, taking amino acids to make proteins such as neurotransmitters, starting to move as much as you can to help lymph flow and improve blood flow to the brain, performing meditation to reduce stress levels, and sleeping 8 hours or more a night to aid in healing and in clearing toxins from the brain.[98]

It has been found that supplements such as lithium orotate can help to protect the brain from toxins, improve thinking, elevate mood, and decrease anxiety and nervous system irritability.[99] Amino acids may also help to restore healthy protein levels in the body, and those such as 5-HTP and L-tyrosine may help to improve cognitive function as well as assist in regulating mood, energy, and sleep.[100] Acetyl-L-carnitine (ALCAR) is another amino acid that might prove worthwhile[101] as it supports healthy acetycholine levels in the brain, which is integral to healthy memory, learning, analysis, perception, and other cognitive functions, with increased levels of it potentially able to improve synaptic flexibility and memory formation. It also possesses antioxidant capabilities, and while supporting blood flow to the brain, it can help in removing toxins from it. Additionally, Choline, a water soluble essential micronutrient, may also be useful since it can aid in cognition, mental processing, and memory, and is important for nerve function as well as muscle movement, brain development, liver function, and supporting energy levels and a healthy metabolism.[102] It is available as a cream or in a capsule, and you can get it from 'brain foods' like eggs, or from meat such as shrimp. Vinpocetine may also be helpful as it increases oxygen and blood flow to the brain, improves glucose utilization, and increases brain cell energy (ATP) production while also protecting from free radical overexposure which can damage neurons as well as dysregulate mitochondrial function and neuronal metabolism.[103]

Buhner identifies a number of mushrooms and plants as important for neuroborreliosis to be taken in tincture or powdered form along with supplements in doses that form his protocol.[104] He views Chinese cat's claw (*Uncaria rhynchophylla*) as the most essential as it is anti-inflammatory (particularly for arthritic conditions), provides

Chapter 10: Immune Support | 143

immune stimulation, and works as a neurological protectant.

A few others of note include:
- Ashwagandha (*Withania somnifera*), an adaptogen that can help the body manage stress, regulate hormones, and protect the brain from degeneration.[105]
- Caterpillar fungus (*cordyceps*), an anti-inflammatory with many benefits including that of immune system and detoxification support.[106]
- Chinese skullcap (*Scutellaria baicalensis*), an anti-inflammatory, neuroprotective, and anti-convulsive, which has a number of other health supporting properties.[107]
- Golden root (*Rhodiola rosea*), an adaptogen that can help regulate cortisol, increase neuron sensitivity including neurotransmitters for dopamine and serotonin, and potentially increase focus and improve memory and mood.[108]
- Gotu kola/Pennywort (*Centella asiatica*), a plant that can help boost memory and cognition by reducing inflammation in the brain, can calm the central nervous system by modulating adrenaline and cortisol release, and can promote brain health by increasing cerebral circulation and blood flow.[109]
- Lion's mane (*Hericium erinaceus*), a neuroprotective with the ability to help

restore myelin along the axons of the brain and to promote nerve regeneration.[110]
- Maidenhair tree (*Ginkgo biloba*), a plant extract which has been studied largely for anti-inflammatory, antioxidant, and circulation-boosting effects, along with its ability to improve cognitive function, mood, energy, and memory.[111]
- Motherwort (*Leonurus cardiaca*), a neuroprotective that provides mitochondrial protection, and works to reduce anxiety and sleeplessness.[112]
- Waterhyssop (*Bacopa monniera*), an adaptogen that can help alleviate stress, and reduce anxiety and depression, provide learning and memory improvement, and among other things, help dementia decline in Alzheimer's patients, help alleviate seizures related to epilepsy and be useful for chronic pain management.[113]

It is recognized that *Borreliosis* can seriously compromise and/or damage the nervous and hormonal (neuro-endocrine) systems.[114] Additionally, the chronic stress of infection may be depleting hormones as well as the essential elements necessary for hormonal balance in the body,[115] so it could be important to work with your clinician to balance your hormones, such as those associated with the thyroid or adrenals for example, as hormones can play a critical role in health and disease, affect mood and other brain functions, as well as overall health and immunity, and drive responses to inflammation, energy levels, and many other different processes in the body.[116] This could be an important step in healing as hormonal issues, like dental health, can sometimes become overlooked when chronically ill.

Dental Health.

Optimizing oral health can play a critical role in sustaining whole-body wellbeing that is often overlooked. The oral cavity is a breeding ground for microorganisms that can cause caries, gingivitis (gum inflammation/infection), and periodontitis (inflammation/infection affecting the gums and bones around the teeth, eventually leading to tooth loosening and loss). There is also growing evidence for a link between periodontitis and several systemic diseases like diabetes mellitus, cardiovascular risk, and Alzheimer's disease.[117,118] Oral symptoms of Lyme disease can include:[119]

- Dry mouth
- Pain in chewing muscles
- Pulpitis (inflammation of the pulp)
- Temporomandibular joint pain
- Tooth sensitivity

For those with Lyme and its co-infections, it is important to understand that *Borrelia* can reside in the dental tubules of the teeth (each tooth has 2 to 3 miles of microscopic tubules). Dead teeth and root canal treated teeth have lost their blood and nerve supply to the tubules, and these tubules can become hiding places for bacterial and fungal microorganisms, feeding on the necrotic debris. It will particularly take refuge in eight teeth – the upper and lower centrals, and the upper and lower first molars.[120] To help heal from Lyme, as many impediments to proper immune function as possible need to be eliminated. In the mouth, this would include the promotion of oral hygiene, reducing inflammation from gingivitis, attending to caries, removing amalgams and any dead teeth, and addressing periodontitis and other chronic infections like those of the jawbone.[121]

Oral Hygiene. There are a number of nutrients that can be used to help in the upkeep of oral hygiene[122] which include coenzymeQ10 (coQ10), green tea, and pomegranate. Vitamins B, C, and D, along with lactoferrin and xylitol, are also beneficial. Vitamin B (folic acid) can reduce redness and bleeding and support gingival health,[123] while vitamin C is important for the maintenance of healthy connective tissue such as gums.[124] There is also a significant association between periodontal health and vitamin D levels, likely due to its ability to act as an anti-inflammatory agent and to stimulate antimicrobial peptides, along with its role in promoting bone metabolism.[125] CoQ10, when applied topically, can also improve symptoms of periodontitis[126] and promote healing[127] by potentially reducing the oxidative stress associated with low-grade inflammation.[128] Lactoferrin has also been seen to stop the bacteria responsible for periodontitis,[129] while xylitol has been useful in the prevention of tooth decay[130] by breaking down the biofilms (dental plaque) within which bacteria and fungi hide and proliferate. Green tea catechins are effective in killing the bacteria that cause periodontitis preventing *Streptococcus mutans* activity, and stopping bacteria from sticking to the teeth.[131-134] Pomegranite extract[135] and rinsing with sugar-free pomegranate juice[136] is effective against dental plaque, suppressing the ability of microorganisms to adhere to the surface of teeth.[137] This is important as plaque is a biofilm, and biofilms serve as protective environments where *Borrelia* can hide from immune cells, antibodies, and antibiotics.[138-140] Another method for controlling plaque levels is oil pulling[141] which has its tradition in the Ayurveda medical system that originated in India. It involves vigorously swishing around one or two teaspoons

(5 to 10 milliliters) of oil, such as coconut or sesame oil, for 20 minutes before spitting out and rinsing the mouth well with warm water then brushing the teeth as usual. It is reported to provide significant oral and general health benefits,[142] particularly for decreasing plaque and plaque induced gingivitis.[143] This could be followed up later in the day with consumption of fermented foods and foods containing probiotics to help establish an abundance of good bacteria in the oral cavity and digestive tract.[144] Thirty minutes after eating, particularly acidic foods, it is important to floss your teeth, and then brush them.[145] In this case you may want to consider using a waterpik if flossing with a cord is causing any problems at the gum line.

Root Canals, Cavitations, and Extractions. Root canals are not advised for those with Lyme and its co-infections as they, along with improper extractions, can weaken the competency of the immune system.[146] Root canals and other cavitations can become sites of infection where bacteria are able to evade the immune system as the teeth no longer have a blood supply. From here, they can then release toxins into the body, and go on to infect the surrounding jawbone.[147,148] Also, traditional Chinese medicine meridian theory[149] holds that each tooth corresponds to an organ of the body, and any cavitations harboring infection may impact these meridians and impair overall health recovery.[150] Therefore, an extraction may be preferred. However, with extractions, it is important to ensure correct healing otherwise the site can fill with fatty tissue, dead bone, or infected material. To remedy this, the socket would need cleaning out and debriding, and removal of the ligament that holds the tooth in place along with the dense bony lining of the socket would then be necessary.[151] In any case, it is recommended that a skilled biological dentist, or a dentist that regularly engages in professional development, perform any such procedures.[152]

Mixed Metals, Toxicity, and Galvanization. Dental amalgams, metal-based crowns, implants, and braces can all lead to potential health issues. Perhaps the result of galvanization, the production of an electrical current from two different metals (such as gold, copper, mercury, nickel, silver, tin, or titanium) placed in an electrolyte solution (like saliva) that creates an electrical charge (like a battery). Although most people will be oblivious to galvanic current, others will have unexplained nerve shocks, ulcerations, a metallic taste, burning in the mouth, or at times receive tissue damage.[153] The presence of any metal in the mouth will also see those metals release ions that will then be transported around the body and bind to proteins, which can cause damage. For example, tin released by metal corrosion of amalgams in the presence of titanium causes a corrosion current that can be tasted and tissue damage if the body is not able to generate a high enough level of pH around the titanium. This could be overlooked as it does not leave any evidence in the actual form of corrosion.[154]

Unfortunately, too, dental amalgams continually off-gas in the mouth, and can leech methyl-mercury into the body and brain causing toxicity.[155] For this reason, it is often advised that those with Lyme and its co-infections have any metal removed from their mouth.[156] Due to the hazardous nature of methyl mercury, amalgam fillings need to be removed using specialized equipment and particular precautions,[157] although not all dentists may use them or know of them.[158] If possible, it would be best to commission a skilled biological dentist or a dentist that regularly engages in professional development to perform any procedure. Of interest, mercury in the body can actually lower inflammation, so those people with high levels of toxicity with this metal may actually experience reduced levels of pain and less symptoms of Lyme and its co-infections until it is removed.[159] This can potentially lead to a flare when the amalgams are replaced. Titanium implants are also known to suppress immune cells (e.g., T-cells, and white blood cells), create oxidative stress, and lead to diseases similar to those of root canals.[160] Some people will be more susceptible to the resulting inflammation, autoimmune response, or allergies, and a blood test might be required to determine this. If any of these procedures become necessary, the use of zirconium filings, implants, and crowns may be the better choice, as this material is considered highly biocompatible.[161] This now leads us into the need to consider the importance of our environment for health and the impact of exposure to metals, mold, and man-made electromagnetic fields (EMF) and radio frequency (RF) radiation.

A View from the Field – The Environment: Metal Toxicity; Combating Mold Exposure; and, Minimizing the Impact of Man-Made Electromagnetic Fields (EMF) and Radio Frequency (RF) Radiation

Metal Toxicity.

Exposure to toxic metals from the environment (like air pollution, rain water, drinking water, antiperspirants, secondhand smoke), foods (like fish), and from dental and medical procedures (like amalgams, flu shots, or vaccinations) can be another problem leading to lower levels of health in those with Lyme and its co-infections. For some, the removal of these metals from the body may be a very important part of the recovery process, as their presence in the body has been linked to chronic infections, illness, and pain.[162] Although mercury levels in fish are high, recommendations for limiting the amount eaten have long been in place, since high amounts can poison the kidney and the nervous system, with a total ban on consumption recommended for women who are nursing, pregnant, or planning to become pregnant within a year.[163] Perhaps the metal to be most wary of for those with Lyme and its co-infections is aluminum. This is a neurotoxic metal that is known to cause several neurodegenerative disorders including Alzheimer's disease.[164] It has also been shown that nanonized aluminum is found to be the most abundant form of the metal in the bodies of people with Lyme and its co-infections,[165] and it is this form of aluminum that can cause wide-spread inflammation, as well as mitochondrial and endothelial dysfunction.[166-168]

Endothelial cells that comprise the wall of blood vessels and the lymphatic system are a favored residence for Lyme and its co-infections,[169] more so than connective tissue, and the neurons of the nervous system where it can also reside.[170] This is important, because it is now known that aluminium settles largely in the endothelium, and once there, it can serve to protect Lyme and its co-infections from the immune system.[171] So removal of it from the body, along with detox from any other metal or chemical contamination (from pesticides, rain water, and other environmental exposure) is worth considering, particularly since the body, when burdened with metals, tends to focus on metabolizing those metals over fighting infections.[172]

A popular chelation[****] method for toxic metals is that of the Cutler protocol, developed specifically in response to mercury poisoning from dental amalgams.[173] Other useful techniques for assisting in the removal of toxic metals from the body (such as aluminum, cadmium, lead, mercury, and nickel) include the use of sauna, binders, supplements, intravenous (IV) chelation, and ionic foot baths.[174] Although the color of the water after an ionic foot bath is not deemed relevant, it is recommended for 30 minutes twice weekly after dinner along with regular intake of a cilantro tincture (two droppers in water before meals).[175] In this combination, it has been shown (through urine and hair samples) to effectively remove metals from the body with particularly higher levels excreted on the third day after the foot bath.[176] However, it is advised that those with dental amalgams not use cilantro.[177] Sauna use can also stimulate detoxification pathways, which leads cells to excrete toxins ranging from chemicals, metals, and plastics.[178] Some research suggests that it can also promote the leeching of spirochetes from tissues into the bloodstream where they can then be attacked with antimicrobials.[179] The use of binders can also be beneficial for removing metals and other toxins

---

[****] *Chelation* (pronounced as *key-lay-shun*) therapy is the process used to remove heavy metals from the blood.

from the gut,[180] but they do tend to bind everything, so they are likely best taken apart from food, supplements, and medication. Other supplements like glutathione in liposomal form and cilantro in tincture form can also promote heavy metal removal.[181] Your clinician is likely to advise of the best for your situation and if there is a need for the use of any IV chelation methods. No matter the method chosen, you may require a test to determine your level of toxicity, what metals need to be chelated first, and in what order. Genetic testing may also be useful to determine if you have the MTHFR***** gene mutation or other SNPs (single-nucleotide polymorphism) which can impair the methylation cycle, which reduces the body's ability to remove toxins and also makes people more susceptible to environmental stressors including that of mold.[182] It may also be very well time to let go of the use of aluminum foil and pie plates, purchase aluminum free baking soda, reduce the use of toxic cleaning supplies, forget about getting a tattoo, give up smoking, purchase cosmetics, lipsticks, and body lotions that are free of metals, and limit the consumption of certain foods that are high in toxic metals.[183] Avoiding any unnecessary exposure to mold may also need to become a new priority.

***** *Methylene tetrahydrofolate reductase* (MTHFR) is the rate-limiting enzyme in the methylation cycle, and it is encoded by the MTHFR gene.

Combating Mold Exposure.

Mold toxicity can play a huge role in chronic illness, and those with a weakened immune system can be more susceptible to the effects of mold. Mycotoxins (poisonous substances that the mold makes to prevent other molds growing on its patch) can also disturb the hormonal balance of the body and reduce the ability to handle stressors.[184] Exacerbating the issue is that mold toxicity and the impact of mycotoxins can produce very similar symptoms to that of Lyme and its co-infections, and so distinguishing between them is not always easy.[185,186] However, a free preliminary online screening test, called the Visual Contrast Sensitivity (VCS) test, is available.[187] VCS measures inflammation in the small nerves of the eye that are needed for good contrast resolution. An abnormal score at different contrast frequencies can suggest some underlying causes[188] (i.e., nutrient deficiency, smoking, toxicity). If necessary, more comprehensive body fluid tests can be performed as a follow up. Discovering if mold toxicity is a problem is important as it is considered by many clinicians to be the single most inhibiting factor in patient recovery from Lyme and its co-infections.[189]

Any attack on mold will likely require three major steps. Mold is not always visible, and so the home, workplace, and car may all need testing for contamination, perhaps starting out by collecting dust samples and using an environmental relative moldiness index (ERMI) test.[190] Any mold that becomes evident then needs to be removed or cleaned out, ideally professionally. If this is not possible, or the mold contamination is substantial, then you may have to move. However, the mold problem if in the body (i.e., dental disease, gastrointestinal tract, sinuses) will also be moving with you, and spores could also be transported on any personal items such as clothing and bedding. Secondly, any mold this is present in the body can, like metals, be bound with binders in the gut to reduce reabsorption (entero-hepatic recirculation) and increase excretion in the stool. Binders include some food substances that are high in dietary fiber, and supplements such as glutathione, chlorella, bentonite clay, and activated charcoal.[191] The strongest binders are some proprietary activated silicas, Welchol and particularly cholestyramine. Third, the mycotoxins that enter the blood stream causing systemic symptoms, along with any places mold has colonized in the body, need to be targeted.[192] The Shoemaker Protocol for biotoxins and mold is perhaps one of the most well-known for treatment.[193]

A MARCoNS (multiple antibiotic resistant coagulase negative *staphylococci*) test may also be required to check for an antibiotic-resistant staph infection in the sinus which can form biofilms that can protect it, and mold, from any treatment. Also of concern may be *Candida albicans*, which is actually a yeast and part of the fungi family, as it can also form biofilms in the mucosal layers which can then act as reservoirs to seed and cloak infections.[194] *Candida* is found in everyone's gut flora but it can be problematic for those with Lyme and its co-infections because it is opportunistic, meaning it can grow out of control when undertaking long-term antimicrobial and/or antibiotic treatment.[195] *Candidiasis* can then result from this dysbiosis (imbalance) with many symptoms reflecting those of Lyme[196] – for example: allergy and sinus issues, brain fog, digestive problems, joint pain, and fatigue. Excessive levels of *Candida* may also be accompanied with cravings for carbohydrates and sugars, but these are the types of foods that are best avoided with such an overgrowth as they can support further increase.[197] A specific diet[198] or medication might then be needed to help reduce *Candida* loads in the body. In addition, the use of pre- and pro-biotics can help to eliminate fungus and mold in the gut.[199] It may also prove beneficial to purchase fresh produce, and avoid processed meats, peanuts, grains, dried fruits, dried beans, dairy products, and any other foods that can all harbor mold.[200] Furthermore, time in the sauna can potentially be a good method for *Candida*[201] and mold[202] detoxification, helping to mitigate their effects, while the use of high efficiency particulate air (HEPA) filters can help to reduce, but not eradicate, mold spores in the home, car, and work environments. Another way of reducing potential mold growth is to reduce exposure to man-made electromagnetic fields (EMF).[203]

Minimizing the Impact of Man-Made Electromagnetic Fields (EMF) and Radio Frequency (RF) Radiation.

The body is an electric machine, and electricity is vital to life.[204] Digestion through to brain activity relies on the biochemical reactions of charged particles with the electrical activity of the heart easily measured by electrocardiography (ECG), the brain by electroencephalograph (EEG) and the muscles by electromyography (EMG). Even nerves relay signals transmitted by electric impulses, and as a result, both electric and magnetic fields can impact our bodies.[205] The term electrosensitive (ES), electromagnetic hypersensitivity (EHS), or microwave syndrome[206] refers to those who are greatly impacted by the effects of electromagnetic fields (EMF), also known as electromagnetic radiation (EMR).

EMFs are present everywhere in the environment. Some sources are natural, like that in the ionosphere, those produced by the earth, or those radiating from the sun, while others are man-made. Some countries enforce areas of national radio quiet zones (NRQZ) for the purposes of limiting cellphone service, Wi-Fi, and other radio transmissions in order to facilitate scientific research (with, for example, radio telescopes).[207] Daily exposure to man-made radiofrequency (RF) radiation, including radio waves and microwaves, as well as EMFs, can come from a variety of sources such as any Bluetooth device, computers, cellphones, cellphone towers and repeaters, cordless phones, electric blankets, electric toothbrushes, electric razors, electrical substations, hairdryers, lighting circuits and dimmer switches, fluorescent or halogen lights, microwaves, photocopiers, power lines, refrigerators, smart meters, televisions, Wi-Fi, Wi-Fi hotspots, and Wi-Fi routers. These non-native, man-made EMFs now cover the entire surface of the Earth, and are much stronger than the Earth's natural EMF, within which we evolved.[208,209] Interestingly, the *theta* waves (4 to 8 hertz) of optimal brain creativity, emotional connection, intuition and relaxation mimic the Schuman resonance (7.83 hertz), the Earth's principal background electromagnetic frequency in the 3 to 60 hertz spectrum.[210] The higher amplitude and frequency of man-made EMR have been shown to, among other things, damage the protective blood-brain barrier and stimulate voltage-gated calcium channels on nerve cells, both promoting damaging neuro-excitation and neuro-toxicity.[211] Today, it is estimated that the radio waves that surround the planet are one billion times the amount that naturally reach us from the sun, and that within the first mile above the earth's surface, there is 2 million times the amount of EMF than there was in 1900.[212]

Although the impact of 'electrosmog' (man-made EMFs and RFs) on humans remains a topic of controversy, limiting exposure may be important for some people[213] including those with Lyme and its co-infections, particularly because these frequencies can be immunosuppressive and drive the growth of microbes in the body,[214] with negative effects being cumulative (meaning they are felt over time) rather than instantaneous. Continued exposure to man-made EMFs can also decrease mitochondrial efficiency which can lead to higher blood sugar levels,[215] damage myelin (the lining of the nerves),[216] potentially contribute to the development of neurodegenerative diseases,[217,218] produce widespread neuropsychiatric effects,[219] lead to DNA strand breaks,[220] and increase levels of oxidative stress,[221] which contribute to cancer development. Of note also, pregnant women who are exposed to magnetic field non-ionizing radiation are at a higher risk of miscarriage than those who are not, [222] and surviving fetus' have an increased risk of neurodevelopmental disorders and autism.[223]

Although there is much research to support safe levels and times of exposure to electrosmog for healthy adults (particularly for the thermal radiation that is produced by cellphones), in 2011 the International Agency for Research on Cancer (IARC) classified radiofrequency electromagnetic fields (including those produced when using cellphones) as Group 2B – possibly carcinogenic.[224] It is therefore advised to follow manufacturer guidelines for the use of cellphones,[225] including keeping phones a safe distance away from the body when worn or carried in order to meet the FCC exposure guidelines on the specific absorption rates (SAR) of heat from radiation exposure.

Overexposure for extensive periods of time, specifically to cellphone radiation, may cause health-related problems,[226] particularly if the phone is held to the head,[227] tucked into a bra,[228] or placed in the front pockets of trousers.[229] Instead of holding a cellphone to the side of your head you may consider talking hands-free or using airtube-type headphones. You may also want to invest in a radiation blocking sleeve, and carry the cellphone in a bag instead of on your person. It would also be wise to leave the cellphone off or in airplane mode when not in use, and keeping it out of the bedroom when you sleep. Limiting child use of cellphones and tablets may also be important, as they are at a greater risk of absorbing this radiation[230] (particularly in the head and the bone marrow of the skull); and of experiencing 'digital dementia'[231] (hampering of brain development impacting memory, and attention span). Evidence also shows that living close to cellphone towers (within around 550 yards, or 500 meters) can substantially increase the prevalence of cancer and neurobehavioural symptoms in individuals.[232-234]

Potential risks of frequencies used in each new generation of wireless technology, and devices that rely on the internet of things (IoT) network may also prove damaging to the health of some individuals, particularly as the roll out of these devices, including that of smart meters, is at a much larger scale than for previous generations of wireless technology. This is expected to bring with it issues which may include blood-brain barrier leakiness, DNA damage, melatonin reduction, memory disturbances, mitochondrial disruption, and nerve cell damage.[235] With increasing use of millimeter waves, which have shallow penetration that can affect the skin surface and surface of the eye (the cornea), this can have a major impact on individuals, as stimulating skin receptors can potentially affect nerve signaling responses leading to a whole body response through the nervous system.[236] In animals, this is seen to produce health problems including lens opacity which predisposes cataract development,[237] heart arrhythmias,[238] heart rate variability changes,[239] and immune system changes.[240] Changes to the sensitivity of bacteria to antibiotics,[241] and changes to gene expression in humans,[242] have also been observed.

While in operation, microwave ovens can produce a large field around them, and you may want to remain outside this area of exposure when you are healing. Over time, door seals may also weaken causing some microwave energy to leak out.[243]

Further, cooking with microwave ovens, as with any method using high heat, can lower the nutritional value of foods. Steaming has found to be the best method of retention, aside from preparing food raw, particularly for broccoli.[244] Also, garlic when microwaved for 60 seconds (or oven cooked for 45 minutes) can negate its anticancer properties,[245] while heating breast milk in the microwave can destroy any disease-fighting agents withn.[246] As such, preparing food raw or relying on gentler heating methods may then be preferred. The type of container used when heating foods is also important to consider as toxins can leak from the packaging of microwave foods, with plastics also releasing toxic chemicals and carcinogens into food when heated.[247] Glass or ceramic containers are a better option.

Other concerns from the environment could be related to flying, particularly when taking long-haul flights, as these can be very stressful on the body. They can be dehydrating,[248] and lead to deep vein thrombosis (DVT) and pulmonary embolisms due to blood clots forming as a result of sitting for long periods of time in a confined space.[249] Frequent jet lag has also been linked to increased cancer risk,[250] and for those flying commercial routes in Europe and North America, exposure to cosmic radiation levels are higher than the annual dose limits recommended by the International Commission on Radiological Protection.[251] Further concerns may also be the radiation exposure from the full body scanners at security checkpoints, which emit exceedingly low levels of ionizing radiation that is considered negligible,[252] but frequent-flyers and those who are radiation sensitive may have a higher probability of developing ill health effects from them.[253] On-board Wi-Fi and other devices used by passengers in-flight may also be problematic for passengers, flight crew, and those with Lyme and its co-infections due to reflection and resonance effects within the aircraft interior leading to exposure exceeding recommended levels[254] (Faraday cage effect).

Thankfully, several devices are available that allow you to measure your exposure to EMFs and RFs, including the Cornet and Trifield meters, which measure alternate current (AC) magnetic and electric fields, as well as microwave radiation (radio fields). These devices can help you identify the strength of these fields in your environment, and they can show you where to position furniture so that you are not constantly exposed. A variety of microwave radiation and EMF shielding paints, curtains, and other products like radiation limiting sleeves, and pads for laptops, tablets, and cellphones also exist. It may also be necessary to invest in smart meter blocking devices to put between the wall of the home and the device, along with netting to create a faraday cage sleep canopy over the bed to keep out EMFs and RFs, but be careful not to use any electronic devices within as it will trap any frequencies being put out. Exposure to Wi-Fi can also be limited in the home by using Ethernet cables (a hard-wired connection), with EMFs further reduced by replacing cordless devices with corded ones, and turning off circuit breakers to

Chapter 10: Immune Support | 165

the bedroom (or the entire house) at night in order to provide a solid digital detox.

References

1. Erasmus, S. (2014). *Can you really boost your immune system?* Health24. Retrieved from https://m.health24.com/Diet-and-nutrition/The-immune-system/Immune-system-boosters-fact-or-fiction-20140514
2. McFadzean, N. (2010). *The Lyme diet: Nutritional strategies for healing from Lyme disease.* San Diego: Legacy Line Publishing.
3. Horowitz, R. I. (2017). *How can I get better?: An action plan for treating resistant Lyme & chronic disease.* New York: St. Martin's Press.
4. IQWIG. (2016). *How does the immune system work?* Informed Health Online. PubMed Health. Institute for Quality and Efficiency in Health Care. Retrieved from https://www.ncbi.nlm.nih.gov/pubmedhealth/PMH0072548/
5. Ober, C., Sinatra, S., & Zucker, M. (2010). *Earthing: The most important health discovery ever?* California, USA: Basic health Publications, Inc.
6. Chevalier, G., et al. (2012). Earthing: Health implications of reconnecting the human body to the Earth's surface electrons. *Journal of Environmental and Public health,* 291541. doi: 10.1155/2012/291541

7. Sokal, K., & Sokal, P. (2012). Earthing the human organism influences bioelectrical processes. *Journal of Alternative and Complementary Medicine: Research on Paradigm, Practice, and Policy, 18*(3), 229-234. doi: 10.1089/acm.2010.0683
8. Oschman, J. (2007). Can electrons act as antioxidants? A review and commentary. *The Journal of Alternative and Complementary Medicine: Research on paradigm, practice, and policy, 13*(9), 955-967. doi: 10.1089/acm.2007.7048
9. Asprey, D. (2016). *Head strong: The bulletproof plan to activate untapped brain energy to work smarter and think faster – in just two weeks.* USA: HarperWave.
10. Asprey, D. (2016). *Ibid.*
11. Oschman, J. (2007). *Op. cit.*
12. Sinatra, S., et al. (2017). Electric nutrition: The surprising health and healing benefits of biological grounding (earthing). *Alternative Therapies in Health and Medicine, 23*(5), 8-16.
13. Ghaly, M., & Teplitz, D. (2004). The biologic effects of grounding the human body during sleep as measured by cortisol levels and subjective reporting of sleep, pain, and stress. *The Journal of Alternative and Complementary Medicine: Research on paradigm, practice, and policy, 10*(5), 767-776. doi: 10.1089/acm.2004.10.767
14. Chevalier, G., et al. (2013). Earthing (grounding) the human body reduces blood viscosity – a major factor in cardiovascular disease. *Journal of Alternative and Complementary Medicine, 19*(2), 102-110. doi: 10.1089/acm.2011.0820

Chapter 10: Immune Support | 167

15. Brown, R., & Chevalier, G. (2015). Grounding the human body during yoga exercise with a grounded yoga mat reduces blood viscosity. *Open Journal of Preventative Medicine,* 5(4). doi: 10.4236/ojpm.2015.54019
16. Brown, R., Chevalier, G., & Hill, M. (2015). Grounding after moderate eccentric contractions reduces muscle damage. *Open Access Journal of Sports Medicine,* 21(6), 305-317. doi: 10.2147/OAJSM.S87970
17. Chevalier, G. The effect of grounding the human body on mood. *Psychological Reports,* 116(2), 534-542. doi: 10.2466/06.PR0.116k21w5
18. Sokal, K., & Sokal, P. (2011). Earthing the human body influences physiologic processes. *The Journal of Alternative and Complementary Medicine,* 17(4), 301-308. doi: 10.1089/acm.2010.0687
19. Sokal, P., & Sokal, K. (2011). The neuromodulative role of earthing. *Medical Hypotheses,* 77(5), 824-826. doi: 10.1016/j.mehy.2011.07.046
20. Oschman, J., Chevalier, G., & Brown, R. (2015). The effects of grounding (earthing) on inflammation, the immune response, wound healing, and prevention and treatment of chronic inflammatory and autoimmune diseases. *Journal of Information Research,* 2015(8), 83-96. doi: 10.2147/JIR.S69656
21. Minkoff, D. (2016). Chapter Four – David Minkoff, MD, in C. Strasheim, *New paradigms in Lyme disease treatment: 10 top doctors reveal healing strategies that work.* California, USA: BioMed Publishing Group, LLC.
22. Mercola, J. (2009). *Feasting on sunshine.* Take Control of Your Health. Retrieved from https://articles.mercola.com/sites/articles/archive/2009/01/08/feasting-on-sunshine.aspx

[23.] Mainster, M., & Turner, P. (2006). Retinal injuries from light: Mechanisms, hazards, and prevention, in Ryan, S., et al., *Retina*, (4th ed.). Elsevier, Mosby.

[24.] Holick, M., & Jenkins, M. (2005). *The UV advantage (2nd ed.)*. USA: IBooks, Inc.

[25.] Cao, R., et al. (2015). Light-regulated translational control of circadian behavior be eIF4E phosphorylation. Nature Neuroscience, 18, 855-862. doi: 10.1038/nn.4010

[26.] NIH. (2017). *Circadian rhythms*. National Institute of General Medical Sciences. Retrieved from https://www.nigms.nih.gov/education/pages/Factsheet_CircadianRhythms.aspx

[27.] Massachusetts Institute of Technology. (2013). *The link between circadian rhythms and aging: Gene associated with longevity also regulates the body's circadian clock.* Science Daily. Retrieved from https://www.sciencedaily.com/releases/2013/06/130620132320.htm

[28.] Walton, A. (2012). *Your body's internal clock and how it affects your overall health.* The Atlantic. Retrieved from https://www.theatlantic.com/health/archive/2012/03/your-bodys-internal-clock-and-how-it-affects-your-overall-health/254518/

[29.] Carnegie Mellon University. (2003). *The sun and its energy.* Environmental Decision making, science, and technology. Retrieved from http://environ.andrew.cmu.edu/m3/s2/02 sun.shtml

[30.] Fell, G., et al. (2014). Skin beta-endorphin mediates addiction to UV light. *Cell, 157*(7), 1527-1534 doi: 10.1016/j.cell.2014.04.032

31. Taylor, S., et al. (2009). Pilot study of the effect of ultraviolet light on pain and mood in fibromyalgia syndrome. *The Journal of Alternative and Complementary Medicine: Research on Paradigm, Practice, and Policy, 15*(1), 15-23. doi: 10.1089/acm.2008.0167
32. Holick, M. (2016). Biological effects of sunlight, ultraviolet radiation, visible light, infrared radiation and vitamin D for health. Anticancer Research, 36(3), 1345-1356.
33. Wilson, L. (2016). *Sauna therapy for detoxification and healing*, (3rd ed.). USA: L.D. Wilson Consultants, Inc.
34. Hamblin, M. (2016). Shining light on the head: Photobiomodulation for brain disorders. BBA Clinical, 6, 113-124. doi: 10.10.16/j.bbacli.2016.09.002
35. Pollack, G. (2013). The fourth phase of water: Beyond solid, liquid, and vapor. Seattle, WA: Ebner and sons publishers.
36. Mercola, J. (2013). *The fourth phase of water – what you don't know about water, and really should*. Take Control of Your Health. Retrieved from https://articles.mercola.com/sites/articles/archive/2013/08/18/exclusion-zone-water.aspx
37. Asprey, D. (2016). *Op. cit.*
38. Asprey, D. (2016). *Ibid*.
39. Mercola, J. (2015). *Sunlight – it does your body good*. Take Control of Your Health. Retrieved from https://articles.mercola.com/sites/articles/archive/2015/12/27/vitamin-d-sunlight.aspx
40. Phan, T., et al. (2016). Intrinsic photosensitivity enhances motility of T lymphocytes. *Scientific Reports 6*, 39479. doi: 10.1038/srep39479

41. Heiting, G. (2017). *Blue light: It's both bad and good for you.*
Blue Light. Retrieved from http://www.allaboutvision.com/cvs/blue-light.htm
42. Mercola, J. (2016). *How LED lighting may compromise your health.* Take control of your health. Retrieved from
https://articles.mercola.com/sites/articles/archive/2016/10/23/near-infrared-led-lighting.aspx
43. Jaadane, I., et al. (2017). Effects of white light-emitting diode (LED) exposure on retinal pigment epithelium in vivo. *Journal of Medicine and Biochemistry, 21*(12), 3453-3466. doi: 10.1111/jcmm.13255
44. Van der Lely, S. (2015). Blue blocker glasses as a countermeasure for alerting effects of evening light-emitting diode screen exposure in male teenagers. *Journal of Adolescent Health Care, 56*(1), 113-119. doi: 10.1016/j.jadohealth.2014.08.0 02
45. Anderson, D. (2012). UV light killed drug-resistant bacteria in hospital rooms. Healio: Infectious Disease News. Retrieved from https://www.healio.com/infectious-disease/nosocomial-infections/news/print/infectious-disease-news/%7Be3f422e9-da66-45bd-8b87-6a391fac0
83a%7D/uv-light-killed-drug-resistant-bacteria-in- hospital-rooms
46. Lam, R., et al. (1991). Ultraviolet versus non-ultraviolet light therapy for seasonal affective disorder. *The Journal of Clinical Psychiatry, 52*(5), 213-216.

47. Liu, D., et al. (2013). UVA lowers blood pressure and vasodilates the systemic arterial vasculature by mobilisation of cutaneous nitric oxide stores. *Journal of Investigative Dermatology, 133*, s209-s221. doi:10.1038/ji d.2013.104
48. Liu, D., et al. (2014). UVA irradiation of human skin vasodilates arterial vasculature and lowers blood pressure independently of nitric oxide synthase. *Journal of Investigative Dermatology, 134*(7), 1839-1846. doi:10.1038/jid.2014.27
49. Morison, W. (1985). What is the function of melanin? *Archives of Dermatology, 121*(9), 1160-1163. doi: 10.100 1/archderm.1985.01660090074017
50. Bogdan, C. (2001). Nitric oxide and the immune response. *Nature Immunology, 2*(10), 907-916. doi: 10.1038/ni1001-907
51. Rizk, M., Witte, M., & Barbul, A. (2004). Nitric oxide and wound healing. *World Journal of Surgery, 28*(3), 301-306. doi: 10.1007/s00268-003-7396-7
52. Holick, M. (2016). *Op. cit.*
53. McDonnell, S., et al. (2016). Serum 25-Hydroxyvitamin D concentrations ≥40 ng/ml are associated with >65% lower cancer risk: Pooled analysis of randomized trial and prospective cohort study. *PLoS One, 11*(4). doi: 10.1371/journal.pone.0152441
54. Mercola, J. (2016). *New discoveries may unlock the link between vitamin D deficiency and autism.* Take Control of Your Health. Retrieved from https://articles.mercola.com/sites/articles/archive/2016/02/14/vitamin-d-autism.aspx

55. Mercola, J. (2017). *How sun exposure improves your immune function.* Take Control of Your Health. Retrieved from https://articles.mercola.com/sites/articles/archive/2017/01/23/how-sun-exposure-improves-immune-function.aspx
56. Aquilla, S., et al. (2009). Human male gamete endocrinology: 1alpha, 25-dihydroxyvitamin D3 (1,25(OH)2D3) regulates different aspects of human sperm biology and metabolism. *Reproductive Biology and Endocrinology, 7,* 140. doi: 10.1186/1477-7827-7-140
57. Krysiak, R., Gilowska, M., & Okopien, B. (2016). Sexual function and depressive symptoms in young women with low vitamin D status: A pilot study. *European Journal of Obstetrics & Gynaecology and Reproductive Biology, 204,* 108-112. doi: 10.1016/j.ejogrb.2016.08.001
58. Marques, C., et al. (2010). The importance of vitamin D levels in autoimmune diseases. *Revista Brasileira de Reumatologia, 50*(1). doi: 10.1590/S0482-50042010000100007
59. French, A., et al. (2013). Time outdoors and the prevention of myopia. *Experimental Eye Research, 114,* 58-68. doi: 10.1016/j.exer.2013.04.018
60. Axe, J. (2017). *Top 10 vitamin D rich foods.* Food is Medicine. Retrieved from https://draxe.com/top-10-vitamin-d-rich-foods
61. Rawls, W. (2017). *Unlocking Lyme: Myths, truths, & practical solutions for chronic Lyme disease.* USA: FirstDoNoHarm Publishing.
62. Rawls, W. (2017). *Ibid.*
63. Aberdour, S. (2017). Natural sun protection from the inside out. Alive – your complete source for natural health and wellness. Retrieved from https://www.alive.com/ health/natural-sun-protection

64. Gunnars, K. (2015). *Does all disease really begin in the gut? The surprising truth.* HealthLine Newsletter. Retrieved from https://www.healthline.com/nutrition/does-all-disease-begin-in-the-gut
65. Horowitz, R. (2017). *Op. cit.*
66. Strasheim, C. (2017). *Healing the gut: a crucial component of recovery from Lyme disease.* ProHealth. Retrieved from http://www.prohealth.com/library/showarticle.cfm?libid=30494
67. Horowitz, R. (2017). *Op. cit.*
68. Mayer, E. (2016). *The Mind-Gut Connection: How the hidden conversation within our bodies impacts our mood, our choices, and our overall health.* USA: Harper Wave.
69. Mohle, L. Ly6C[hi] monocytes provide a link between antibiotic-induced changes in gut microbiota and adult hippocampal neurogenesis. Cell Reports, 15(9), 1945-1956. doi: 10.1016/j.celrep.2016.04.074
70. Horowitz, R. (2017). *Op. cit.*
71. Yan, F., & Polk, D. (2011). Probiotics and immune health. *Current Opinion in Gastroenterology, 27*(6), 496-501. doi: 10.1097/IMOG.0b013e32834baa4d
72. Kelesidis, T., & Pothoulakis, C. (2012). Efficacy and safety of the probiotic Saccharomyces boulardii for the prevention and therapy of gastrointestinal disorders. Therapeutic Advances in Gastroenterology, 5(2), 111-125. doi: 10.1177/1756283X11428502
73. Horowitz, R. (2017). *Op. cit.*
74. Strasheim, C. (2017). *Op. cit.*

75. CDSA. (2018). Identify problems with your gut health with the comprehensive digestive stool analysis test (CDSA). Planet Naturopath. Retrieved from https://www.planetnaturopath.com/clone-cdsa-test-au/?gclid=CjwKCAiA4vbSBRBNEiwAMorER72cA5NQzrYKLi8v_wAl3GD7KlD-5jxWhMstTWfztHBvNCTaIRO17BoCaiMQAvD_BwE

76. Streisham, C. (2017). *Five supplements that improve cognitive function in Lyme disease*. ProHealth. Retrieved from http://www.prohealth.com/lyme/library/showarticle.cfm?libid=30627

77. Jemmott, J. (2018). Meet the Lyme disease experts: Dr. Robert Bransfield: Lyme disease and the brain. Lyme Connection. Retrieved from http://lymeconnection.org/news_publications/meet_the_lyme_disease_experts.html/title/dr-robert-bransfield-lyme-disease-and-the-brain-

78. Mayne, P. (2015). Clinical determinants of Lyme borreliosis, babesiosis, bartonellosis, anaplasmosis, and ehrlichiosis in an Australian cohort. *International Journal of General Medicine, 8*, 25-26. doi: 10.2147/IJGM.S75825

79. Schaller, J. (2007). Do Bartonella infections cause agitation, panic, disorder, and treatment-resistant depression? *Medscape General Medicine, 9*(3), 54.

80. Balakrishnan, N. (2016). Vaculitis, cerebral infarction and persistent Bartonella henselae infection in a child. *Parasites & Vectors, 9*, 254. doi: 10.1186/s13071-016-1547-9

81. Logigian, E., et al. (1990). Chronic neurologic manifestations of Lyme disease. *New England Journal of Medicine, 323*, 1438-1444. doi: 10.1056/NEJM/199011223232102

82. McFadzean Ducharme, N. (2016). *Lyme brain: The impact of Lyme disease on your brain, and how to reclaim your smarts.* USA: BioMed Publishing Group.
83. Global Lyme Alliance. (2017). *Living with Lyme brain.* Global Lyme Alliance. Retrieved from https://globallymealliance.org /living-lyme-brain
84. Sherr, V. (2015). The agony of Lyme brain: Mainstream medicine misses psychiatric symptoms of Neuroborreliosis. *The Lyme Times, 27*(3), 24.
85. Miklossy, J. (2011). Alzheimer's disease – a neurospirochetosis. Analysis of the evidence following Koch's and Hill's criteria. *Journal of Inflammation, 8*, 90. doi: 10.1186/1742-2094-9-90
86. Kristoferitsch, W. (1993). Neurologic manifestations in Lyme borreliosis. *Clinics in Dermatology, 11*(3), 393-400. doi: 10.1016/0738-081X(93)90095-T
87. Fallon, B., & Nields, J. (1994). Lyme disease: a neuropsychiatric illness. *The American Journal of Psychiatry, 151*(11), 1571-1583. doi:10.1176/ajp.151.11.1571
88. Rhee, H., & Cameron, D. (2012). Lyme disease and pediatric autoimmune neuropsychiatric disorders associated with streptococcal infections (PANDAS): an overview. *International Journal of General Medicine, 5*, 163-174. doi: 10.2147/IJGM.S24212
89. Grab, D., et al. (2005). Borrelia burgdorferi, host-derived proteases, and the blood-brain barrier. *Infection and Immunity, 73*(2), 1014-1022.
90. Horowitz, R. (2017). *Op. cit.*
91. Anderson, W. (2016). Chapter One – Wayne Anderson, ND, in C. Strasheim, *New paradigms in Lyme disease treatment: 10 top doctors reveal healing strategies that work.* California, USA: BioMed Publishing Group, LLC.

92. Forsgren, S. (2008). Candida related complex: A complicating factor in Lyme disease. Public Health Alert. Retrieved from http://www.publichealthalert.org/candida-related-complex-a-complicating-factor-in-lyme-disease.html
93. Jockers, D. (2018a). *CBS mutation and low sulfur diet.* Supercharge Your Health. Retrieved from https://drjockers.com/cbs-mutation-low-sulfur-diet
94. Jernigan, D. (2007). Lyme toxins the primary cause of your symptoms. *Townsend Letter for Alternative Medicine: The Examiner of Alternative Medicine,* April, 141-149.
95. Jockers, D. (2018a). *Op. cit.*
96. Harvard Medical School. (2018). *Healthy Sleep.* Division of Sleep Medicine at Harvard Medical School in Partnership with WGBH Educational Foundation. Retrieved from http://healthysleep.med.harvard.edu/healthy/matters
97. Horowitz, R. (2017). *Op. cit.*
98. Xie, L., et. al. (2013). Sleep drives metabolite clearance from the adult brain. *Science, 342*(6156), 373-377. doi: 10.1126/science.1241224
99. Ross, M. (2018). *Lithium orotate.* The Treat Lyme Book. Retrieved from http://www.treatlyme.net/treat-lyme-book/lithium-orotate-5mg
100. Streisham, C. (2017). *Op. cit.*
101. BrainMD. (2014). *How acetyl-carnitine helps produce energy.* BrainMD Health. Retrieved from https://www.brainmdhealth.com/blog/acetyl-l-carnitine-the-dark-horse-brain-health-supplement-that-you-need-to-know
102. Axe, J. (2018). *What is choline? Benefits, sources, and signs of choline deficiency.* Food is Medicine. Retrieved from https://draxe.com/what-is-choline

[103] Streisham, C. (2017). *Op. cit.*

[104] Buhner, S. (2013). *Healing Lyme co-infections: Complimentary and holistic treatments for Bartonella and Mycoplasma.* Vermont: Healing Arts Press.

[105] Axe, J. (2018). *Ashwagandha benefits thyroid and adrenals.* Food is Medicine. Retrieved from https://draxe.com/ashwagandha-proven-to-heal-thyroid-and-adrenals

[106] Axe, J. (2018). *Cordyceps for anti-aging and exercise performance.* Food is Medicine. Retrieved from https://draxe.com/cordyceps

[107] Mercola, J. (2018). *Skullcap: Why this hooded herb deserves your attention.* Take Control of Your Health. Retrieved from https://articles.mercola.com/herbs-spices/skullcap.aspx

[108] Axe, J. (2018). *Rhodiola benefits: Burning fat for energy and beating depression.* Food is Medicine. Retrieved from https://draxe.com/rhodiola-benefits-burning-fat-for-energy-and-beating-depression

[109] White, S. (2016). *Herbs and supplements for memory and cognitive support during Lyme treatment.* ProHealth. Retrieved from http://www.prohealth.com/lyme/library/showArticle.cfm?libid=29499

[110] White, S. (2016). *Ibid.*

[111] Axe, J. (2018). *Ginkgo biloba benefits energy, mood and memory.* Food is Medicine. Retrieved from https://draxe.com/ginkgo-biloba-benefits

[112] Buhner, S. (2013). *Op. cit.*

[113] Axe, J. (2018). *Bacopa: The brain-boosting alternative treatment to psychotropic drugs.* Food is Medicine. Retrieved from https://draxe.com/bacopa

114. Nathan, N. (2016). Chapter Three – Neil Nathan, MD. in C. Strasheim, *New paradigms in Lyme disease treatment: 10 top doctors reveal healing strategies that work*. California, USA: BioMed Publishing Group, LLC.

115. Anderson, W., & Gitlin, R. (2014). Lyme, neurotoxins, and hormonal factors: An interview with Nancy Faass. *Townsend Letter: The Examiner of Alternative Medicine, July*. Retrieved from http://www.townsendletter.com/July2014/lymeneuro0714.htm

116. Mercola, J. (2014). *The fantastical world of hormones*. Take Control of Your Health. Retrieved from https://articles.mercola.com/sites/articles/archive/2014/09/27/fantastical-world-hormones.aspx

117. Williams, R., et al. (2008). The potential impact of periodontal disease on general health: A consensus view. *Current Medical Research and Opinion, 24*(6), 1635-1643. doi: 10.1185/03007990802131215

118. Abbayya, K., et al. (2015). Association between periodontitis and Alzheimer's disease. *North American Journal of Medical Sciences, 7*(6), 241-246. doi: 10.4103/1947-2714.159325

119. Russell, A. (2017). Ticks, Lyme disease, and your oral health. Western Pennsylvania Oral & Maxillofacial Surgery PC. Retrieved from http://www.westernpaoms.com/ticks-lyme-disease-oral-health

120. Budinger, M. (2009). Interview: Biological dentist Dr. Andrew Landerman, DDS, Lyme disease often resides in the mouth. Public Health Alert: Investigating Lyme and Chronic Illness. Retrieved from http://www.publichealthalert.org/lyme-disease-often-resides-in-the-mouth

121. Budinger, M. (2009). *Ibid*.

122. Kiefer, D. (2008). Disease prevention begins in the mouth. *Life Extension Magazine*, September. Retrieved fromhttp://www.lifeextension.com/Magazine/2008/9/Disease-Prevention-Begins-in-the-Mouth/Page-01

123. Pack, A. (1984). Folate mouthwash: Effects on established gingivitis in periodontal patients. *Journal of Clinical Periodontology, 11*(9), 619-628. doi:10.1111/j.1600-051X.1984.tb00914

124. Chambial, S., et al. (2013). Vitamin C in disease prevention and cure: An overview. *Indian Journal of Clinical Biochemistry, 28*(4), 314-328. doi: 10.1007/s12291-013-0375-3

125. Stein, S., & Tipton, D. (2011). Vitamin D and its impact on oral health – an update. *The Journal of the Tennessee Dental Association, 91*(2), 30-33.

126. Hanioka, T., et al. (1994). Effect of topical application of coenzyme Q10 on adult periodontitis. *Molecular Aspects of Medicine, 15*, s241-s248.

127. Wilkinson, E., et al. (1975). Bioenergetics in clinical medicine. II. Adjunctive treatment with coenzyme Q in periodontal therapy. *Research Communications in Chemical Pathology and Pharmacology, 12*(1), 111-123.

128. Battino, M., et al. (2005). Antioxidant status (CoQ10 and Vit. E levels) and immunohistochemical analysis of soft tissues in periodontal diseases. *Biofactors, 25*(1-4), 213-217. doi: 10.1002/biof.5520250126

129. Kalfa, S., et al. (1991). Human lactoferrin binding to Porphyromonas gingivalis, Prevotella intermedia and Prevptella melaninogenica. *Oral Microbiology and Immunology, 6*(6), 350-355. doi: 10.1111/j.1399- 302X.1991.tb00506.x

130. Lynch, H., & Milgrom, P. (2003). Xyitol and dental caries: An overview for clinicians. *Journal of the Californian Dental Association, 31*(3), 205-209.

131. Hirasawa, M., et al. (2002). Improvement of periodontal status by green tea catechin using a local delivery system: A clinical pilot study. *Journal of Periodontal Research, 37*(6), 433-438. doi: 10.1034/j.1600-0765.2002.01640.x

132. Hamilton-Miller, J. (2001). Anti-cariogenic properties of tea (Camellia sinensis). *Journal of Medical Microbiology, 50*(4), 299-302. doi: 10.1099/0022-1317-50-4-299

133. Cabrera, C., Artacho, R., & Gimenez, R. (2006). Beneficial effects of green tea – a review. Journal of the American College of Nutrition, 25(2), 79-99. doi: 10.1080/07315724.2 006.10719518

134. Jayakeerthana, S. (2016). Benefits of green tea: A review. *Journal of Pharmaceutical Sciences and Research, 8*(10), 1184-1187.

135. Menzes, S., Cordeiro, L., & Viana, G. (2006). Punica granatum (pomegranate) extract is active against dental plaque. *Journal of Herbal Pharmacotherapy, 6*(2), 79-92. doi: 10.1080/J157v06n02_7

136. Kote, S., Kote, S., & Nagesh, L. (2011). Effect of pomegranate juice on dental plaque microorgansims (Streptococci and Lactobacilli). *Ancient Science of Life, 31*(2), 49-51. doi: 10.4103/0257-7941.107364

137. Vasconcelos, L., et al. (2006). Minimum inhibitory concentration of adherence of Punica granatum Linn (pomegranate) gel against S. mutans, S. mitis and C. albicans. *Brazillian Dental Journal, 17*(3), 223-227. doi: 10.1590/S0103-64402006000300009

138. Jefferson, K. (2004). What drives bacteria to form a biofilm? *FEMS Microbiology Letters, 52*(4), 917-924.

139. Sapi, E. (2008). Biofilms: A hideout for Borrelia burgdorferi. *The Lyme Times, 54*, 15-16.
140. Ross, M. (2016). *Biofilms: Lyme disease gated communities*. The Treat Lyme Book. Retrieved from http://www.treat lyme.net/treat-lyme-book/biofilms-lyme-disease-gated-communities
141. Nagilla, J., et al. (2017). Comparative evaluation of antiplaque efficacy of coconut oil pulling and a placebo, among dental college students: A randomized controlled trial. *Journal of clinical and diagnostic research, 11*(9), zc08-zc11. doi: 10.7860/JCDR/2017/26656.10563
142. Naseem, M., et al. (2017). Oil pulling and importance of traditional medicine in oral health maintenance. *International Journal of Health Sciences, 11*(4), 65-70.
143. Peedikayil, F., et al. (2015). Effect of coconut oil in plaque related gingivitis – a preliminary report. *Nigerian Medical Journal: Journal of the Nigeria Medical Association, 56*(2), 143-147. doi: 10.4103/0300-1652.153406
144. Lin, S. (2018). *The Dental Diet: The Surprising Link Between Your Teeth, Real Food, and Life-changing Natural Health*. USA: Hay House, Inc.
145. Salinas, T. When and how often should you brush your teeth? Mayo Clinic. Retrieved from https://www.mayo clinic.org/healthy-lifestyle/adult-health/expert- answers/ brushing-your-teeth/faq-20058193
146. Budinger, M. (2009). *Op. cit.*
147. Kulacz, R., & Levy, J. (2014). *Toxic Tooth: How a Root Canal Could be Making You Sick*. Nevada, USA: Medfox publishing.
148. Meinig, G. (2008). *Root Canal Cover-Up*, (9th ed.). USA: Price Pottenger Nutrition.

149. Wang, G., Ayati, M., & Zhang, W. (2010). Meridian studies in China: A systematic review. *Journal of Acupuncture and Meridian Studies, 3*(1), 1-9. doi: 10.1016/S2005-2901(10)600 01-5
150. Patel, R. (2016). Chapter Five – Raj Patel, MD, in C. Strasheim, *New paradigms in Lyme disease treatment: 10 top doctors reveal healing strategies that work*. California, USA: BioMed Publishing Group, LLC.
151. Budinger, M. (2009). *Op. cit.*
152. Strasheim, C. (2016). *New paradigms in Lyme disease treatment: 10 top doctors reveal healing strategies that work*. California, USA: BioMed Publishing Group, LLC.
153. Stoep, C. (2014). *Safer and healthier alternatives to root canals and other common, yet harmful, tooth restoration techniques*. Take Control of Your Health. Retrieved from https://articles.mercola.com/sites/articles/archive/2014/05/03/root-canal-alternative.aspx
154. Ravnholt, G. (1988). Corrosion current and pH rise around titanium coupled to dental alloys. *Scandinavian Journal of Dental Research, 96*(5), 466-472.
155. Strasheim, C. (2016). *Op. Cit.*
156. Minkoff, D. (2016). *Op. cit.*
157. Matheson, M. (2016). Chapter Nine – Marie Matheson, ND, in C. Strasheim, *New paradigms in Lyme disease treatment: 10 top doctors reveal healing strategies that work*. California, USA: BioMed Publishing Group, LLC.
158. Minkoff, D. (2016). *Op. cit.*
159. Klinghardt, D. (2016). Chapter Two – Dietrich Klinghardt, MD, PhD, in C. Strasheim, *New paradigms in Lyme disease treatment: 10 top doctors reveal healing strategies that work*. California, USA: BioMed Publishing Group, LLC.
160. Stoep, C. (2014). *Op. cit.*

Chapter 10: Immune Support | 183

161. Hisbergues, M., Vendeville, S., & Vendeville, P. (2009). Zirconia: Established facts and perspectives for a biomaterial in dental implantology. *Journal of Biomedical Materials Research. Part B, Applied Biomaterials, 88*(2), 519-529. doi: 10.1002/jbm.b.31147
162. Klinghardt, D. (2016). *Op. cit.*
163. NRDC. (2017). *Mercury Guide: Whether you're getting dental fillings or ordering sushi, keep these tips in mind to avoid exposure.* National Resources Defense Council. Retrieved from https://www.nrdc.org/stories/mercury-guide
164. Lukiw, J., Percy, M., & Kruck, T. (2005). Nanomolar aluminium induces pro-inflammatory and pro-apoptotic gene expression in human brain cells in primary culture. *Journal of Inorganic Biochemistry, 99*(9), 1895-8. doi: 10.1016/j.jinorgbio.2005.04.021
165. Klinghardt, D. (2016). *Op. cit.*
166. Pineton de Chambrun, G., et al. (2014). Aluminum enhances inflammation and decreases mucosal healing in experimental colitis in mice. *Mucosal Immunology, 7*(3), 489-601. doi: 10.1038/mi.2013.78
167. Yamamoto, Y., et al. (2002). Aluminum toxicity is associated with mitochondrial dysfunction and the production of reactive oxygen specials in plant cells. Plant physiology, 128(1), 63-72. doi: 10.1104/pp.010417
168. Martinez, C., et al. (2017). Aluminum exposure at human dietary levels promotes vascular dysfunction and increases blood pressure in rats: A concerted action of NAD(P)H oxidase and COX-2. *Toxicology, 390*, 10-21. doi: 10.1016/j.tox.2017.08.004
169. Lidar, M., et al. (2009). The infectious etiology of vasculitis. *Autoimmunity, 42*(5), 432-438.
170. Klinghardt, D. (2016). *Op. cit.*
171. Klinghardt, D. (2016). *Ibid.*

172. Matheson, M. (2016). *Op. cit.*
173. Cutler, A. (1999). *Amalgam illness, diagnosis and treatment: What you can do to get better, how your doctor can help.* USA: Andrew Hall Cutler.
174. Klinghardt, D. (2016). *Op. cit.*
175. Klinghardt, D. (2016). *Ibid.*
176. Griesz-Brisson, M., in Klinghardt, D. (2016). *Ibid.*
177. Rainville, A. (2017). *Refresher Lecture.* Klinghardt Lyme Solutions 2017.
178. Wilson, L. (2016). *Sauna therapy for detoxification and healing,* (3rd ed.). USA: L.D. Wilson Consultants, Inc.
179. Matheson, M. (2016). *Op. cit.*
180. Patel, R. (2016). *Op. cit.*
181. McFadzean-Ducharme, N. (2016). Chapter Six – McFadzean-Ducharme, ND, in C. Strasheim, *New paradigms in Lyme disease treatment: 10 top doctors reveal healing strategies that work.* California, USA: BioMed Publishing Group, LLC.
182. McFadzean-Ducharme, N. (2016). *Op. cit.*
183. Cosentino, B. (2015). Heavy metals, Lyme disease and parasites. Real Food Rebel: Natural Solutions for Better Health. Retrieved from http://realfoodrebel.com/heavy-metals-lyme-disease-and-parasites/
184. Rawls, W. (2017). *Op. cit.*
185. Patel, R. (2016). *Op. cit.*
186. Rawls, W. (2017). *Op. cit.*
187. VCST. (2017). Visual Contrast Sensitivity Test. VCSTest.com. Retrieved from https://www.vcstest.com
188. Anderson, W. (2016). *Op. cit.*
189. Strasheim, C. (2016). *New paradigms in Lyme disease treatment: 10 top doctors reveal healing strategies that work.* California, USA: BioMed Publishing Group, LLC.

[190] Patel, R. (2016). *Op. cit.*
[191] Rawls, W. (2017). *Op. cit.*
[192] Anderson, W. (2016). *Op. cit.*
[193] Shoemaker, R. (2017). Treatment. Surviving Mold. Retrieved from http://www.survivingmold.com/treatment
[194] Gulati, M., et al. (2017). Visualization of biofilm formation in Candida albicans using an automated microfluidic device. *Journal of Visualized Experiments, 14*(13). doi: 10.3791/56743.
[195] Buttaccio, J. (2016). *Six ways to combat Candida during Lyme treatment.* Prohealth. Retrieved from http://www.prohealth.com/lyme/library/showarticle.cfm?libid=29775
[196] Forsgren, S. (2008). Candida related complex: A complicating factor in Lyme disease. Public Health Alert. Retrieved from http://www.publichealthalert.org/candida-related-complex-a-complicating-factor-in-lyme-disease.html
[197] Axe, J. (2018). 9 Candida symptoms and 3 steps to treat them. Food is Medicine. Retrieved from https://draxe.com/candida-symptoms
[198] Boroch, A. (2009). *The Candida cure: Yeast, fungus and your health – the 90-day Program to beat Candida and restore vibrant health*. California, USA: Quintessential Healing, Inc.
[199] Douwes, F. (2016). Chapter Eight – Fridrich Douwes, MD, in C. Strasheim, *New paradigms in Lyme disease treatment: 10 top doctors reveal healing strategies that work*. California, USA: BioMed Publishing Group, LLC.
[200] Rawls, W. (2017). *Op. cit.*
[201] Richards, L. (2018). *Sauna can relieve Candida Symptoms.* Perfect Health. Retrieved from https://www.thecandidadiet.com/sauna-for-candida

[202] McFadzean-Ducharme, N. (2016). *Op. cit.*

[203] Klinghardt, D. (2016). *Op. cit.*

[204] Becker, R., & Selden, G. (1998). The body electric: electromagnetism and the foundation of life. New York: Morrow.

[205] WHO. (2018a). What are electromagnetic fields? World Health Organization. Retrieved from http://www.who.int/peh-emf/about/WhatisEMF/en /index1.html

[206] Carpenter, D. (2015). The microwave syndrome or electro-hypersensitivity: historical background. *Reviews on Environmental Health, 30*(4), 217-22. doi: 10.1515/reveh-2015-0016

[207] Woody, P. & Murphy, D. (2016). *National radio quiet zone.* National Radio Astronomy Observatory: Enabling forefront research into the universe at radio wavelengths. Retrieved from https://science.nrao.edu /facilities/gbt/int erference-protection/nrqz

[208] WHO. (2018b). Natural background and human-made sources and exposure. World Health Organization. Retrieved from http://www.who.int/peh- emf/publications/3_EHC_232_Sources_and_Exposure.pdf

[209] WHO. (2018a). *Op. cit.*

[210] Cherry, N. (2003). Human intelligence: The brain, an electromagnetic system synchronized by the Schumann Resonance signal. *Medical hypotheses, 60*(6), 843-844. doi: 10.1016/S0306-9877(03)00027-6

[211] Pall, M. (2013). Electromagnetic fields act via activation of voltage-gated calcium channels to produce beneficial or adverse effects. *Journal of Cellular and Molecular Medicine, 17*(8), 958-965. doi: 10.1111/jcmm.12088

212. Kruse, J. (2013). EMF 5: What are the biologic effects of EMF? Reversing Disease for Optimal Health. Retrieved from https://www.jackkruse.com/emf-5- what-are-the-biologic-effects-of-emf

213. Marshall, T., & Rumann Heil, T. (2017). Electrosmog and autoimmune disease. *Immunologic Research, 65*(1), 129-135. doi: 10.1007/s.12026-016-8825-7

214. Klinghardt, D. (2016). *Op. cit.*

215. Meo, A., et al. (2015). Association of exposure to radio-frequency electromagnetic field radiation (RF-EMFR) generated by mobile phone base stations with glycated hemoglobin (HbA1c) and risk of type 2 diabetes mellitus. *International Journal of Environmental Research and Public Health, 12*(11), 14519-14528. doi: 10.3390/ijerph121114519

216. Redmayne, M., & Johansson, O. (2014). Could myelin damage from radiofrequency electromagnetic field exposure help explain the functional impairment electrohypersensitivity? A review of the evidence. *Journal of toxicology and environmental health. Part B, critical reviews, 17*(5), 247-258. doi: 10.1080/10937404.2014.923356

217. Consales, C., et al. (2012). Electromagnetic fields, oxidative stress, and neurodegeneration. *International Journal of Cell Biology, 2012*. doi: 10.1155/20 12/683897

218. Dasdag, S., et al. (2015). Effects of 2.4 Ghz radiofrequency radiation emitted from Wi-Fi equipment on microRNA expression in brain tissue. *International Journal of Radiation Biology and Related Studies in Physics, Chemistry, and Medicine, 91*(7), 555-561. doi: 10.3109/09553002.2015

219. Pall, M. (2016). Microwave frequency electromagnetic fields (EMFs) produce widespread neuropsychiatric effects including depression. *Journal of Chemical Neuroanatomy, 75,* part B, 43-51. doi: 10.1016/j.chemneu.2015.08.001

220. Mihai, C., et al. (2014). Extremely low-frequency electromagnetic fields cause DNA strand breaks in normal cells. *Journal of Environmental Health Science & Engineering, 12*(15). doi: 10.1186/2052-336X-12-5

221. Yakymenko, I, et al. (2016). Oxidative mechanisms of biological activity of low-intensity radiofrequency radiation. *Electromagnetic biology and medicine, 35*(2), 186-202. doi: 10.3109/15368378.2015.1043557

222. Li, D., et al. (2017). Exposure to magnetic field non-ionizing radiation and the risk of miscarriage: A prospective cohort study. *Scientific Reports, 7,* 17541. doi: 10.1038/s41598-017-16623-8

223. Sage, C., & Carpenter, D. (Eds.). (2012). Bioinitiative report: A rationale for a biologically-based public exposure standard for electromagnetic radiation. Bioinitiative 2012. Retrieved from http://bioinitiative.info /bioInitiativeReport2012.pdf

224. WHO. (2011). IARC classifies radiofrequency electromagnetic fields as possibly carcinogenic to humans. *World Health Organization press release No. 208.* International Agency for Research on Cancer. Retrieved from http://www.iarc.fr/en/media-centre/pr/2011/pdfs/pr208_E.pdf

225. Apple. (2018). iPhone X RF exposure information. Apple, Inc. Retrieved from https://www.apple.com/legal/rfexposure/iphone10,3/en/

226. Naeem, Z. (2014). Health risks associated with mobile phone use. *International Journal of health Sciences, 8*(4), v-vi.

227. Kesari, K., et al. (2013). Cell phone radiation exposure on brain and associated biological systems. Indian Journal of Experimental Biology, 51(3), 187-200.

228. West, J., et al. (2013). Multifocal breast cancer in young women with prolonged contact between their breasts and their cellular phones. Case Reports in Medicine, 2013, 354682. doi: 10.1155/2013/354682

229. Zilberlicht, A., et al. (2015). Habits of cell phone usage and sperm quality – does it warrant attention? *Reproductive Biomedicine Online, 31*(3). 421-426. doi: 10.1016/j.rbmo.2015.06.006

230. Ghandi, O., et al. (2012). Exposure limits: The underestimation of absorbed cell phone radiation, especially in children. *Electromagnetic biology and medicine, 31*(1), 34-51. doi: 10.3109/15368378.2011.622827

231. Dossey, L. (2014). FOMO, digital dementia, and our dangerous experiment. *Explore: The Journal of Science and healing, 10*(2), 69-73. doi: 10.1016/j.explore.2013.13.008

232. Gandhi, G., Kaur, G., & Nisar, U. (2015). A cross-sectional case control study on genetic damage in individuals residing in the vicinity of a mobile phone base station. *Electromagnetic Biology and Medicine, 34*(4), 344-354. doi: 10.3109/15368378.2014.933349

233. Khurane, V. et al, (2010). Epidemiological evidence for a health risk from mobile phone base stations. *International Journal of Occupational and Environmental Health,* 16(3), 263-267. doi: 10.1179/107735210799160192

234. Levitt, B., & Lai, H. (2010). Biological effects from exposure to electromagnetic radiation emitted by cell tower base stations and other antenna arrays. *Environmental reviews, 18*(NA), 369-395. doi: 10.1139/A 10-018
235. Sage, C., & Carpenter, D. (Eds.). (2012). *Op. cit.*
236. Russell, C., (2017). A 5G wireless future: Will it give us a smart nation or contribute to an unhealthy one? *The Bulletin*, January/February, 20-23. Retrieved from https://ecfsapi.fcc.gov/file/10308361407065/5%20G%20Wireless%20Future-SCCMA%20Bulletin_Feb%202017_pdf.pdf
237. Prost, M., et al. (1994). Experimental studies on the influence of millimeter radiation on light transmission through the lens. *Klinika Oczna, 96*(8-9), 257-259.
238. Chernyakov, G., et al. (1989). Reactions of biological systems of various complexity to the action of low-level EHF radiation, in N. Devyatkov. *Millimeter Waves in Medicine and Biology*. Moscow: Radioelectronica.
239. Potekhina, I., et al. (1992). Effects of low-intensity electromagnetic radiation in the millimeter range on the cardio-vascular system of the white rat. *Journal of Physiology of USSR, 78*, 35-41.
240. Kolomytseva, M., et al. (2002). Suppression of nonspecific resistance of the body under the effect of extremely high frequency electromagnetic radiation of low intensity. *Biofizika, 47*(1), 71-77.
241. Soghomonyan, D., et al. (2016). Millimeter waves or extremely high frequency electromagnetic fields in the environment; What are their effects on bacteria? *Applied Microbiology and Biotechnology, 100*(11), 4761-4771. doi: 10.1007/s00253-016-7538-0

Chapter 10: Immune Support | 191

[242] Habauzit, D. et al. (2014). Transcriptome analysis reveals the contribution of thermal and the specific effects in cellular response to millimeter wave exposure. PLos One, 9(10), e109435. doi: 10.137/journal.pone.0109435

[243] Lahham, A., & Sharabati, A. (2013). Radiofrequency radiation leakage from microwave ovens. *Radiation Protection Dosimetry, 157*(4), 488-490. doi: 10.1093/rpd/nct173

[244] Yuan, G., et al. (2009). Effects of different cooking methods on health-promoting compounds of broccoli. *Journal of Zhejiang University Science B, 19*(8), 580-588. doi: 10.1631/jzus.B0920051

[245] Song, K., & Milner, J. (2001). The influence of heating on the anticancer properties of garlic. *Journal of Nutrition, 131*(3s), 1054S-1057S.

[246] Quan, R., et al. (1992). Effects of microwave radiation on anti-infective factors in human milk. *Pediatrics, 89*(4), 667-669.

[247] Lefferts, L., & Schmidt, S. (1990). *Microwaves: The heat is on (microwaveable packaging & Cookware may be releasing harmful substances into food)*. Nutrition Action Newsletter. Retrieved from https://www.highbeam.com/doc/1G1-8811061.html

[248] Shepherd, L., & Edwards, S. (2004). The effects of flying: Processes, consequences and prevention. *British Journal of Nursing, 13*(1), 19-29. doi: 10.12968/bjon.2004.13.Sup4.163 47

[249] CDC. (2016). *Blood clots and travel: What you need to know*. Centers for Disease Control and Prevention. Retrieved from https://www.cdc.gov/ncbddd/dvt/travel.html

250. Iwamoto, A., et al. (2014). Effects of chronic jet lag on the central and peripheral circadian clocks in CBA/N mice. *Chronobiology International, 31*(2), 189-198. doi: 10.3109/07420528.2013.837478

251. Alvarez, L., Eastham, S., & Barret, S. (2016). Radiation dose to the global flying population. Journal of Radiological Protection, 36(1), 93-103. doi: 10.1088/0952-4746/36/1/93

252. Mehta, P., & Smith-Bindman, R. (2011). Airport full body screening: What is the risk? *Archives of Internal Medicine, 171*(12), 1112-1115. doi: 10.1001/architernmed.2011.105

253. Accardo, J., & Chaudhry, A. (2014). Radiation exposure and privacy concerns surrounding full-body scanners in airports. *Journal of Radiation Research and Applied Sciences, 7*(2), 198-200. doi: 10.1016/j.jrras.2014.02.005

254. Crofton, K. (2015). Wi-Fi in the sky – convenient and in-demand – is it safe? Towards better health. Retrieved from http://mieuxprevenir.blogspot.com/2015/11/wifi-in-sky-convenient-and-in-demand-is.html

11. How Do You Detox From The Treatment Of Lyme And/Or Its Co-infections?

Detoxification, or *detox* for short, is the term used to refer to the process of toxin removal from the body. This is a continual and ongoing process which the body naturally undertakes using the colon, kidneys, liver, lymph, lungs, and skin,[1,2] but the process can be assisted.[3,4]

Detoxification

There are a number of methods available for helping the body with detox. Some methods are found steeped in folklore, simply accepted due to tradition, and employed due to historical use, and it is not often clear why each method is meant to be valuable. Taking this into account, the benefits of a handful of detoxification methods will be explored in detail. These include cupping therapy, the use of Epsom salt, exercise, lemon water, massage therapy, and sauna. A major reason why detoxification during treatment of Lyme disease and its co-infections is important is that it can be used to alleviate symptoms of a Jarisch-Herxheimer Reaction,[5] or *herx* for short, and this is also discussed.

Several approaches to help alleviate a Jarisch-Herxheimer reaction, and to further assist with detoxification, are then introduced.

Cupping Therapy.

This is one of the world's oldest healing modalities, with a long and well-documented history in ancient Chinese, as well as ancient Egyptian medical practices.[6] It involves the use of glass, bamboo, earthenware, or silicone cups, to create suction on the skin over an acupuncture point or an area of pain, and it comprises of either dry or wet cupping techniques.[7] Wet cupping pulls the skin into the cup after laceration so that blood is drawn into the cup, while dry cupping pulls the skin into the cup without laceration. Both methods break superficial blood vessels in the uppermost layer of the skin, and leave marks which disappear over several days. Wet cupping has been traditionally used for detoxification of the blood,[8] with cup fluid reportedly high in toxins,[9] for alleviating pain,[10,11] and for increasing health-related quality of life for patients with chronic conditions.[12] Cupping is associated with the acupuncture tradition, as is moxibustion* which can help to strengthen immunity,[13] while acupuncture has been found to help alleviate inflammation in the body in animal and human studies.[14]

---

* *Moxibustion* is a form of heat therapy where dried mugwort, *moxa*, is burned on or near the surface of the skin.

Epsom Salt.

This salt takes its name from a spring in Epsom (Surrey, England), where it was first distilled from water,[15] and it has been used for a variety of purposes throughout time (like boosting plant growth, or cleaning tiles).[16] It is different from other salts as it is a mineral compound of magnesium and sulfate, unlike table salt which is sodium chloride. Today, Epsom salt is commonly used in foot baths and full-body baths to help relax muscles, ease pain, assist with fatigue, and to enhance circulation and detoxification.[17] Foot baths are said to help magnesium absorb thorough the soles, and full-body baths can help magnesium absorb through the skin, into tissues and cells, pushing out heavy metals, toxins, and chemicals, as well as breaking down yeast toxins.[18] The magnesium component of Epsom salt can also help with fatigue, particularly for those deficient in the macromineral, and this is noteworthy as nearly 48% of people in the United States consume less than the required amount of magnesium from food.[19] In the body, sulfate is also a key component for several biological processes, and supports an important detox pathway for the liver.[20] Sulfur can increase bile production, which is important because bile is the means for transporting toxins from the liver to the colon for expulsion.[21] One to two cups of Epsom salts (8 to 16 ounces or 240 to 480 grams) is a common recommendation per twenty-minute warm bath,[22] with bathing of two or three times per week using 500 to 600 grams considered optimal.[23]

Exercise.

Exercising while ill with any disease might prove difficult if bed-bound, couch-bound, or even just house-bound, but movement can help to engage the circulatory and lymph systems,[24] thus promoting oxygenation of the tissues, delivery of nutrients to the body, and the removal of toxins from the body.[25] Exercise can be as strenuous as rebounding to support the circulatory system and the movement of lymph.[26] Getting the lymph flowing is important as it transports waste products from cells and the extra cellular matrix to the blood and on to the detoxification organs. Benefits of hydration, particularly during exercise, is also important, and along with proteolytic enzymes between meals (i.e., serrapeptase), it can help to thin the lymph for easy flow. As an aerobic activity, walking could help counteract the impact of a sedentary lifestyle.[27,28] Exercise can also mean performing breathing exercises as a relaxation technique to reduce the impact of stress[29,30] and for pain management,[31] or engaging in a gentle restorative yoga program to help in stress reduction as well as to increase flexibility, build up lost strength, and help to reduce pain.[32] Ultimately, the key is doing what is possible, when it is possible.[33] Even simply spending time in nature can lead to increased psychological and physiological benefits, including a reduction in stress levels.[34] Stress reduction is important, as stress can lead to inflammation in the body.[35]

Lemon Water.

This is essentially the juice of lemons, and perhaps the rind, added to water, and a variety of recipes for it exist.[36,37] The total quantity of water required by a person per day, obtained from food, water, and other beverages, varies with age, weight, and gender,[38] and lemon water can aid in reaching that amount. Citrus fruits and their juices can also play a preventative role in many diseases,[39] with many of the medicinal properties of lemons stemming from the flavonoids** that they contain.[40] Drinking water[41] with added lemon juice[42] can stimulate the production of bile in the liver, serving to keep food moving along the gastrointestinal tract for expulsion. The vitamin C content obtained from lemons can also enhance the immune system.[43] Lemon water may also promote a more alkaline environment in the body,[44] which helps to maintain a blood pH balance that is beneficial for metabolic functioning, and it can potentially be used to alleviate a Jarisch-Herxheimer reaction,[45]

** Plants provide vitamins, minerals, and phytonutrients. *Flavonoids* are one class of phytonutrients, and are thought to provide health benefits through cell signaling pathways and antioxidant effects.

particularly at the high ratio of one to two lemons' worth of juice (1.5 ounces or 45 milliliters) to a glass (8 ounces or 240 milliliters) of water.[46]

Massage Therapy.

This therapy for Lyme disease shows some promise for the relief of pain, fatigue, and impaired concentration.[47] Lymphatic drainage may also help increase the flow of lymph, and in turn assist in the removal of toxins from the body.[48] This is because, along with facilitating absorption of fats and fat-soluble nutrients and balancing fluid in the blood versus tissues, the lymphatic system forms part of the body's immune system.[49] Techniques for performing lymphatic drainage, along with detoxification are discussed by Prilutsky,[50] where he suggests undergoing lymphatic drainage every fifth treatment if getting a weekly massage.

Sauna.

The use of sauna has long been recognized as a therapeutic tool,[51,52] and it can enhance blood flow in as little as 15 minutes,[53] with sweating a useful body mechanism for the elimination of toxins[54] such as heavy metals[55] and chemicals.[56] Sauna use can also reduce the risk of fatal heart attacks,[57] and reduce the onset of dementia and Alzheimer's disease.[58] A wide variety of saunas exist – full-spectrum, near-, mid-, and far-infrared, wet/dry Finnish, smoke, steam, and portable – each with their own heating mechanisms and potential health benefits.[59,60] Wilson[61] goes into more detail, and provides several recommendations for sauna use which include starting slow; drinking lots of water before, during, and after; using a towel to wipe sweat from the body while in the sauna; limiting sessions to 20 minutes; and showering afterwards.

A View from the Field – Additional Detoxification Methods and Jarisch-Herxheimer Reaction Relief

A Jarisch-Herxheimer reaction, or herx for short, can occur when disease symptoms flare, perhaps due to spirochete lysis,*** and release of bacterial toxins into the blood and tissues resulting in inflammation and pain.[62] It is also known as JHR, herxing, or a Herxheimer reaction, and is a typical *die-off* response to therapy, occurring between 48 to 72 hours after treatment. It is not specific to the treatment of Lyme disease or its co-infections, as it is the result of the body's inability to process the number of endotoxins released as the microbes are being killed with treatment.[63] Interestingly, it was first described in the literature in relation to syphilis,[64,65] which is another spirochete and the

---

*** *Lysis* is the rupturing of the cell wall or membrane, leading to disintegration of the cell.

original 'great imitator.'[66] Adverse reactions to medication or to herbal treatments may also promote the same bodily reactions as a herx, and might be confused with a JHR,[67] so it is always prudent to update the treating physician concerning any symptom changes.

A number of detoxification methods can offer near immediate relief from a herx while others will work over the long term by helping to continuously cleanse the body of endotoxins in small amounts. For fast relief, Horowitz[68] specifically recommends an Alka-Seltzer Gold, glutathione, lemon water combination, with 70% of people feeling better within hours after taking it.[69] The suggested dosage is 2 Alka-Seltzer Gold tablets in 8 ounces (240 milliliters) of water with the juice of one lemon (2 ounces or 60 milliliters) for alkalization and vitamin C. Prior to drinking it, 1,500 milligrams of liposomal glutathione should be taken to support detoxification, and then the concoction should be sipped slowly over several minutes.

Other methods to help alleviate a herx and to aid in the process of detoxification might include the use of: algae, herbs and herbal tinctures, foods, plants, and seeds, clays and minerals, homeopathic-spagyric medication, prescription-based products, over-the-counter drugs, and supplements, as well as the use of castor oil packs, colonics and coffee enemas, cold showers, or dry skin brushing.[70,71]

Algae, Herbs and Herbal Tinctures, Foods, Plants and seeds.

Algae.

Chlorella. These algae being rich in minerals, proteins, and vitamins can support the immune system.[72] They have been found to relieve symptoms and normalize body functions in patients with fibromyalgia,[73] while also reducing the heavy metal burden of the digestive tract.[74] They can also prove useful for removing environmental chemicals and pesticides, as well as mold toxins from the body.[75] Taking the broken cell wall form will aid in better digestion of the algae.

Herbs and Herbal Tinctures.

Herbs.

Red Root. This herb can help clear dead cellular tissue from the lymph system while protecting the spleen from microbial damage, but it is contraindicated in pregnancy.[76]

Smilax. This herb is useful for binding neurotoxins, and supporting detoxification and herxes, while also acting as a general anti-inflammatory.[77] It is known for its antimicrobial properties, attributed to its ability to bind endotoxins.[78]

Turmeric (curcumin). The active ingredient in turmeric (curcumin) contains anti-inflammatory properties which can help reduce the symptoms of a herx.[79] Turmeric can also assist in detoxification of the liver as it can increase bile production, with bile the means of transporting toxins from the liver to the colon.[80,81]

Herbal Tinctures. There are several Nutramedix herbal tinctures, part of the Cowden Protocol,[82] that are available separately and are designed to help with detoxification and in alleviating a herx. These are: *burbur-pinella*, *parsley*, and *sparga*.

Burbur-Pinella. The *burbur* component assists in cleansing the blood, kidneys, liver, and lymph, while the *pinella* component is said to help reduce brain fog and toxin induced seizures.[83,84] If experiencing a herx the protocol suggests a recommended dose of 20 drops in 2 ounces (60 milliliters) of water every 10 minutes for up to 2 hours.

Parsley. It is said that this herbal tincture can assist in reducing a herx by helping drain the lymph system, and by supporting detoxification of the liver, gall bladder, and kidneys. It is recommended to take 8 to 10 drops in a ¼ cup (2 ounces or 60 milliliters) of water every 10 to 15 minutes until symptoms subside (typically 1 to 2 hours).[85]

Sparga. This herbal tincture is an extract from the root of asparagus. It is designed to help remove excess sulfites and sulfa drugs (sulfonamide) from the body which can be absorbed when eating animals that have been dosed with antibiotics, as well as from the direct intake of medication.[86] Consuming this tincture is useful as the cells can then begin to take in appropriate sulfur amino acids, and can more efficiently produce glutathione, an antioxidant important for detoxification. However, those with the cystathionine beta synthase (CBS) and sulfite oxidase (SuOx) gene mutations may require molybdenum for efficient processing of the sulfites being removed through any use of sparga.[87]

Foods, Plants, and Seeds.
Foods.
Apple Cider Vinegar. There is evidence for the antioxidant,[88] antibacterial, antifungal, antiviral, and cytotoxicity of apple cider vinegar,[89] and for these reasons, it may actually induce a herx. However, like the use of lemon water, using it for promoting an alkaline balance in the body may prove beneficial in the detoxification process.

Cruciferous Vegetables. Broccoli, Brussel sprouts, cabbage, and cauliflower are the types of foods that can provide a range of nutrients[90] that can specifically support the body as it performs its natural detoxification process.[91]

Plants.
Dandelion. This flowering plant contains a number of vitamins and nutrients that can support the liver

to work properly, support the proper flow of bile, help with mineral absorption, and reduce inflammation.[92] Dandelion tea is also a particularly good choice as an alternative to coffee.

Seeds.
Milk Thistle. *Silymarin*, the main component of milk thistle seeds, supports healthy liver and kidney function, stimulates bile production and flow, acts as an immune stimulant, and as an anti-inflammatory for both the liver and the spleen.[93] It primarily helps with phase I detoxification, but can be combined with liposomal glutathione to support phase II.[94,95] Phase I detoxification relies on chemical reactions to make toxic chemicals less harmful. Phase II, the conjugation pathway, further processes the toxic chemicals so that they become harmless and water soluble. Phase III detoxification then removes these water-soluble toxins from the cells and the body.[96]

Clays and Minerals.
Clays.
Bentonite. This is an edible clay composed of the ash from volcanos that can be taken to help bind chemicals and heavy metals for removal from the body. It can be used externally on the skin, in a bath, or taken once per day as a drink by mixing ½ to 1 teaspoon (about 2 to 4 grams) in water.[97] It is also known as Montmorillonite clay, and it is thought to

work by producing an electrical charge when in contact with liquid that then attracts toxins that can be removed from the gut, skin, and mouth.[98] Clays have been known to heal skin infections, and to serve as antibacterial agents since the earliest times of recorded history,[99] with clay eating (*geophagia*) part of traditional medicine treatments for a variety of illnesses.

Minerals.

Fulvic Acid. Supplementing with fulvic acid can produce humoral immune stimulation,[100] while use of a fulvic mineral complex can provide nutrients to deep tissues.[101] Obtaining minerals and trace minerals from supplements is important today, as many foods are devoid of micronutrients,[102] and they are important to the methylation cycle which is responsible for among other things, dealing with inflammation, energy production and mitochondrial health, immune responses, and assisting with the detoxification of hormones, chemicals, and heavy metals.[103]

Molybdenum. This is an essential trace element that can be found in a variety of foods (like legumes, leafy vegetables, and nuts). It is also a co-factor for sulfite oxidase, which is necessary for metabolizing sulfur-containing amino acids, and it serves as an enzyme catalyst contributing to the antioxidant capacity of the blood, helps in the metabolism of drugs and toxins, and in expediting the removal of certain toxic substances from the body.[104] If you are suffering from *Candida* die-off, it is an important mineral as it can convert the toxin acetaldehyde to acetic acid for removal by the body.[105] If you have the CBS gene mutation, then it can also be used to bring down excess sulfites.[106]

Zeolites. These are minerals which are formed after molten lava comes into contact with a water source, and they have been used as a binder for heavy metals and chemicals particularly ammonia.[107] It can provide some anti-inflammatory effects, support intestinal wall integrity,[108] and alleviate oxidative stress,[109] and as such may play a useful part in any detox regime.

Homeopathic-Spagyric Medication, Prescription-Based Products, Over-The-Counter Drugs, and Supplements.

Homeopathic-Spagyric Medication

Pekana Products. Only available with a doctor's note or after a consultation, Pekana products consist of a variety of homeopathic-spagyric remedies.[110] For those interested in this method or protocol, the products for detoxification are: Apo-Hepat (for the liver), Itires (for the lymph), and Renelix (for the kidney).[111]

Prescription-Based Products.

Cholestyramine. The strongest binders are some proprietary activated silicas, like cholestyramine (particularly for mold).[112] It is available by prescription and binds so well that nothing can be taken an hour prior and four to six hours after ingesting it, otherwise nutritional deficiencies could result.[113] An alternative is the supplement modified citrus pectin.

Over-The-Counter Drugs.

Benadryl. This over-the-counter drug is widely available in a number of countries. The active ingredient diphenhydramine produces an antihistamine effect, and the medication can also be useful for promoting relaxation and for falling asleep.[114] It may prove useful short-term as a herx reaction can cause a release of histamine,[115] but it would be best not to rely on it long-term.

Supplements.

Activated charcoal. In capsule, powder, or tablet form, activated charcoal works by a process of adsorption, with endotoxins responsible for a herx binding to it as it travels through the intestinal tract. It is able to reduce the toxic load of the body by over 60% with daily use,[116] and it is best taken in a natural form (like that derived from coconut husk).[117] If combined with magnesium citrate, a charcoal/magnesium flush developed as part of the

Yasko protocol for autism can be undertaken to help reduce ammonia levels in the body.[118] This is important for those with Lyme and its co-infections, particularly for those with the CBS gene mutation which can lead to high levels of ammonia, taurine, and sulfur building up in the body.[119] High levels of ammonia can be toxic and inflammatory, seeing a reduction in the production of usable energy (ATP, or adenosine triphosphate) and leading to symptoms such as fatigue, muscle weakness, nausea, and back pain, while also being damaging to the brain and leading to symptoms that include insomnia, the inability to concentrate, and mood disturbances.[120] High amounts of stress can also increase the levels of ammonia in the body. Normally it is removed as part of the urea or ornithine cycle, and flushed out in urine.[121]

Alpha Lipoic Acid. This antioxidant is naturally made by the body, as well as obtained from foods like broccoli, spinach, and red meat (particularly organ meat).[122] For those with Lyme and its co-infections it may be important as it can help the body recycle the antioxidant glutathione, reduce inflammation in the body, and serve to protect mitochondria while providing support for cellular and liver detoxification.[123] It is also a chelator,[124] can be useful for mold related issues, but is perhaps best avoided by those with the CBS gene mutation (along with chlorella, glutathione, and methyl-folate among others) or those with dental amalgams.[125]

Glutathione. This antioxidant is important as it serves to protect all cells in the body from oxidative stress, supports detoxification via the liver, and promotes heavy metal detoxification.[126] It is also known as the body's master antioxidant, as it plays a role in maintaining all other essential antioxidants in their active forms.[127]

L-Ornithine. This amino acid supplement has been shown to have anti-fatigue effects as a result of increasing the efficiency of energy production as well as being responsible for assisting in the excretion of ammonia.[130]

Methyl-Guard. This supplement may prove useful for those with the methylene tetrahydrofolate reductase (MTHFR) gene mutation, as it provides the active form (folate) rather than the inactive form (folic acid) of vitamin B9 which can help produce the antioxidant glutathione in the methylation cycle. This is important as the methylation cycle, among other things, deals with inflammation, energy production and mitochondrial health, immune responses, and assists with the detoxification of hormones, chemicals, and heavy metals from the body.[129]

Modified Citrus Pectin. This supplement is derived from the peel and pulp of citrus fruit, and can be used as a detoxifier for heavy metals, binding to these metals in the digestive tract and helping to prevent their reabsorption into the bloodstream, leading to a 74% decrease in toxicity.[130] It can also help with constipation.[131]

Castor Oil Packs, Colonics and Coffee Enemas, Cold Showers, and Dry Skin Brushing.

Castor Oil Packs.

The external use of castor oil packs was popularized by Edgar Cayce for a variety of ailments,[132] and in fact the topical application of castor oil has been found to produce analgesic and anti-inflammatory effects[133] as well as working as an antitoxin and having an impact on the lymphatic system by enhancing immunologic function.[134] It has also been said that castor oil packs can support the detoxification process, likely as a result of helping to expel waste from the body, as they have been shown to reduce constipation,[135] with castor oil also producing a laxative effect and inducing labor when taken internally.[136] The packs can be made using castor oil and flannel placed onto the skin above the liver (or other area of concern), then covered with a plastic wrap before a gentle heat source (like a hot water bottle) is placed on top for half an hour or so.[137] As a relaxing process, it may also help to reduce levels of stress with the heat assisting with circulation.

Colonics and Coffee Enemas.

As part of the Gerson therapy, coffee enemas have been used in the fight against cancer.[138] It is considered beneficial in the detoxification process as it is said to produce the antioxidant glutathione, but this is not necessarily supported by the literature.[139] There is also a lack of literature in support of colonics,[140] even though these are widely reported to provide health benefits, with some Lyme practitioners recommending them.[141]

Cold Showers.

Cold bathing is a common cultural custom in a number of countries, particularly seeing people alternating between warm, hot, and cold plunge pools in spas, and using it or a cold shower to finish off a sauna session.[142] It is claimed that it can potentially boost the immune system, raise the metabolic rate of the body, and increase blood and lymph flow, but true associations are still unclear.[143] For detox it might be helpful as muscle contractions during a short cold shower could help in moving toxins along pathways for processing and removal from the body.

Dry Skin Brushing.

The purpose behind dry skin brushing is to stimulate the skin as well as the lymphatic system of the body by increasing blood flow, and thereby supporting detoxification.[144] It is performed in combination with the use of a specific brush designed for the purpose, typically with a long handle, and can also help in exfoliating the skin. It can take as little as 5 to 15 minutes to complete, starting at the top of the body and working down, with all brush strokes firm and going towards the heart using long motions and avoiding cuts or wounds. Follow the process with a bath or a shower.[145]

It may not always be possible to prevent a Herxheimer reaction during treatment for Lyme and its co-infections,[146] but steps can be taken to minimize the severity of the reaction through any number of detoxification methods, or a combination thereof. Though finding a balance is going to be key, as too much detoxification applied too quickly can be as bad as not enough, or going too slowly, as each could end up making you feel worse. The type of diet can also impact upon the process of detoxification,[147-149] and a change in diet could help those living with Lyme and co-infections as they heal.

References

1. Slaga, T. (2003). *The detox revolution: A powerful new program for boosting your body's ability to fight cancer and other diseases*. New York: McGraw Hill.
2. Gonzalez, D. (2014). *Organs that detox the body*. Family Health Chiropractic. Retrieved from http://www.famiIyhealthchiropractic.com/organs-that-detox-your-body
3. Fitzgerald, P. (2007). Incorporating circulatory therapy into a comprehensive detoxification program. *The Lyme Times: Alternative Medicine 49*, 11-12.
4. Muran, P. (2008). Lyme disease – A functional medicine approach. *The Lyme Times, 54*, 3-5.
5. Horowitz, R. (2017). *How can I get better?: An action plan for treating resistant Lyme & chronic disease*. New York: St. Martin's Press.
6. Qureshi, N., et al. (2017). History of cupping (hijama): A narrative review of literature. *Journal of Integrative medicine, 15*(3), 172-181. doi: 10.1016/S2095-4964(17)60339-X
7. Chirali, I. (2014). *Traditional Chinese medicine cupping therapy*, 3rd ed. London: Churchill Livingstone Elsevier.
8. El Wakil, A. (2011). Observations of the popularity and religious significance of blood-cupping (al-hijama) as an Islamic medicine. *Contemporary Islamic Studies, 2*, doi: 10.5339/cis.2011.2
9. Schockert, T. (2009) Observations on cupping. High toxin concentration in blood from cupping. *MMW Fortschritte Der Medizin, 151*(23), 20.

10. Kwon, Y., & Cho, H. (2007). Systematic review of cupping including bloodletting therapy for musculoskeletal diseases in Korea. *Korean Journal of Oriental Physiology & Pathology, 21*, 789-793. Retrieved from http://www. hantopic.com/kjopp/ 2103/33.pdf

11. Lee, M., Kim, J., & Ernst. (2011). Is cupping an effective Treatment? An overview of systematic reviews. *Journal of Acupuncture and Meridian Studies, 4*(1), 1-4. doi: 10.1016/S2005-2901(11)60001-0

12. Al Jaouni, S., et al. (2017). The effect of wet cupping on quality of life of adult patients with chronic medical conditions in King Abdulaziz University Hospital. *Saudi Medical Journal, 38*(1), 53-62. doi: 10.15537/smj.2017.1.15154

13. Myoung, H., & Lee, K. (2014). A unique electrical thermal stimulation system comparable to moxibustion of subcutaneous tissue. *Evidence-Based Complementary and Alternative Medicine, 2014*. doi: 10.1155/2014/518313

14. McDonald, J. Cripps, A., & Smith, P. (2015). Mediators, receptors, and signaling pathways in the anti-inflammatory and antihyperalgesic effects of acupuncture. *Evidence-Based Complementary and Alternative Medicine, 2015*. doi: 10.1155/2015/975632

15. Axe, J. (2017). *Epsom salt – The magnesium-rich, detoxifying, pain reliever*. Food is Medicine. Retrieved from https://draxe. com/epsom-salt

16. Rudolf, R. (1917). The use of Epsom salts, historically considered. *Canadian Medical Association Journal, 7*(12), 1069-1071.

17. Fitzgerald, P. (2007). *Op. cit.*

18. Rippey, M (2014). *Episode 20: Dr. Carolyn Dean explains the power of old fashioned Epsom salt baths*. Lyme Ninja Radio. Retrieved from https://lymeninjaradio.com/dr carolyndean

[19] Rosanoff, A., Weaver, C., & Rude, R. Suboptimal magnesium status in the United States: Are the health consequences underestimated? *Nutrition Reviews*, 70(3), 153-164. doi: 10.1111/j.1753-4887.2011.00465.x

[20] Elliot, E. (2007). Guide to detoxification. *The Lyme Times: Alternative Medicine 49*, 13-16.

[21] Slaga, T. (2003). *Op. cit.*

[22] Brusie, C. (2017). *Epsom salt detox: What are the benefits?* Healthline. Retrieved from http://www.healthline.com/health/epsom-salt-detox#overview1

[23] Waring, R. (2015). Report on absorption of magnesium sulfate (Epsom salts) across the skin. UK: School of Biosciences, University of Birmingham. Retrieved from http://www.epsomsaltcouncil.org/wp-content/uploads/2015/10/report_on_absorption_of_magnesium_sulfate.pdf

[24] Fitzgerald, P. (2007). *Op. cit.*

[25] Elliot, E. (2007). *Op. cit.*

[26] Walker, M. (2005). *Jumping for health: A guide to rebounding aerobics*. New York: KE Publishing.

[27] Hamilton, M., et al. (2012). Too little exercise and too much sitting: Inactivity physiology and the need for new recommendations on sedentary behavior. *Current Cardiovascular Risk Reports, 2*(4), 292-298. doi: 10.1007/s12170-008-0054-8

[28] Tschentscher, M, Niederseer, D., & Niebauer, J. (2013). Health benefits of Nordic walking: A systematic review. *American Journal of Preventative Medicine, 44*(1), 76-84. doi: 10.1016/j.amepre.2012.09.043

29. Nogawa, M., et al. (2007). Assessment of slow-breathing relaxation technique in acute stressful tasks using a multipurpose non-invasive beat-by-beat cardiovascular monitoring system. *Proceedings of the Annual International Conference of the IEEE Engineering in Medicine and Biology Society*, 5323-5325. August, 22-26. France: Lyon.

30. Brown, R., & Gerbarg, P. (2009). Yoga breathing, meditation, and longevity. *Annals of the New York Academy of Sciences, 1172*, 54-62. doi: 10.1111/j.1749-6632.2009. 04394.x

31. Miller, K. (1987). Deep breathing relaxation: A pain management technique. *AORN Journal, 45*(2), 484, 486-488.

32. Meltzer, D. (2007). Acupuncture, qigong, and yoga for Lyme disease. *The Lyme Times: Alternative Medicine 49*, 32-33.

33. Oderberg, N. (2009). Managing the stresses of chronic illness: Focused attention affirmations, exercises, and activities promote physical and mental wellness. *The Lyme Times, 55*, 22-23.

34. Hansen, M., Jones, R., & Tocchini, K. (2017). Shinrin-yoku (forest bathing) and nature therapy: A state-of-the-art review. *International Journal of Environmental Research and Public Health, 14*(8), 851. doi: 10.3390/ijerph14080851

35. Kiecolt-Glaser, J. (2010). Stress, food, and inflammation: Psychoneuroimmunology and nutrition at the cutting edge. *Psychosomatic Medicine, 72*(4), 365-369. doi: 10.1097/PSY.0b013e3181dbf489

36. Olena. (2015). *How to make lemon water*. iFoodreal. Retrieved from http://ifoodreal.com/how-to-make-lemon-water

37. Nichols, H. (2017). *35 science-backed health benefits of lemon water*. Well-Being Secrets. Retrieved from http://www.well-beingsecrets.com/lemon-water-benefits/#Why_Choose_Lemon_Water
38. Popkin, B., et al. (2010). Water, Hydration, and Health. *Nutrition Reviews, 68*(8), 439-458. doi: 10.1111/j.1753-4887.2010.00304.x
39. Cirmi, S., et al. (2017). Anticancer potential of citrus juices and their extracts: A systematic review of both preclinical and clinical studies. *Frontiers in Pharmacology, 30*(8), 420. doi: 10.3389/fphar.2017.00420
40. Rio, J., et al. (2007). Citrus Limon: A source of flavonoids of pharmaceutical interest. *Food Chemistry, 84*(3), 457-461. doi: 10.1016/S0308-8146(03)00272-3
41. Ross, M. (2014). Lyme detoxification 101: The basics. *The Treat Lyme Book*. Healing Arts Partnership. Retrieved from http://www.treatlyme.net/treat-lyme-book/lyme-detoxificati on- 101-the-basics
42. Axe, J. (2017). *The benefits of lemon water: Detox your body & skin*. Food is Medicine. Retrieved from https://draxe.com/ benefits-of-lemon-water
43. Wintergerst, E., Maggini, S., & Hornig, D. (2006). Immune-enhancing role of vitamin C and zinc and effect on clinical conditions. *Annals of Nutrition and Metabolism, 50*(2), 85-94.
44. Manoukian, A. (2007). Holistic food basics. *The Lyme Times: Integrative medicine, 47*, 44-46.
45. Horowitz, R. (2017). *How can I get better?: An action plan for treating resistant Lyme & chronic disease*. New York: St. Martin's Press.
46. Horowitz, R. (2017). *Ibid*.

47. Thomason, M., & Moyer, C. (2012). Massage therapy for Lyme disease symptoms: A prospective case study. *International Journal of Therapeutic Massage and Bodywork, 5*(4), 9-14.
48. DeMatteo, L. (2015) *Best massage techniques for clients with Lyme disease*. Institute for Integrative healthcare. Retrieved from http://www.integrativehealthcare.org/ mtarchives/2015/07/best-massage-techniques-for-clients-with-lyme-disease.html/2
49. MacGill, M. (2016). Lymphatic system: Facts, functions, and diseases. *Medical News Today, April* 14, Newsletter.
Retrieved from http://www.medicalnewstoday.com/articles/303087.php
50. Prilutsky, B. (2006). Lymph drainage for detoxification. *Massage Bodywork, June/July*, 40-44. Retrieved from https://medicalmassage-edu.com/wp-content/uploads/20 14/09/LymphDetox.pdf
51. Perasalo, J. (1988). Traditional use of the sauna for hygiene and health in Finland. *Annals of Clinical Research, 20*(4), 220-223.
52. Valtakari, P. (1988). The sauna and bathing in different countries. *Annals of Clinical Research, 20*(4), 230-235.
53. Crinnion, W. (2007). Components of practical clinical detox programs – Sauna as a therapeutic tool. *Alternative Therapies in Health and Medicine 13*(2), 154-156.
54. Genuis, S., et al. (2011). Blood urine, and sweat (BUS) study: Monitoring and elimination of bioaccumulated toxic elements. *Archives of Environmental Contamination and Toxicology, 61*(2), 344-357. doi: 10.1007/s00244-010-9611-5

55. Stauber, J., & Florence, T. (1988). A comparative study of copper, lead, cadmium, and zinc in human sweat and blood. *Science of the Total Environment, 74,* 235-247. doi: 10.1016/0048-9697(88)90140-4

56. Cecchini, et al. (2006). Chemical exposures at the World Trade Center: Use of the Hubbard sauna detoxification regimen to improve the health status of New York City rescue workers exposed to toxicants. *Townsend Letter: The Examiner of Alternative medicine, 273,* 58-65. Retrieved from http://arthritistrust.info/wpcontent/u pl oads/2013/03/Chemical-Exposure-at-World-Trade-Center.pdf

57. Laukkanen, T., et al. (2015). Association between sauna bathing and fatal cardiovascular and all-cause mortality events. *JAMA Internal Medicine, 175*(4), 542-548. doi: 10.1001/jamainternmed.2014.8187

58. Laukkanen, T., et al. (2017). Sauna bathing is inversely associated with dementia and Alzheimer's disease in middle-aged Finnish men. *Age and Aging, 46*(2), 245-249. doi: 10.1093/ageing/afw212

59. Mercola, J. (2016). Some like it hot – The many health benefits of sauna bathing. *Peak Fitness.* Retrieved from http://fitness.mercola.com/sites/fitness/archive/2016/0 9/09/sauna-bathing.aspx

60. Wilson, L. (2016). *Sauna therapy for detoxification and healing,* (3rd ed.). USA: L.D. Wilson Consultants, Inc.

61. Wilson, L. (2017). *Sauna therapy.* Wilson Consultants, Inc. Retrieved from http://drlwilson.com/Articles/sau na_therapy.htm

62. Burrascano, J. (2008). *Diagnostic hints and treatment guidelines for Lyme and other tick borne illnesses,* (16th ed). Advanced Topics in Lyme Disease. Retrieved from http://www.lymenet.org/ BurrGuide200810.pdf

63. Marshall, T., & Marshall, F. (2004). Sarcoidosis succumbs to antibiotics – Implications for autoimmune disease. *Autoimmunity Reviews, 3*(4), 295-300. doi: 10.1016/j.autrev.2003.10.001
64. Jarisch, A. (1895). Therapeutische versuche bei Syphilis. *Wiener Medizinische Wochenschrift, 45*, 721-742.
65. Herxheimer, K., & Krause, D. (1902). Uber eine bei Syphilitischen vorkommende Quecksilberreaktion. *Deutsch Medizinische Wochenschrift, 28(5),* 895-897. doi: 10.1055/s-0028-1139096
66. Fitzgerald, F. (1982). The great imitator, Syphilis. *The Western Journal of Medicine, 134*(5), 424-432.
67. Philip, J. (1990). Allergic drug reactions. In H. Walker., W. Hall., J. Hurst (Eds.), *Clinical Methods: The History, Physical, and Laboratory Examinations*, (3rd ed). Boston: Butterworths. Retrieved from https://www.ncbi.nlm.nih.gov/books/NBK32 7
68. Horowitz, R. (2010). *Co-infections*. ILADS 2010 Lyme Conference. International Lyme and Associated Diseases Society.
69. Mutzel, D. (2014). *The role of inflammation in Lyme and chronic disease with Richard Horowitz, MD*. High Intensity health. Retrieved from https://highintensityhealth.com/the-role-of-inflammation-in-lyme-and-chronic-disease-with-richard-horowitz-md
70. Tired of Lyme. (2017). *Detoxing: Cleaning up the mess left by dead spirochetes*. Tired of Lyme. Retrieved from http://www.tiredoflyme.com/detox-methods.html
71. Strasheim, C. (2016). *New paradigms in Lyme disease treatment: 10 top doctors reveal healing strategies that work*. California, USA: BioMed Publishing Group, LLC.

72. Axe, J. (2018). 7 proven chlorella benefits (#2 is best). Food is Medicine. Retrieved from https://draxe.com/7-proven-chlorella-benefits-side-effects
73. Merchant, R., & Andre, C. (2001). A review of recent clinical trials of the nutritional supplement Chlorella pyrenoidosa in the treatment of fibromyalgia, hypertension, and ulcerative colitis. *Alternative Therapies in Health and Medicine, 7*(3), 79-91.
74. Uchikawa, T., et al. (2011). Enhanced elimination of tissue methylmercury in parachlorella beijerinckii fed mice. *The Journal of Toxicological Sciences, 36*(1), 121-126. doi: 10.2131/jts.36.121
75. Strasheim, C. (2017). *Chlorella: A powerful detox agent and amazing superfood.* ProHealth. Retrieved from http://www.prohealth.com/lyme/library/showarticle.cfm?libid=30378
76. Shanks, K. (2017). *Cruciferous vegetables: Powerful detoxification medicine.* Heart, Hope, Healing. Retrieved from http://www.karynshanksmd.com/2017/01/20/cruciferous-vegetables-powerful-detoxification-medicine
77. Buhner, S. (2013). *Op. cit.*
78. McFadzean-Ducharme, N. (2016). Chapter Six – McFadzean-Ducharme, ND, in C. Strasheim, *New paradigms in Lyme disease treatment: 10 top doctors reveal healing strategies that work.* California, USA: BioMed Publishing Group, LLC.
79. Hughes, R. (2017). *Benefits of sarsaparilla (smilax).* Live Strong. Retrieved from https://www.livestrong.com/article/312826-benefits-of-sarsaparilla-smilax
80. Jurenka, J. (2009). Anti-inflammatory properties of curcumin, a major constituent of Curcuma longa: A review of preclinical and clinical research. *Alternative Medicine Review, 14*(2), 141-153.

81. Rivetty, D. (2017). *Turmeric and liver detox*. Live Strong. Retrieved from https://www.livestrong.com/article/108918-cleanse-human-liver-toxins
82. Nutramedix. (2017). *Cowden support program*. Nutramedix. Retrieved from https://www.nutramedix.com/products/cowden-support-program
83. Cowden, W. (2016). *Burbur detox*. YouTube. Retrieved from https://www.youtube.com/watch?v=3r8DM90xxT8
84. Cowden, W. (2009). *Pinella brain nerve cleanse*. YouTube. Retrieved from https://www.youtube.com/watch?v=PPB0DIQ3WaM
85. Cowden, W. (2016). *Parsley detox*. YouTube. Retrieved from https://www.youtube.com/watch?v=zlVZr7RkSV4
86. Cowden, W. (2016). *Sparga sulphur detox*. YouTube. Retrieved from https://www.youtube.com/watch?v=h4AsXJov_90
87. Tired of Lyme. (2017). *Op. cit.*
88. Sarich, C. (2015). How drinking this orange tea can detox your liver. Natural Society: Transform Your Health naturally. Retrieved from http://naturalsociety.com/how-drinking-this-orange-tea-can-detox-your-liver
89. Naziroglu, M., et al. (2014). Apple cider vinegar modulates serum lipid profile, erythrocyte, kidney, and liver membrane oxidative stress in ovariectomized mice fed high cholesterol. *The Journal of Membrane Biology, 247*(8), 667-673. doi: 10.1007/s00232-014-9685-5

90. Gopal, J., et al. (2017). Authenticating apple cider vinegar's home remedy claims: Antibacterial, antifungal, antiviral properties and cytotoxicity aspect.
Natural Product Research, 11, 1-5. doi: 10.1080/14786419.2017.1413567

91. Nho, C., & Jeffrey, E. (2001). The synergistic upregulation of phase II detoxification enzymes by glucosinolate breakdown products in cruciferous vegetables. *Toxicology and Applied Pharmacology, 174*(2), 146-152. doi: 10.1006/taap.2001.9207

92. Axe, J. (2018). Dandelion tea for liver detox, healthy skin and stomach. Food is Medicine. Retrieved from https://draxe.com/dandelion-tea

93. Buhner, S. (2013). *Op. cit.*

94. Tired of Lyme. (2017). *Op. cit.*

95. Grant, D. (1991). Detoxification pathways in the liver. *Journal of Inherited Metabolic Disease, 14*(4), 421-430.

96. Liska, D. (1998). The detoxification enzyme systems. *Alternative Medicine Review, 3*(3), 187-198.

97. Axe, J. (2018). 10 bentonite clay benefits and uses. Food is Medicine. Retrieved from https://draxe.com/10-bentonite-clay-benefits-uses

98. Moosavi, M. (2017). Bentonite clay as a natural remedy: A brief review. *Iranian Journal of Public Health, 46*(9), 1176-1183.

99. Williams, L., & Haydel, S. (2010). Evaluation of the medicinal use of clay minerals as antibacterial agents. International Geology Review. doi: 10.1080/00206811003679737

100. Vucskits, A., et al. (2010). Effect of fulvic and humic acids on performance, immune response and thyroid function in rats. *Journal of Animal Physiology and Animal Nutrition, 94*(6), 721-728. doi: 10.1111/j.1439-0396.2010.01023.x

101. Meena, H., et al. (2010). Shilajit: A panacea for high-altitude problems. *International Journal of Ayurveda Research, 1*(1), 37-40. doi: 10.4103/0974-7788.59942

102. Thomas, D. (2003). A study on the mineral depletion of the foods available to us as a nation over the period 1940 to 1991. *Nutrition and Health, 17*(2), 85-115. doi: 10.1177/026010600301700201

103. Pratt, S. (2016). *What is the big deal about the methylation cycle?* Seeking Health Educational Institute. Retrieved from https://seekinghealth.org/physicianpost/big-deal-methylation-cycle

104. Curinga, K. (2017). What are the health benefits of molybdenum? Live Strong. Retrieved from https://www.livestrong.com/article/361012-what-are-the-health-benefits-of-molybdenum/

105. Schmitt, W., et al. (1991). The art of getting well molybdenum for Candida albicans: Patients and other problems. *The Digest of Chiropractic Economics, 31*(4), 56-63.

106. Tired of Lyme. (2017). *Op. cit.*

107. Burgess, R., et al. (2004). Use of zeolite for removing ammonia and ammonia-caused toxicity in marine toxicity identification evaluations. *Archives of environmental contamination and toxicology, 47*(4), 440-447. doi: 10.1007/s00244-004-4003-3

[108.] Lamprecht, M. (2015). Effects of zeolite supplementation on parameters of intestinal barrier integrity, inflammation, redoxbiology and performance in aerobically trained subjects. *Journal of the International Society of Sports Nutrition, 12*, 40. doi: 10.1186/s12970-015-0101-z

[109.] Montinaro, M., et al. (2013). Dietary zeolite supplementation reduces oxidative damage and plaque generation in the brain of an Alzheimer's disease mouse model. *Life Sciences, 92*(17-19), 903-910. doi: 10.1016/j.l f s.2013.03.008

[110.] Anderson, W. (2016). *Op. cit.*

[111.] Tired of Lyme. (2017). *Op. cit.*

[112.] Nathan, N. (2016). Chapter Three – Neil Nathan, MD. in C. Strasheim, *New paradigms in Lyme disease treatment: 10 top doctors reveal healing strategies that work*. California, USA: BioMed Publishing Group, LLC.

[113.] Tired of Lyme. (2017). *Op. cit.*

[114.] RxList. (2018). B*enadryl*. RxList, Inc. Retrieved from https://www.rxlist.com/benadryl-drug.htm

[115.] Loveday, C., & Bingham, J. (1985). Changes in intravascular complement, kininogen, and histamine during Jarisch-Herxheimer reaction in secondary syphilis. *Genitourinary Medicine, 61*(1), 27-32.

[116.] Derlet, R., & Albertson, T. (1986). Activated charcoal – past present, and future. *Western Journal of Medicine, 145*(4), 493-496.

[117.] Axe, J. (2018). Top 10 activated charcoal uses and benefits. Food is medicine. Retrieved from https://draxe.com/activated-charcoal-uses

[118.] Yasko, A. (2014). *Feel good nutrigenomics: Your roadmap to health*. USA: Neurological Research Institute, LLC.

[119] Jockers, D. (2018a). *CBS mutation and low sulfur diet.* Supercharge Your Health. Retrieved from https://drjockers.com/cbs-mutation-low-sulfur-diet

[120] Jockers, D. (2018a). *Ibid.*

[121] Cheriyedath, S. (2016). *What is the urea cycle?* News Medical Life Sciences. Retrieved from https://www.news-medical.net/health/What-is-the-Urea-Cycle.aspx

[122] Keifer, D. (2016). *Alpha-Lipoic Acid.* WebMD Medical Reference. Retrieved from https://www.webmd.com/diet/supplement-guide-alpha-lipoic-acid#1

[123] Jockers, D. (2018b). 7 supplements to detoxify your body. Supercharge Your Health. Retrieved from https://drjockers.com/7-supplements-to-detoxify-your-body

[124] Suh, J., et al. (2005). Dietary supplementation with (R)-alpha-lipoic acid reverses the age-related accumulation of iron and depletion of antioxidants in the rat cerebral cortex. *Redox report: Communications in free radical research,* 10(1), 52-60. doi: 10.1179/135100005X21624

[125] Jockers, D. (2018b). *Op. cit.*

[126] McFadzean-Ducharme, N. (2016). *Op. cit.*

[127] Jockers, D. (2018b). *Op. cit.*

[128] Sugino, T., et al. (2008). L-ornithine supplementation attenuates physical fatigue in healthy volunteers by modulating lipid and amino acid metabolism. *Nutrition Research,* 28(11), 738-743. doi:10.1016/j.nutres.2008.08.008

[129] Pratt, S. (2016). *Op. cit.*

[130] Eliaz, I., Weil, E., & Wilk, B. (2007). Integrative medicine and the role of modified citrus pectin/alginates in heavy metal chelation and detoxification – Five case reports. *Research in Complementary Medicine, 14*(6), 358-364. doi: 10.1159/0000109829

[131] Anderson, W. (2016). Chapter Two – Wayne Anderson, ND. in C. Strasheim, *New paradigms in Lyme disease treatment: 10 top doctors reveal healing strategies that work.* California, USA: BioMed Publishing Group, LLC.

[132] Edgar Cayrce's A.R.E. (2017). *Edgar Cayce health database therapies.* Edgar Cayce's A.R.E. Association for Research and Enlightenment. Retrieved from https://www.edgarcayce.org/the-readings/health-and-wellness/holistic-health-database/therapies-castor-oil-packs/

[133] Vieira, C., et al. Effect of ricinoleic acid in acute and subchronic experimental models of inflammation. *Mediators of Inflammation, 9,* 223-228.

[134] Grady, H. (1999). Immunomodulation through castor oil packs. *Journal of Naturopathic Medicine, 7*(1), 84-89.

[135] Arslan, G., et al. (2011). An examination of the effect of castor oil packs on constipation in the elderly. *Complementary Therapies in Clinical Practice, 17*(1), 58-62. doi: 10.1016/j.ctcp.2010.04.004

[136] Tunaru, S., et al. (2012). Castor oil induces laxation and uterus contraction via ricinoleic acid activating prostaglandin EP_3 receptors. *Proceedings of the National Academy of Sciences of the United States of America, 109*(23), 9179-9184. doi: 10.1073/pnas.1201627109

[137] Edgar Cayrce's A.R.E. (2017). *Op. cit.*

[138] Gerson Institute. (2018). *The Gerson therapy*. The Gerson Institute. Retrieved fromhttps://gerson.org/gerpress/the-gerson-therapy

[139] Teekachunhatean, S., et al. (2012). Antioxidant effects after coffee enema or oral coffee consumption in healthy Thai male volunteers. *Human and experimental toxicology, 31*(7), 643-651. doi: 10.1177/0960327111432499

[140] Acosta, R., & Cash, B. (2009). Clinical effects of colonic cleansing for general health promotion: A systematic review. *The American Journal of Gastroenterology, 105*(5), 1214. doi: 10.1038/ajg.2009.494

[141] Klinghardt, D. (2016). Chapter Two – Dietrich Kinghardt, MD, PHD. in C. Strasheim, *New paradigms in Lyme disease treatment: 10 top doctors reveal healing strategies that work*. California, USA: BioMed Publishing Group, LLC.

[142] Pilch. W., et al. (2013). Effect of a single Finnish sauna session on white blood cell profile and cortisol levels in athletes and non-athletes. *Journal of Human Kinetics, 39*, 127-135. doi: 10.2478/hukin-2013-0075

[143] Buijze, G., et al. (2016). The effect of cold showering on health and work: A randomized controlled trial. *PLoS One, 11*(9), e0161749. doi: 10.1371/journal.pone.0161749

[144] Mercola, J. (2014). Dry skin brushing: Benefits and how to. Take Control of Your Health. Retrieved from https://articles.mercola.com/sites/articles/archive/2014/02/24/dry-skin-brushing.aspx

[145] Mayne, D. (2017). *Dry brush detox*. Live Strong. Retrieved fromhttps://www.livestrong.com/article/104702-dry-brush-detox

[146] Horowitz, R. (2017). *Op. cit.*

[147] Cline, J. (2015). Nutritional aspects of detoxification in clinical practice. *Alternative Therapies in Health and Medicine, 21*(3), 54-62.

[148] Hodges, R., & Minich, D. (2015). Modulation of metabolic detoxification pathways using foods and food-derived components: A scientific review with clinical application. *Journal of Nutrition and Metabolism, 2015*. doi: 10.1155/ 2015/760689

[149] Klein, J. (2006). The immune system as a regulator of thyroid hormone activity. *Experimental Biology and Medicine, 231*(3), 229-236.

12. What Should(n't) You Eat With Lyme And/Or Its Co-infections?

Lyme and its co-infections can prove to be very disempowering,[1] but diet is one thing that can be actively controlled. Taking control of eating patterns, and enjoying certain foods while avoiding others can also be an important first step toward taking control of the healing journey. This control can be gained by focusing on what not to eat, as well as what to eat, and when to eat it.

Diet

Diet is important for people with Lyme and/or its co-infections because the foods that we eat can support detoxification,[2] reduce inflammation, boost the immune system,[3-5] and reduce the impact of stressors on the body when healing.[6,7] Essentially then, the aim of a 'Lyme Diet' is to eat to:
- Reduce inflammation
- Boost the immune system
- Reduce body burdens

Foods to Include.

The type of food a person eats can help reverse disease and create health,[8] with the building blocks required to repair years of cellular damage from being ill coming from a nutritionally dense supportive diet. However, trying to overhaul dietary habits when chronically ill can be a massive challenge, so it is probably best to take small steps at a time.

Reducing Inflammation. To help reduce inflammation, Elliot[9] suggests eating whole foods rich in nutrients and vitamins, along with a diet rich in antioxidants and essential fatty acids. When the omega-3 to omega-6 ratio is out of balance in the body it can contribute to inflammation and therefore to increased pain levels.[10] It is important then to increase fatty acid consumption, such as omega-3 from fish or vegetable sources and omega-9 from nuts and oils, while decreasing omega-6 fatty acid consumption from sources such as dairy and meat.[11] That said, grass-fed and finished meats have much lower pro-inflammatory omega-6 fatty acids than grain fed animals, and provide good sources of saturated fats and amino acids needed for tissue repair[12]. Similarly, reducing industrial seed oils (canola, soy, rapeseed) will decrease omega-6's. An increased intake of fruit and vegetables along the lines of a Mediterranean diet,[13] a Ketogenic,[14,15] or a Paleo diet[16] can also potentially lead to the lowering of inflammation, as can spices like curcumin, and ginger.[17] The Wahls Paleo Diet[18] helped its creator reverse her symptoms of MS (multiple sclerosis),[19] and it is a protocol that patients such as Cosentino[20] have had success in following.

Boost the Immune System. The gastrointestinal system plays an important role in ensuring homeostasis of the immune system,[21] and contains bacterial colonies that exert a major impact over immune functions.[22] Nutrition can therefore play a pivotal role in offsetting antibiotic side effects, strengthening the immune system, supporting detoxification, reducing inflammation, preventing the overgrowth of candida, alkalinizing the blood, and healing the gut.[23] It may also be important to include foods like fermented vegetables such as kimchi, miso, and sauerkraut into the diet, because these kinds of foods can support gut flora which is important for assisting the immune system in functioning at its peak.[24]

Reduce Body Burdens. Reducing stressors includes taking into account methods to help lower the body burden of heavy metal toxins through detoxification, addressing hormonal and other imbalances, and addressing inadequate nutrition while maintaining adequate hydration.[25]

Detoxification. Foods high in sulfur, such as garlic, cabbage, broccoli, and cauliflower, can assist the liver in the detoxification process, as can amino acids from protein-rich foods.[26] Leafy greens contain antioxidants, carotenoids, and flavonoids which can help protect against cellular damage[27] and disease,[28] and potentially assist in inducing enzymes to support detoxification,[29] while potentially helping to alleviate joint pain and other Lyme symptoms because they are also anti-inflammatory.[30]

Hormonal Imbalance. It is important to keep hormones in balance when ill because they all serve to regulate various functions throughout the body.[31,32] Sea vegetables are rich in iodine and can help to support the thyroid, but keep in mind that different types of seaweed, along with the cooking or preparation process, will influence the amount of iodine content they contain.[33]

Inadequate Nutrition. Essential nutrients and vitamins from a variety of foods are important to obtain.[34] Traditionally, when an animal was killed all of it was eaten,[35] with the offal consisting of blood, bone marrow, brain, ear, eye, face, foot, gizzard, heart, intestines, kidney, liver, lungs, sexual organs, skin, spleen, sweetbreads (pancreas/thymus), tail, tendon, tongue, and the stomach lining/small intestine,[36] leading to food such as blood sausage, tripe, pigs tongue, and ox tail, as well as broths, soups, stews, and stocks.[37] Due to their water, mineral, and vitamin content, the latter can be very nourishing and easy to consume while ill,[38,39] while the former can provide a range of different nutrients, as can eating a diversity of foods.[40-42]

Hydration. Water is an essential nutrient. Remember the survival rule of three: you can live for 3 minutes without oxygen in an emergency or in icy water; 3 hours without shelter in a harsh environment, hot or cold; 3 days without potable water if sheltered from a harsh environment; and 3 weeks without food if shelter and potable water are available.[43] The human body is between 58% to 70% water,[44] and among other things, water is important for maintaining the moisture level of the body's bones, blood, organs, and tissues.[45,46] Drinking water continuously throughout the day helps all these functions, and helps with staying hydrated, but it is also important to consider the source of the water.[47] Drinking good quality mineral water can be beneficial as the minerals in the water are bioavailable and supplemental to that obtained from normal nutrition.[48] Water is also viewed as an important part of some Lyme treatment protocols.[49]

Foods to Avoid.

Nutrition can control how our genes behave,[50] and as a result, there are a number of foods that health professionals[51,52] suggest are best avoided. Some of these are:
- Foods that provoke any allergy/sensitivity/intolerance
- Alcohol
- Caffeine
- Dairy
- Gluten

- Genetically modified (GM) foods
- Hydrogenated fats/oils
- Soy
- Sugar
- Table salt

Foods that Provoke Any Allergy/Sensitivity/Intolerance. All foods that provoke an allergy, sensitivity, or an intolerance need to be taken into consideration when ill.[53] Everyone is perhaps familiar with the need to conceivably go dairy-free if you are lactose-intolerant, or gluten-free if you are celiac, but most people may not realize that wheat gluten and wheat lectin can be pro-inflammatory for almost everyone.[54] So these foods, along with others that the body may react to, should be avoided, particularly when healing.[55] The impact of pesticides and chemicals, as well as antibiotics and hormones, throughout the food production process, along with cross-contamination when food products are packaged and processed at the same facility, can also impact, either by allergy or sensitivity, on how the body reacts when certain foods are eaten.[56,57] This also needs to be taken into account when purchasing food for nutrition and healing. Ultimately, a food sensitivity test might be the best means of finding out if there is an allergy, sensitivity, or intolerance to anything you might wish to eat. Alternatively, if this is unaffordable, you may decide to try a physician-suggested elimination diet as part of the healing process.[58]

Alcohol. Drinking alcohol while ill with Lyme and/or its co-infections can be problematic. It can tax the liver,[59] it is associated with increasing markers of inflammation,[60] and it can compromise the immune response.[61] Alcohol can also interact dangerously with some medications, rendering them useless, or cause severe illness or organ damage.[62] Since alcohol should perhaps be avoided, even when healthy, there are essentially no alternatives for it. However, you might choose alternates, such as a good quality mineral water[63] or even lemon water,[64] if you have been used to drinking alcohol before becoming ill.

Caffeine. The consumption of caffeine can put the body into a mild state of fight-or-flight as it stimulates the adrenal glands to release cortisol,[65] and draining the adrenals in this way can lead to fatigue. Wilson[66] also thinks that caffeine impacts the adrenals more negatively than a variety of other foods including sugar and wine. Some alternatives are Rooibos tea, Teeccino, or dandelion root tea which can support the liver with detoxification.[67,68]

Dairy. Food products made from dairy are, for many, difficult to digest. Around 65%[69] of the human population, after infancy, lose the ability to digest lactose which is a sugar found in dairy products. Casein at 80% is one of two proteins found in milk, the other being whey at 20%.[70] Many people do tolerate whey, but have a reaction toward

Casein.[71] A1 beta-casein can also take a long time to digest,[72] and as a result, puts a strain on the digestive system. Alternative choices might be the use of nut butters, nut milks, and coconut milk yogurt or coconut kefir.

Gluten. Regardless of intolerance gluten has been shown to cause inflammation in the human body,[73] with grains also linked to the cause of leaky gut and brain diseases.[74] Tapioca flour, nut flours, or coconut flours, are some alternatives.

Hydrogenated Fats/Oils. Appearing in around 90% of all processed foods,[75] hydrogenated fats/oils are trans fatty acids (TFA). TFAs should be avoided because the refining process impairs the nutritional value of these oils by either destroying or removing beneficial plant components, they are inflammatory, and the adverse effects of their consumption is well documented.[76] Other fats like saturated ones coming from sources such as dairy or red meat can also be problematic as they too can be pro-inflammatory. Fats have a major impact on human health, leading to acute as well as chronic inflammatory responses that can lead to various disease states.[77] Alternatives are the unsaturated fats, such as the omega-3, omega-6, and omega-9 fatty acids, but an imbalance of these can also lead to inflammation. Omega-3 is often the most focused upon due to its health benefits,[78] and because it is perceived to be the one that most people lack due to eating more foods containing omega-6 and omega-9.[79] There are three kinds of omega-3 fats – two can be found in animals (EPA/DHA, eicosapentaenoic acid/docosahexaenoic acid) and one in vegetables (ALA, alphalinolenic acid), with the body using ALA to make EPA/DHA.[80]

Genetically Modified (GM) Foods. GM produce, in terms of the compositional, metabolic, nutritional, and toxicological differences between them and organically grown crops, and the longitudinal impact that this may have on human health, is of a large concern to many people.[81,82] Recently, glyphosate has received a lot of attention for being found at above acceptable levels in the North American food supply,[83] as it can impact humans and animals, show disruption of brain development in mice,[84] and cause enzyme disturbances leading to sulfate sensitivities.[85] In addition, non-organic diary, eggs, meats, and poultry contain antibiotics and hormones that are used while raising the animals, which can then be absorbed by the human body when these types of foods are eaten.[86] The non-therapeutic use of these antibiotics contributes to resistance and health dangers for humans,[87] with ongoing risk assessment being important.[88] The International Agency for Research on Cancer (IARC),[89] the cancer agency of the World Health Organization (WHO), has also classed all processed meats as a carcinogen (Group 1), and red meats as probably carcinogenic (Group

2A). As they have found that 1.7637 ounces or 50 grams of processed meat, eaten daily, increases colorectal cancer risk by 18%, and that overall, the consumption of red meats (beef, goat, horse, lamb, pork) increases the risk for colorectal, pancreatic, and prostate cancer. Alternatives include eating leaner meats, or meats containing good fats which can lower inflammation and potentially dampen responses to endotoxins,[90] as opposed to eating a 'Westernized diet' (high in red and processed meats along with refined grains, sweets, and take-away foods).[91]

Soy. When soy is used as animal fodder this can see residual phytoestrogens and their active metabolites ingested when those animals are later consumed,[92] and this can lead to potentially feminizing effects in humans.[93] However, soy is viewed as a good source of protein, and there is evidence it can prevent chronic diseases.[94] Fermented soybean paste, like the Korean *doenjang*, has also been reported to wield anti-carcinogenic, anti-diabetic, anti-inflammatory, and anti-mutagenic effects,[95] with the fermentation, heating, and soaking of soy possibly reducing the amount of antinutrients that it contains.[96]

Sugar. Limiting the effectiveness of the immune system by reducing the ability of white blood cells to kill pathogens[97,98] sugar can also lead to a number of health problems,[99] including issues with the gall bladder and the formation of gallstones.[100] The consumption of sugar can also lead to yeast and bacterial overgrowth, particularly in the gastrointestinal tract.[101] A lot of foods contain added sugar, even ones that you may not suspect, and particularly those marked low-fat.[102] Giving up sugar may be the hardest part of a Lyme diet because it can induce cravings comparable to that of an addictive drug.[103] Reducing sugar also means reducing some 'healthy' foods that are high in sugar, and foods with a high glycemic index, as they can raise blood sugar (glucose) levels.[104] This can stimulate high insulin release leading to a higher circulating level of insulin in the blood stream, facilitating the release of inflammatory cytokines that can lead to increased pathological pain,[105] and also overtaxing of the metabolism.[106] This applies to all kinds of sugar (including honey), along with simple carbohydrates that can readily convert to sugar (including cereals, cakes, pasta, refined bread, sweets, and white rice).[107] It has also been found that absorption of vitamin C can be prohibited when there is an excess amount of sugar in the gut.[108] An alternative to sugars or artificial sweeteners is the use of Stevia, of which extract of the whole leaf has gotten attention for killing Lyme *in vitro*.*[109]

---

* *in vitro* describes a process taking place in a test tube, a culture dish, or elsewhere outside of a living organism.

Table Salt. As a refined product table salt has had all of its trace minerals removed and chemical agents added, which can cause a ratio imbalance of potassium to sodium in the heart, and lead to hypertension or high blood pressure.[110] High sodium diets have also been linked to deaths from cardiovascular disease, chronic kidney disease, and stomach cancer.[111] An alternative is the use of unrefined sea salt such as gray Celtic salt or pink Himalayan salt.

A View from the Field – Fasting

Fasting is a bit contentious as many people may think that it means 'nil by mouth' for a very extended period of time. However, a fast could be simply not eating for as short as 16 hours, or it might mean undertaking one of a variety of other fasts. These include water only, juice, bone-broth, or an intermittent fast. The benefits of fasting are documented for health,[112] when fighting cancer,[113] and in bolstering brain power.[114,115] Fasting can also promote autophagy,**[116] and life-extension,[117] and help dampen inflammation as well as pain.[118] Yet, no matter the fast, certain medications and other prescribed supplements must be taken with food,

---

** *autophagy* is from the Greek, *auto,* meaning 'self', and *phagein,* 'to eat' – the process where degraded matter (e.g., organelles, proteins, cell membranes) are broken down for recycling by the body.

and fasting while ill would require medical supervision.

Intermittent fasting is a popular way of getting both the benefits of a fast along with nutrition from food,[119,120] because it is essentially time-shifting the same amount of food and calories that would normally be eaten over breakfast, lunch, and dinner to either dinner only, or breakfast and lunch, or to within a specific time-window. For example: eating an early dinner then not eating 3 hours prior to sleep, and then fasting for the following 16 hours. It is important to realize that engaging in an intermittent fast is not starving or refusing to eat; it is just eating differently.

Intermittent fasting has been used for weight-loss,[121] with the 5:2 diet becoming a popular 'fad' where people eat normally for five days, and then go into a calorie restricted diet for two days.[122] No matter the fast, if this is the route a medical professional advises, then to undertake it, you must be physically and mentally prepared before being able to perform it. Ultimately, different diets work for different people, and it comes down to what works best for the individual.[123]

References

[1.] Rippey, M. (2015). *Episode 27: Lyme expert – Dr. Nicola McFadzean Ducharme – Author, naturopath.* Lyme Ninja Radio. Retrieved from http://lymeninjaradio.com/nicola_ducharme

2. Elliot, E. (2007). Guide to detoxification. *The Lyme Times: Alternative Medicine 49*, 13-16.
3. Chandra, R. (1997). Nutrition and the immune system: An introduction. *The American Journal of Clinical Nutrition, 66*(2), 460S-363S.
4. Wahls, T. (2014). *The Wahls protocol: A radical new way to treat all chronic autoimmune conditions using paleo principles*. USA: Avery.
5. Colbert, D. (2015). *Let food be your medicine: Dietary changes proven to prevent or reverse disease*. USA: Worthy Publishing.
6. Muran, P. (2008). Lyme disease – A functional medicine approach. *The Lyme Times, 54*, 3-5.
7. McFadzean, N. (2010). *The Lyme diet: Nutritional strategies for healing from Lyme disease*. San Diego: Legacy Line Publishing.
8. Rippey, M. (2016). *Episode 97: Dr. Terry Wahls – Using the Wahl's protocol for Lyme disease*. Lyme Ninja Radio. Retrieved from http://lymeninjaradio.com/97-dr-terry-wahls
9. Elliot, E. (2007). *Op. cit.*
10. McFadzean, N. (2012). *The beginner's guide to Lyme disease: Diagnosis and treatment made simple*. USA: BioMed Publishing Group.
11. Horowitz, R. (2017). *How can I get better?: An action plan for treating resistant Lyme & chronic disease*. New York: St. Martin's Press.
12. Daley, C., et al., (2010). A review of fatty acid profiles and antioxidant content in grass-fed and grain-fed beef. *Nutrition Journal, 9*(10). doi: 10.1186/1475-2891-9-10
13. Horowitz, R. (2012). Pain-management strategies in the chronically ill Lyme disease patient. *Pharmaceutical and Therapeutics, 37*(4), 247-248.

14. Levendusky, A. (2017). Rese*arching the ketogenic diet.* My Life with Lyme. Retrieved from http://annieslyme.blogspot.com/2017/02/researching-ketogenic-diet.html
15. Scott, K. (2017). *Five eating plans every Lyme patient should consider.* Lyme Warrior: Fighting for a Cure. Retrieved from http://lymewarrior.us/lymeology/2017/5/22/5-eating-plans-every-lyme-patient-should-consider
16. Wahls, T., & Adamson, E. (2017). *The Wahls protocol cooking for life: The revolutionary modern Paleo plan to treat all chronic autoimmune conditions.* USA: Avery.
17. Jurenka, J. (2009). Anti-inflammatory properties of curcumin, a major constituent of Curcuma longa: A review of preclinical and clinical research. *Alternative Medicine Review, 14*(2), 141-153.
18. Wahls, T. (2014). *Op. cit.*
19. Wahls, T. (2011). *Minding your mitochondria.* TEDx Talk. Retrieved fromhttps://www.youtube.com/watch?v=KLjg BL wH3Wc
20. Cosentino, B. (2015). Success with Wahls Paleo diet for Lyme disease. Real Food Rebel: Natural Solutions for Better Health. Retrieved from http://realfoodrebel.com/wahls-paleo-diet-for-lyme-disease
21. Vighi, G., et al., (2008). Allergy and the gastrointestinal system. *Clinical and Experimental Immunology, 15,*(s1), 3-6. doi: 10.1111/j.1365-2249.2008.03713.x
22. Suzuki, K., et al. (2007). Intestinal IgA synthesis: A primitive form of adaptive immunity that regulates microbial communities in the gut. *Seminars in Immunology, 19*(2), 127-135. doi: 10.1016/j.smim.2006.10. 001

23. Harris, S. (2010). *Foreword*. In N. McFadzean, The Lyme diet: Nutritional strategies for healing from Lyme disease, (iv-v). USA: BioMed Publishing Group.
24. Paddock, C. (2014). *Gut bacteria essential for immune cell development*. Medical News Today. Retrieved from http://www.medicalnewstoday.com/articles/273958.php
25. McFadzean, N. (2010). *Op. cit.*
26. Elliot, E. (2007). *Op. cit.*
27. Slaga, T. (2003). *The detox revolution: A powerful new program for boosting your body's ability to fight cancer and other diseases*. New York: McGraw Hill.
28. Pandey, K., & Rizvi, S. (2009). Plant polyphenols as dietary antioxidants in human health and disease. *Oxidative Medicine and Cellular Longevity, 2*(5), 270-278. doi: 10.416/oxim.2.5.9498
29. Rose, P., Ong, C., & Whiteman, M. (2005). Protective effects of Asian green vegetables against oxidant induced cytotoxicity. *World Journal of Gastroenterology, 11*(48), 7607-7614. doi: 10.3748/wjg.v11.i48.7606
30. Basu, A., Devaraj, S., & Jialal, I. (2006). Dietary factors that promote or retard inflammation. *Arteriosclerosis Thrombosis and Vascular Biology, 26*(5), 995-1001.
31. Bhalla, A. (1989). Hormones and the immune response. *Annals of the Rheumatic Diseases, 48*, 1-6.
32. Klein, J. (2006). The immune system as a regulator of thyroid hormone activity. *Experimental Biology and Medicine, 231*(3), 229-236.
33. Zava, T., & Zava, D. (2011). Assessment of Japanese iodine intake based on seaweed consumption in Japan: A literature-based analysis. *Thyroid Research,* 4,14. doi: 10.1186/1756-6614-4-14

34. Jayathilakan, J., et al. (2012). Utilization of by products and waste materials from meat, poultry, and fish processing industries: A Review. *Journal of Food Science and Technology, 49*(3), 278-293. doi: 10.1007/s13197-011-0290-7
35. Jayathilakan, J., et al. (2012). *Ibid.*
36. Sietsema, R. (2015). *The offal-eater's handbook: Untangling the myths of organ meats.* Eater. Retrieved from https://www.eater.com/2015/6/16/8786663/offal-organ-meat-handbook-cuts-sweetbreads-tripe-gizzard
37. Jayathilakan, J., et al. (2012). *Op. cit.*
38. Axe, J. (2017). *Offal: Are organ meats healthy to eat?* Food is Medicine. Retrieved from https://draxe.com/offal
39. Mercola, J. (2013). *The health benefits of consuming organ meats.* Take Control of Your Health. Retrieved from http://articles.mercola.com/sites/articles/archive/2013/12/30/eating-organ-meats.aspx
40. Mercola, J. (2013). *Bone broth – One of your most healing diet staples.* Take Control of Your Health. Retrieved from http://articles.mercola.com/sites/articles/archive/2013/12/16/bone-broth-benefits.aspx
41. Mercola, J. (2015). *Is bone broth the new super food?* Take Control of Your Health. Retrieved from http://articles.mercola.com/sites/articles/archive/2015/02/23/bone-broth-superfood.aspx
42. Axe, J. (2017). *Bone broth benefits for digestion, arthritis, and cellulite.* Food is Medicine. Retrieved from https://draxe.com/the-healing-power-of-bone-broth-for-digestion-arthritis-and-cellulite
43. Airservices Australia. (2012). *En route supplement Australia.* ERSA – Effective 23 August 2012.

44. Mitchell, H. H., et al. (1945). The chemical composition of the adult human body and its bearing on the biochemistry of growth. *Journal of Biological Chemistry, 158*(3), 625-637.
45. Ross, M. (2014). Lyme detoxification 101: The basics. *The Treat Lyme Book*. Healing Arts Partnership. Retrieved from http://www.treatlyme.net/treat-lyme-book/lyme-detoxificati on-101-the-basics
46. Laskey, J. (2015). *The health benefits of water: We all need water to survive, but how exactly does it help?* Everyday Health. Retrieved from https://www.everydayhealth.com/water-health/water-body-health.asp
47. Giglio, D., et al. (2015). Mineral water or tap water? An endless debate. *Annali di Igiene, Medicina Preventiva e di Communita, 27*(1), 58-65. doi: 10.7416/ai.2015.2023
48. Marktl, W. (2009). Health-related effects of natural mineral waters. *Wien Klin Wochenschrift, 121*(17-18), 544-550. doi: 10.1007/s00508-009-1244-1
49. Cowden, W. (2007). Herbal treatment for Lyme disease: An integrated approach. *The Lyme Times: Alternative Medicine, 49*, 19-20.
50. Campbell, C., & Campbell, T. (2016). *The China study: Revised and expanded edition. The most comprehensive study of nutrition ever conducted and the startling implications for diet, weight loss, and long-term health.* USA: BenBella Books.
51. Kinderlehrer, D. (2007). Food sensitivities. *The Lyme Times: Alternative Medicine 49*, 3-4.
52. Burrascano, J. (2008). *Diagnostic hints and treatment guidelines for Lyme and other tick borne illnesses* (16th ed.). Advanced Topics in Lyme Disease. Retrieved from http://www.lymenet.org/BurrGuide200810.pdf
53. Colbert, D. (2015). *Op. cit.*

54. Punder, K., & Pruimboom, L. (2013). The dietary intake of wheat and other cereal grains and their role in inflammation. *Nutrients,* 5(3), 771-787. doi:10.3390/nu50307771
55. McFadzean, N. (2012). *Op. cit.*
56. Taylor, S., & Baumert, J. (2010). Cross-contamination of foods and implications for food allergic patients. *Current Allergy and Asthma Reports,* 10(4), 265-270. doi: 10.1007/ s11882-010-0112-4
57. McDermott, L. (2017). How can I get better from allergies – Dr. Richard Horowitz. Lillian McDermott Radio Show. Retrieved from https://www.youtube.com/watch?v=K7B C9 E4vw_g
58. Pastorello, E., et al. (1989). Role of the elimination diet in adults with food allergy. *The Journal of Allergy and Clinical Immunology,* 84(4), 475-483.
59. Szabo, G., & Mandrekar, P. (2010). Focus on: Alcohol and the liver. *Alcohol Research and Health,* 33(1-2), 87-96.
60. Lu, B., et al. (2010). Alcohol consumption and markers of inflammation in women with pre-clinical rheumatoid arthritis. *Arthritis and Rheumatism,* 62(12), 3554-3559. doi: 10.1002/art.27739
61. MacGreggor, R., & Louria, D. (1997). Alcohol and infection. *Current Clinical Topics in Infectious Diseases,* 17, 291-315.
62. Moore, A., Whiteman, E., & Ward, K. (2007). Risks of combined alcohol-medication use in older adults. *The American Journal of Geriatric Pharmacotherapy,* 5(1), 64-74.
63. Marktl, W. (2009). *Op. cit.*
64. Horowitz, R. (2017). *Op. cit.*
65. Wilson, J. (2014). *Adrenal fatigue: The 21st century stress syndrome.* USA: Smart Publications.

66. Wilson, J. (2014). *Ibid*.
67. LaValle J. B., et al. (2000). *Natural Therapeutics Pocket Guide, 200-2001*. USA: LexiComp Inc.
68. Sweeney, B., et al. (2005). Evidence-based systematic review of dandelion (*Taraxacum officinale*) by natural standard research collaboration. *Journal of Herbal Pharmacotherapy*, 5(1), 79-93.
69. GHR. (2017). *Lactose intolerance*. Genetics home reference: Your guide to understanding genetic conditions. U.S. National Library of Medicine. Retrieved from https://ghr.nlm.nih.gov/condition/lactose-intolerance#statistics
70. Jenness, R. (1979). Comparative aspects of milk proteins. *Journal of Dairy Research*, 46(2), 197-210.
71. Hochwallner, H., et al. (2014). Cow's milk allergy: From allergens to new forms of diagnosis, therapy and prevention. *Methods*, 66(1), 22-23. Doi: 10.1016/j.ymeth.2 013.08.005
72. Pal, S., et al. (2015). Milk intolerance, beta-casein, and lactose. *Nutrients*, 7(9), 7285-7297.
73. Jamnik, J., et al. (2015). Gluten intake is positively associated with plasma a2-macrogobulin in young adults. *The Journal of Nutrition*. doi:10.3945/jn.115.212 829
74. Perlmutter, D. (2013). *Grain brain: The surprising truth about wheat, carbs, and sugar – Your brain's silent killers*. USA: Little, Brown and Company.
75. Manoukian, A. (2007). Holistic food basics. *The Lyme Times: Integrative medicine*, 47, 44-46.

76. Baylin, A. (2013). Secular trends in trans fatty acids: Decreased trans fatty acids in the food supply are reflected in decreased trans fatty acids in plasma. *The American Journal of Clinical Nutrition, 97*, 4, 665-666. doi: 10.3945/ajcn.113.058321
77. Fritsche, K. (2015). The Science of fatty acids and inflammation. *Advances in Nutrition, 6*, 293S-301S.
78. Swanson, D., Block, R., & Mousa, S. (2012). Omega-3 fatty acids EPA and DHA: Health benefits throughout life. *Advances in Nutrition, 3*(1), 1-7. doi: 10.3945/an.111.000893
79. McFadzean, N. (2010). *Op. cit.*
80. Lane, K., Derbyshire, E., & Brennan, C. (2014). *Critical reviews in food science and nutrition, 54*(5), 572-579. doi: 10.1080/10408398.2011.596292
81. Dona, A., & Arvanitoyannis, I. (2009). Health risks of genetically modified foods. *Critical Reviews in Food Science Nutrition, 49*(2), 164-175. doi: 10.1080/10408390701855993
82. Bawa, A., & Anilakumar, K. (2013). Genetically modified foods: Safety, risks, and public concerns – A review. *Journal of Food Science and Technology, 50*(6), 1035-1046.
83. CFIA. (2017). *Safeguarding with science: Glyphosate testing in 2015-2016.* CFIA – Science Branch Survey Report. Food Safety Science Directorate, Canadian Food Inspection Agency.
84. Bali, A., Ba-Mhamed, S., & Bennis, M. (2017). Behavioral and immunohistochemical study of the effects of subchronic and chronic exposure to glyphosate in mice. *Frontiers in Behavioral Neuroscience, 11*, 146. doi: 10.3389/fnbeh.2017.00146

Chapter 12: Diet | 251

85. Rippey, M. (2017). *Episode 149: Stephanie Seneff, PhD – Glyphosate is interfering with your Lyme recovery*. Lyme Ninja Radio. Retrieved from http://lymeninjaradio.com/148-stephanie-seneff-glyphosphate
86. Manoukian, A. (2007). *Op. cit.*
87. Paulson, J., & Zaoutis, T. (2015). *Nontherapeutic use of antimicrobial agents in animal agriculture: Implications for pediatrics*. American Academy of Pediatrics Technical Report. Retrieved from http://pediatrics.aappublications.org/content/pediatrics/early/2015/11/11/peds.2015-3630.full.pdf
88. Jeong, S., et al. (2010). Risk assessment of growth hormones and antimicrobial residues in meat. *Journal of Toxicology and Public Health, 26*(4), 301- 313.doi:10.5487/TR.2010.26.4.301
89. IARC. (2015). *Press Release No. 240*. World health Organization. Retrieved from http://www.iarc.fr/en/media-centre/pr/2015/pdfs/pr240_E.pdf
90. Kiecolt-Glaser, J. (2010). Stress, food, and inflammation: Psychoneuroimmunology and nutrition at the cutting edge. *Psychosomatic Medicine, 72*(4), 365-369. doi: 10.1097/ PSY.0b013e3181dbf489
91. Lopez-Garcia, E., et al. (2004). Major dietary patterns are related to plasma concentrations of markers of inflammation and endothelial dysfunction. *American Journal of Clinical Nutrition, 80*(4), 1029-1035.
92. Jargin, S. (2014). Soy and phytoestrogens: Possible side effects. *German Medical Science, 12*, doc 18. doi: 10.3205/000203
93. Jargin, S. (2014). *Ibid.*
94. Messina, M. (2016). Soy and health update: Evaluation of the clinical and epidemiologic literature. *Nutrients, 8*(12), 754. doi: 10.3390/nu8120754

95. Lee, J., et al. (2017). Effect of fermented soybean products intake on the overall immune safety and function in mice. *Journal of Veterinary Science, 18*(1), 25-32. doi: 10.4142/jvs.2017.18.1.25
96. D'Adamo, C., & Sahin, A. (2014). Soy foods and supplementation: A review of commonly perceived health benefits and risks. *Alternative Therapies in Health and Medicine, 20*(S1), 39-51.
97. Sanchez, A., et al. (1973). Role of sugars in Human Neutrophilic Phagocytosis. *The American Journal of Clinical Nutrition, 26*(11), 1180-1184.
98. Ringsdorf, W., et al. (1976). Sucrose, neutrophilic phagocytosis and resistance to disease. *Dental Survey, 52* (12), 46-48.
99. Taubes, G. (2016). *The case against sugar*. New York: Alfred A. Knopf.
100. Bennet, P., & Barrie, S. (2007). The gallbladder, bile, and gallstones. *The Lyme Times: Alternative Medicine, 49*, 42-43.
101. Manoukian, A. (2007). *Op. cit.*
102. Nguyen, P., Lin, S., & Heidenreich, P. (2016). A systematic comparison of sugar content in low-fat vs regular versions of food. *Nutrition and Diabetes, 6*(1), e193. doi: 10.1038/nutd.2015.43
103. Ahmed, S., Guillem, K., & Vandaele, (2013). Sugar addiction: Pushing the drug-sugar analogy to the limit. *Current opinion in clinical nutrition and metabolic care, 16*(4), 434-439. doi: 10.1097/MCO.0b013e328361c8b8
104. Wilson, J. (2014). *Op. cit.*
105. Zhang, J., & An, (2007). Cytokines, inflammation and pain. *International Anaesthesiology Clinics, 45*(2), 27-37. doi: 10.1097/AIA.0b013e318034194e

[106] Kinderlehrer, D. (2007). Blood sugar and insulin resistance. *The Lyme Times: Alternative Medicine 49*, 39-41.

[107] Manoukian, A. (2007). *Op. cit.*

[108] Wilson, J. (2005). Regulation of vitamin C transport. *Annual Review of Nutrition, 25*, 105-125. doi: 10.1146/annurev.nutr.25.050304.092647

[109] Theophilus, P., et al. (2015). Effectiveness of Stevia rebaudiana whole leaf extract against the various morphological forms of Borrelia burgdorferi in vitro. *European Journal of Microbiology and Immunology, 5*(4), 268-280.

[110] Sarkkinen, E., et al. (2011). Feasibility and antihypertensive effect of replacing regular salt with mineral salt – rich in magnesium and potassium – in subjects with mildly elevated blood pressure. *Nutrition Journal, 10*, 88. doi: 10.1186/1475-2891-10-88

[111] Liu, S., et al. (2017). Deaths and life expectancy losses attributable to diet high in sodium in China. *Zhonghua Liu Xing Bing Xue Za Zhi, 38*(8), 1022-1027. doi: 10.3760/cma.j.issn.0254-6450.2017.08.005

[112] Brandhorst, S., et al. (2015). A periodic diet that mimics fasting promotes multi-system regeneration, enhanced cognitive performance, and healthspan. *Cell Metabolism, 22*, 86-89.

[113] Cheng, C., et al. (2014). Prolonged fasting reduces IGF-1/PKA to promote hematopoietic-stem-cell-based regeneration and reverse immunosuppression. *Cell Stem Cell 14*(6), 810-823.

[114] Li, L., Wang, Z., & Zuo, Z. (2013). Chronic intermittent fasting improves cognitive functions and brain structures in mice. *PLoS One, 8*(6), e66069. doi: 10.1371/journal.pone.0066069

115. Mattson, M. (2014). *Why fasting bolsters brain power: Mark Mattson at TEDx Johns Hopkins University.* TEDx Talk. Retrieved from https://www.youtube.com/watch?v=4UkZAwKoCP8&feature=youtu.be
116. Alirezaei, M., et al. (2010). Short-term fasting induces profound neuronal autophagy. *Autophagy, 6*(6), 702-710.
117. Anton, S., & Leeuwenburgh, C. (2013). Fasting or caloric restriction for healthy aging. *Experimental Gerontology, 48*(10), 1003-1005. doi: 10.1016/j.exger.2013.04.011
118. Longo, V., & Mattson, M. (2014). Fasting: Molecular mechanisms and clinical applications. *Cell Metabolism, 19*(2), 181-192. doi: 10.1016/j.cmet.2013.12.008
119. Marinac, C., et al. (2015). Frequency and circadian timing of eating may influence biomarkers of inflammation and insulin resistance associated with breast cancer risk. *PloS One, 10*(8), e0136240. doi: 10.1371/journal.pone.0136240
120. Patterson, R., et al. (2015). Intermittent fasting and human metabolic health. *Journal of the Academy of Nutrition and Dietetics, 115*(8), 1203-1212. doi: 10.1016/j.jand.2015.02.018
121. Aly, S. (2014). Role of intermittent fasting on improving health and reducing diseases. *International Journal of Health Sciences, 8*(3), v-vi.
122. Harrison, K. (2013) The 5:2 diet: Feast for 5 days, fast for 2 days to lose weight and revitalize your health. USA: Ulysses Press.
123. Manoukian, A. (2007). *Op. cit.*

13. What Does It Feel Like To Have Lyme And/Or Its Co-infections?

While Dana Walsh[1] describes the feeling of living with Lyme as simply, *Pain, pain, pain. Relentless pain, no one would believe it*, others bluntly make statements like, *Lyme turns your body into a torture chamber.*[2,3] Still others describe it as being victimized in at least five different ways:[4]

1. *By the disease itself*
2. *By doctors who turn their backs*
3. *By loved ones who roll their eyes and walk away*
4. *By insurers who refuse to provide coverage*
5. *By the CDC* [Centers for Disease Control and Prevention] *and IDSA* [Infectious Diseases Society of America] *who together say that chronic Lyme does not exist*

It is a disease that requires fighting for healing, fighting for care, fighting socially, fighting financially, fighting for awareness, and fighting for understanding of what it is like to live with it.

Traits when Suffering from Early to Late Disseminated or Chronic Lyme and/or its Co-infections

Ultimately, while Lyme and/or its co-infections can impact everyone differently, there are elements of the illness that everyone with the affliction shares.[5] These are all very real, all very natural, and all very acceptable responses to being chronically ill,[6-8] and they include:

- Disbelief
- Post-traumatic stress disorder (PTSD)
- Isolation
- Emotional and neurological disturbances like *Lyme brain**
- Insomnia
- Pain
- Bouts of rage and irritability
- Anxiety and depression
- Fatigue
- Feelings of grief
- A forever life-changing experience
- Invisibility

Although there are a host of other traits like hallucinations, depersonalization, and obsessive-compulsive disorder (OCD), the ones just

---

* *Lyme brain* includes symptoms such as brain fog, confusion, difficulty retrieving vocabulary, mixing words (word salad), short-term memory loss and word repetition, even anxiety and depression, or rage and irritability.

mentioned are perhaps the most common, and will be the ones touched upon in this chapter. A viewpoint regarding the need for energy management with chronic and invisible illnesses is also discussed.

Disbelief.

You will hear doctors say things like *all the blood tests are normal*, or *you look fit and healthy, nothing could possibly be wrong with you*. When getting responses from health providers like this, you will need support from family members and friends. It is your body, and you know that something is terribly wrong.

> *My doctor's denial of my illness made me feel alone and scared* – Vaccaro.[9]

For the family member or friend, it is crucial at a time like this to advocate, and provide support for the person who is ill. After all, who will you choose to believe: the clinician that was met for perhaps five minutes, or the long-term friend, the person who you have known your whole life, the child who you raised, or the person who you have been married to for decades?

> *I know the truth – that my illness and my pain are real – and that's all that matters* – Gaudian.[10]

Do not discount the extreme importance of needing to work with a medical professional when you are very ill, but try to find one that you can trust and work with together. Be open with your doctor, and be prepared to question and to be questioned, but be aware that if they are not able to answer your questions, they might get angry. It has also long been recognized that frustration is a result of anger,[11] and clinician frustration can also lead to aggression.

> *He slammed his fist down on the table, and said don't talk to me about Lyme anymore!* – Anonymous.[12]

> *It's hard to have a nurse yell at your wife and scream,* **you're making this up, stop shaking***, when you know there's something wrong* – Bridgman.[13]

If not a result of frustration, the doctor may hold a negative bias toward specific health conditions or simply believe that they are fantasies.[14]

> *Time and time again as I searched for answers, I found myself carrying the burden of proof. It should not be this way, we should not have to hide our trauma in order to receive adequate care. We shouldn't have to carry the shame of lack when medical bills can swallow a year's worth of salary in less than 30 days and still*

leave you broken and sick ... The part that grieves my soul the most is that after years of appointments and specialists, when you finally do have 'proof' that something is in fact terribly wrong because you can no longer walk, or think or work, you are told that it is all in your head, or that you are causing it through anxiety, or maybe you want some attention? Our battles, my friends, are not fought in dark parking lots, but within a physician's office. They can leave bruises on your soul that you long to cover up ... Shame in any form does not help you to heal. Instead, it holds you captive. If you are already living within the shackles of chronic illness, don't agree to be shackled yet again by shame – Sanchez.[15]

The medical literature does focus on the requirements of doctors to manage anger and to be empathetic, but it predominantly focuses on the management of patients who are perceived as being difficult.[16] The other side to this, of course, is that a particular doctor is being difficult, frustrating, or simply one that you feel is being incompetent or dismissive, and it may be prudent to fire them.[17] Yes, fire them. Get up, walk out, and ask for a refund or file an official complaint. Remember, doctors are working for you and your health, and quite often, you will need to pay a substantial amount of money out-of-pocket for this. That said, most doctors genuinely do care for their patients, although some may actually forget that they have been commissioned by you. If you are chronically ill, it will be a long journey back to health, and you will need to work with a doctor, or doctors, that you are comfortable with. This is important, for whoever you commission as your physician, because you will likely need to work with them for a very significant amount of time, and you will need to be able to trust and rely on them for medical support.

> *I've been failed too many times by healthcare professionals, [and] I just have a total disregard for many of them now. The 5-minute GP consult is a joke. However, as an expert in my field, I do know that 5 minutes is enough time to make a successful assessment of a person in general, but I am also very aware that it is certainly not enough time to make a very comprehensive assessment of that individual. However, I do trust the physician I work with now. Probably because he is careful, and competent, and he listens, but most likely because I reach my own medical conclusions before seeing him, and largely I have found that he reaches the same ones independently, backing them up with the clinical and professional knowledge that I lack – G.*[18]

Post-Traumatic Stress Disorder (PTSD).

Post-traumatic stress disorder is, unfortunately, something that you will suffer due to the treatment that you receive from many in the medical community,[19] being blamed for your own illness[20] while attempting to obtain a diagnosis and treatment,[21] and from suffering the symptoms of a disease that no one around you can understand.[22]

> ... PTSD from all the horrific things it has done to me ... it has taken my brain to places that have scarred me for life – Noelle.[23]

Although short-term stressors might be beneficial to the immune system, prolonged physical and psychological stress can negatively impact it,[24] and it will have an adverse effect on your healing.[25] This kind of emotional wounding, if not addressed, will also impact on later physician consults.

> I have PTSD symptoms ... from a long battle with being sick; treatment; hospitals; tests; fearing I would be disabled forever; ... doctors; waiting rooms; SEVERE insomnia; 3 PICC line failures; chest port; horrendous depression and PMS ...I find that I very often don't talk about the illness ... – Kayaklove.[26]

Fostering forgiving thoughts rather than rehearsing hurtful memories can promote a lower physiological stress response.[27] It is also important to try and resolve any emotional issues, since psychic trauma also appears to contribute to a relapse in chronic infectious tick-borne disease.[28] Possible ways of achieving this is to engage in religious and spiritual practices such as prayer which has been seen to help move patients towards a positive health outcome.[29,30]

> *My tendency is to grow bitter and become angry, but I know that letting my mind engage in that kind of thinking is never helpful! It is a struggle to do so when symptoms take over, but I never regret taking my pains to the Lord. He is our comforter ...* – M. K.[31]

Approaches like meditation are also beneficial as it can reduce free radical loads[32] which can disrupt mitochondrial integrity and function. It can also promote physical brain changes[33] that can potentially lead to greater intelligence,[34] improve mitochondrial resiliency as a result of improving the production and utilization of mitochondrial energy.[35] It can also help to reduce stress hormone levels in the body, such as cortisol and adrenaline which can negatively impact a number of organs including the brain and adrenals.[36,37]

Meditation can also give you the time and space that you might need to resolve all of the emotions you have experienced while being chronically ill.[38] Spending time meditating might also help you come to feel comfortable with the feelings of isolation that can accompany chronic illness, as it can also help in reducing feelings of loneliness.[39]

> *Chronic illnesses ... are not the flowers and casseroles type of diseases. No one came by to drop off dinner because I was too sick to cook, or dropped off flowers to brighten my day. No one sent me get well cards. No one even came by really much at all* – Milton.[40]

Isolation.

Unfortunately, suffering from late disseminated or chronic Lyme and its co-infections can be very isolating. You will be alone (sometimes), and if housebound or bedridden, you will also be forgotten by many friends who will simply vanish and you will be better for it.

> *People have become accustomed to you not being around. So, you become gradually irrelevant ... chapters of my life came and went without me being fully present* – Sanchez.[41]

Sometimes family members and other loved ones will give up on you. The level of support and continued help required of you as a patient will see all of your relationships fray, and not many will endure.[42] Unfortunately, at times your spouse will also forget that you, as their significant other, are extremely ill ... or worse.

> *The knowledge that a loved one's behavior is caused by a physical disorder takes a back seat ... It was very sad, frustrating and angering to watch my significant other turn into a monster ... I walked out on her* – Ben.[43]

Lyme Brain.

One of the most frequent symptoms of late disseminated or chronic Lyme is that of an infected or inflamed brain as well as an infected nervous system –*encephalitis*[44] but you might simply call it *Lyme Brain*. It includes symptoms such as brain fog, confusion, difficulty retrieving vocabulary, mixing words (word salad), short-term memory loss, and word repetition.[45-47] The neurological effects along with the associated behavioral effects can be devastating, not just for you being ill, but also to your family members, friends, and the significant others that surround you, and they are "some of the most confused with other illnesses."[48]

> *The bacteria burrows deep into brain tissue to avoid being killed by medications that can't cross the blood-brain barrier ... it's so hard to explain to someone without sounding like you've lost your mind* – Starling.[49]

Cognitive impairment can mean that when driving, you might forget the meaning of a signal change from red to green at a traffic light, yet still know that it has significance.[50] You might run out of medications before realizing that you had to order more, or thought that you had already placed the order. You might even end up taking the wrong dose at the right time, or the right dose at the wrong time.

> *I hope that lady that accidentally drank half a bottle of A-Bart, because it was on the counter next to her normal dosage, is okay!* – D.[51]

For many, there is a significant and measurable decline in intellectual acuity similar to that seen with diffuse brain injury, and it can impact all areas of normal functioning.[52] For that same majority, treatment can bring significant improvement,[53,54] and perhaps even resolution. Until then, symptoms of *Lyme brain*, and at times being unable to shut off your brain, may lead you to insomnia.

Insomnia.

Sleep is a critical component in helping your body to heal, but unfortunately, sleep disturbances like initial insomnia (trouble falling asleep), middle insomnia (trouble remaining asleep), and/or terminal insomnia (waking up too early) are all too common with Lyme and its co-infections.[55] Maintaining an adequate circadian rhythm might help you induce a better night of sleep, or in getting to sleep earlier. This is important as long-term circadian misalignment can potentially lead to disease states such as breast cancer, and other negative cardiovascular, physiologic, and metabolic effects.[56,57]

> *No matter what I do I just can't sleep at night ... I'm desperate. I don't know what to do –* O.[58]

Techniques to help maintain a good circadian rhythm include the use of blackout curtains, as artificial light can disrupt sleep patterns,[59] and by implementing a *digital sunset*, as light from electronic devices in the evening can suppress the production of melatonin, phase-shift the biological clock, and increase alertness.[60] Blue blocker glasses can significantly weaken the suppression of melatonin by artificial light,[61] and you may need to start wearing blue blockers in the evening for a few hours before bed. In this way, your body is able to naturally start making the melatonin that it needs to help induce sleep.

Once able to sleep more, symptoms often lessen,[62] because a lack of sleep can negatively impact the immune system and increase inflammation which can then lead to increased pain, increased fatigue, and irritability[63] which often makes it difficult for you to then get to sleep or remain asleep.

> *Even when you feel like you can finally get to sleep, you might not be able to, you will have to force yourself to stay awake, waiting for the timer to countdown to your next intake of pills*
> – D.[64]

Pain.

The key to alleviating chronic pain from late disseminated or chronic Lyme and its co-infections is the simultaneous treatment of infection, inflammation, and immune dysfunction,[65] but until then, you will experience pain and symptoms that will disable you. They will come and go, and they will move around.[66] Lyme disease is known as the great imitator,[67,68] and as it affects everyone differently, the pain for everyone will also be different.[69] You could experience either joint, muscle, or nerve pain, or perhaps all three; it will be influenced by your hormonal cycle (particularly if you are a woman);[70] and, it will present as one or more of over 250 other conditions.[71,72]

> *The pain that I experienced was so horrible and so frightening, all I wanted to do was curl up into a ball and give up* – Vaccaro.[73]

Pain can also come from a Jarisch-Herxheimer reaction** when disease symptoms flare in response

---

** A *Jarisch-Herxheimer reaction* is also known as *JHR, herxing,* a *herx,* or a *Herxheimer reaction.*

to treatment.[74] It is viewed as a typical *die-off* response to therapy, occurring between 48 to 72 hours after treatment, and it is not specific to the treatment of Lyme disease and its co-infections, as it is the result of the body's inability to process the number of endotoxins released as the microbes are being killed.[75]

> *My herx's all start at the same time: 2 AM or 3 AM ... I wake up literally crying in pain. This time my insomnia kept me awake so as I got out of bed to get water at 2 AM, the pain hit me like a ton of bricks ... always amazes me how one moment I can be fine and the next I'm trying to catch my breath because the pain is so bad* – Purpleyogamat.[76]

Depression and anxiety, or any degree of stress, can also lower the pain threshold in the body[77] and exacerbate feelings of pain. Co-infections can also increase pain: *Babesia* is known to increase all Lyme symptoms, while *Bartonella* can lead to neuropathic[***] and encephalopathic[****] issues.[78] The pain may also, at times, cause you to lash out at others in bouts of rage and irritability.

[***] *Neuropathic* meaning disease or dysfunction of peripheral nerves, and this can cause numbness or weakness.
[****] *Encephalopathic* disease where the functioning of the brain is affected.

If I could be out of pain I'd rip a limb off – it's tearing my family apart – M.[79]

Bouts of Rage and Irritability.

Infectious diseases are known to cause a range of mental symptoms,[80] such as sudden-onset OCD[81] as well as hormonal imbalances[82] like low serotonin levels.[83] Combined with this, the impact of late disseminated or chronic Lyme disease on the central nervous system can lead to bouts of rage and irritability.[84] Those living with someone with late disseminated or chronic Lyme and its co-infections may know this well.

> *Both her brain and her hormones were adversely affected, and this wreaked havoc on her psyche. Rarely a day went by when she didn't criticize me about something, and not just normal relationship criticism either. Everything about me bothered her: my eating habits, my favorite TV shows, the way I cut my hair. When I'd wash dishes, she'd get upset because I used **too much soap** on the sponge* – B.[85]

Lyme rage[86,87] appears abruptly and unexpectedly in a sudden explosive burst. You may not even know that you are in a state of rage; anything will trigger you at any time any place – the checkout clerk stops swiping your items to answer a passerby's question, a driver cuts you off in traffic, your child uses one drop too many on a dish sponge. Your rage can become violent when you strike out at someone you love, or perhaps suicidal if you strike out at yourself.

> *I've come very close to hurting someone … when the 'attacks' got really serious, I would … beat the livin' daylights out of some poor tree!!* – Traveler.[88]
> *My son has the Lyme rages. He is 7 and he can get so violent. We had to often restrain him* – Lymemomma.[89]

> *I turn into the 'HULK' as he calls me … when I'm really angry it really is not pretty and I'm afraid that I'll do something that I'll regret* – RainStorm.[90]

> *I could feel my blood starting to boil … I realized what it was and fought … to make myself realize it was the disease …it did subside for me. So, hang in there* – Woodarrows.[91]

Mood swings, irritability, and *Lyme rage* all improve with treatment,[92] but it can often be traced back to pain,[93] such as that resulting from sensitivity to light or noise,[94] or insomnia.[95] It can also stem from issues that lead into anxiety and depression.

Anxiety and Depression.

Resulting from late disseminated or chronic Lyme disease[96] anxiety and depression are often linked,[97,98] and can stem from a multitude of causes,[99,100] both psychological and physical. It is also recognized,[101] that late disseminated or chronic Lyme disease can contribute to suicidality and homicidality in those who have never been suicidal prior to infection. This is not a unique phenomenon as immune system imbalance,[102] parasites,[103] infection,[104] or treatment modalities[105] can all cause alteration of neural circuits.

You are isolated, you are desperately clutching at one treatment after another, you are rejected by the healthcare community, you are abandoned by friends and family, you have a multimicrobial infection, and you have a spirochete residing in your tissues, and it is physically burrowing around inside your brain.[106] Knowing all of this, your feelings of worry, nervousness, and unease can help build your depression, and on top of all the other things (the pain, the insomnia, the financial stress), your thoughts may turn to suicide. They might just be temporary, or they may linger, calling to you. In either case, you need to know that there are many organizations that can help you get through this, and there are many support forums online where other people with Lyme and co-infections know exactly how you feel, no matter the age.

> *The day before a young boy called Shea died from Lyme disease, he asked his mom to pinkie swear that she would never take her own life if something happened to him. She kept that promise, and so too have many others, digitally signing a promise with Shea to never hurt themselves* – Hilton.[107]

Your first step is reaching out. You know that you do not have to become another statistic or a newspaper headline[108] because there is hope – and there is life after Lyme. There are online groups (*Lyme Success Stories*) that detail the many successful stories of recovery from Lyme, and one day you will be able to add your story to it as well.

> *I remember telling myself years ago that when I got better I wouldn't just ride off into the sunset. I promised myself I'd be present to inspire those in the thick of their battle with Lyme disease to keep fighting … I never thought I'd be pain free again, let alone cycling, running, and enjoying vibrant energy. My symptoms were too many to list, but my biggest ones were intense joint pain, nerve pain that felt like I was burning from the inside out (so much so I couldn't even wear clothes some days), crushing fatigue, air hunger, and intense brain fog/confusion … while healing has been slow … I've been symptom free for over 8 months now. Healing*

is possible! Never stop believing! Know that however bad it is right now, you are doing something toward healing. It might not feel like much, if all you can manage as you're stuck in bed is to stretch your arms above your head, or make your way to the kitchen for your next dose of herbals, or it's all you can do to draw yourself a detox bath, you are doing something, you are doing enough, just keep going. ... I know how depressing it can feel ... how much people are suffering. I hope this helps someone know there is a future after Lyme disease, and I KNOW we will all get there one day at a time! – U.[109]

Fatigue.

A bone-numbingly soul-crushing feeling of pure exhaustion doesn't even come close to describing the fatigue that results from Lyme and its co-infections. It is not just being tired, needing another coffee, muscle soreness, or needing an early night, it is literally a fatigue that occurs at the intracellular level with the mitochondria that convert oxygen, along with the sugars, fats, and proteins from food, to usable energy (ATP, or adenosine triphosphate), without which the body would die in seconds.[110] When the mitochondria are damaged by late disseminated or chronic Lyme and its co-infections, it can lead to a kind of fatigue that does not improve.[111] Repair and rebuilding of the mitochondria might then take a significant amount of time, but it can be supported.[112]

> *Well-meaning friends say **I'm tired too**, but then they are working out, or planning a party, but the fatigue of tick-borne diseases can't be fixed with a shot of coffee or a quick nap –* Crystal.[113]

You will find yourself no longer able to keep up with those around you. They will walk up the stairs ten times faster than you, and when they get to the top, they will look back, and wonder where you are, and you, halfway up the stairs, have been forcing yourself to try and keep up.

> *I'm too tired to breathe … the effort required to take a breath is more than I can manage –* Razzie.[114]

You might now also be thought of as a quiet person because you don't say much. It's not because you don't have anything to say, but because you are just too worn out to speak.

> *Chronic illness is not only physically painful but also emotionally exhausting, and small talk, any talk, steals your energy –* A.[115]

Most times, you may not even have the energy to stand up to any discrimination that comes your way, publicly and privately. This point drives home the importance for friends and family to be your advocate, especially when this discrimination is directed towards you by a health provider.

> *You don't know what tired is, you should see my grandmother* – C.[116]

Depending on your age, security might target you, and harass you for loitering in a shopping center or other public place because you are too exhausted to get back to your car or wait in line for a taxi because you feel unable to drive and have to abandon your vehicle. So, you may need to invest in props.

> *Always take a cane with you, even if you don't need it that day* – K.[117]

This simple visual for people has, I am sure, helped to keep many tongues in check. Occasionally, it might even see people offer assistance!

Unfortunately, the impact of late disseminated or chronic Lyme and its co-infections, the time that they take to get diagnosed, and the time that it takes to do anything when you have no energy, will not just get to you, it will also impact on those around you, like your partner. This can lead to grief.

> *I'm so tired all the time, my wife, well ex-wife is too. She just told me she was **tired of dealing with my sickness** and has walked out on me. I don't blame her, it's got to be hard for a woman when they have a man unable to do anything but lay in bed* – T.[118]

Experiencing Stages of Grief and Healing.

Suffering a chronic illness can be emotionally devastating as your self-esteem is stripped away and you no longer have the same sense of purpose as when you were living a normal life[119] – a life that you feel you may very well never be able to live again, but which you must fight hard to return to. In the meantime, learning to live with a chronic illness often means that you will need to say goodbye to your old life, and in saying goodbye, you may need to grieve.[120] Grieve, because you will not only need to come to terms with your illness, but with what that illness now means for your life.

> *If a person lived with tick-borne disease, that person suffered, not just on a physical level – which is tremendous – but on a social level as well. That kind of suffering needs to be acknowledged and grieved for too* – Arnold.[121]

The famous five stages of grief are denial, anger, bargaining, depression, and acceptance.[122] Each can be visited in any order, and perhaps multiple times, as can those described by Greg Kirk in his article *six stages to chronic Lyme healing: discovery; disillusionment; treatment; anger and panic; acceptance; and gratitude*.[123] Let's journey through each of these six stages together.

Discovery leads to relief after a diagnosis, but it may take you years, and relief will really only last until you come to understand what treatment actually involves. During your process of discovery, or even during your treatment, disillusionment may take you over. You will become disillusioned with the medical establishment, companies that should be providing support but don't, and with family members or friends who could once be relied upon during tough times but are now no longer there.

There will be frustration at loss – loss of employment, loss of social life, loss of relationships, and loss of self-esteem.[124] You will find a need to become self-empowered before you will be able to move out of this stage. Self-empowerment will also be crucial during treatment because Lyme is not a one-size-fits-all approach,[125] and you will need to research and come to understand what works for you, and just what kind of treatment you will need to undertake. Your treatment might take you less than a year, or it might take you many years, and it could require many different approaches, leading you to either anger or panic, or to both.

You will express your frustration with the healing process externally as anger or internally as panic. When your anger rises up, you will lash out at those around you, at the frustrations arising from dealing with doctors, from feeling unheard, and from being marginalized. There is a reason for the expressions *Lyme rage* and *Bartonella rage*, and you may come to find it ironic that the Hulk is often depicted as green. You will also panic when you know there is no money left for treatment, when your support system crumbles, or when your partner walks out on you. You will begin to feel hopeless, and you will be left with almost no energy to carry on the fight. It is here where those first thoughts of suicide could greet you, and you will need to be strong enough to realize that both the anger and the panic are taking vital energy away from you. Energy that you need in order to put these things behind you so that you can progress to acceptance.

Reaching acceptance allows for the negative attention you have unwittingly given to your chronic illness a chance to fade, and other more positive aspects of your life will then start to shine through and allow for feelings of gratitude to emerge. Ultimately, you will be thankful for having gone through the previous stages, and you will then be able to move on with your life.

> *The experience can be like a forest fire that burns away all unnecessary elements in your life, while creating space for new growth –* Kirk.[126]

It will be forever life-changing.

Forever Life-Changing.

Brock[127] describes Lyme as a thief that steals bits and pieces of your life. There is a constant falling away of the things that you *used to love most in this world*, and even when not physically alone, you have come to know the feeling of isolation, and that of being alone – alone with pain, alone with the struggle to keep up, and alone with fatigue.

> *Life's precious moments are stolen, and life is on hold indefinitely, until that elusive day comes when perhaps you might be well again –* Buttaccio.[128]

> *For me, I see it as a death, the life I lived before my illness is gone, and I will probably never be able to go back to doing many of the things I used to love, and if so, never with the same intensity. I choose to view myself as being resurrected. I have a new body, and I have the opportunity to live a completely different style of life, and meet and interact with a completely new group of people, in a new way. Today, I live with my illness shrouded in a cloak of invisibility, and if you have Lyme, then you will wear that cloak too –* D.[129]

Invisibility. Many suffering long term from Lyme and co-infection exposure may look normal to the rest of the world,[130] wearing a 'cloak of invisibility'. An invisible illness, or an invisible disability, means to the rest of the world that these people should be performing normally.

> *It's really hard when people don't even acknowledge that you're sick* – Perry.[131]

Looking outwardly normal, but being extremely ill, is one of the most difficult things to deal with for several reasons. You may experience immense pain from normal noises, and have an increased startle response that sends your heart racing at the slightest unexpected noise. You might be sensitive to light, ensuring a need to keep your eyes firmly shut or a need to wear sunglasses indoors. You might even be hypersensitive to touch.

> *Lyme disease has stolen my ability to be hugged … one of my many Lyme symptoms is hypersensitive, painful shoulders. If someone touches them, it feels like I'm being stung by a thousand bees. And the worst part is that people don't understand because I don't look sick* – Leland.[132]

Regardless, you will be expected by others around you to function normally when in public, and you might even be approached by strangers for help, and asked to assist them in tasks which you know that you cannot perform. You might be asked to help with directions but *Lyme Brain* has taken over, and as a woman with a light hair color, you're just another dumb blond. As a man, you might be asked to help lift heavy bags, or you might be ridiculed and verbally attacked for 'forcing' your wife to carry heavy luggage or shopping bags while you hold nothing and are struggling just to walk. You could also be yelled at, or abused for trying to use a toilet that is labeled for those with disabilities, and one that it is clearly 'not for you'.

> *Can the all-knowing bystanders of this world please stop talking now? Because all of us ... living with these illnesses, have had enough of their misinformed views. Serious illness is a completely game changing experience. I know this because I have lived it firsthand. Everything you ever thought was true is no longer. What you thought was possible for you and your life becomes totally rewritten. Your entire belief system, all your relationships, your sense of self ... everything looks completely different* – Hill.[133]

A View from the Field – The Spoon Theory

The spoon theory is an online essay by Christine Miserandino,[134] and it is perhaps one of the best ways for family, friends, and caregivers to understand how difficult it can be to function when a person is very ill but does not look sick. Although she has lupus, her theory can be applied to those who are ill with Lyme and/or its co-infections.

In her essay,[135] Christine details how she used *spoons* as a visual aide to help answer her friends question *What does having lupus feel like?* She gave her friend twelve spoons, and asked her to detail the events of her typical day, taking a spoon away for each activity mentioned. The theory is that the spoons, or units of energy, must be rationed each day to avoid running out of them before the end of the day.

The problem is, you never really know how many spoons you will wake up with on any given day. For someone with a chronic illness, like late disseminated or chronic Lyme and/or its co-infections, simply getting out of bed (one spoon), putting on a shirt (one spoon), brushing hair (one spoon), taking medicine (one spoon), counting drops of a tincture (one spoon) ... shows how easily, and how quickly, the person can run out of spoons. Every action needs to be thought out (one spoon) before being undertaken, nothing can be done on a whim or desire. Sacrifices have to be made, for example: taking medicine or eating, eating or showering, showering or washing up, washing up or doing laundry.

Christine says,
> ... the hardest thing I ever had to learn is to slow down ... I hate feeling left out, having to choose to stay home, or to not get things done ... I miss that freedom. I miss never having to count 'spoons' – Miserandino.[136]

For her, exceeding today's spoons is like taking spoons from tomorrow to use today. Although spoons might be replaced by a good night's rest, or a good night of sleep, many with late disseminated or chronic Lyme and/or its co-infections may not be able to get to sleep, or stay asleep if they do. This lack of sleep can result in a low supply of energy. Interestingly, Brune and Wilson[137] mention that those who are disabled may not actually experience fatigue from the disability itself, that fatigue comes from a constant effort, or a need to mask the disability in order to appear as non-disabled. People with an invisible illness like late disseminated or chronic Lyme and/or its co-infections, that are attempting to function normally in order to keep a job, appease a spouse, or meet life expectations, might also be included in this category.

The spoon theory has been discussed in relation to Lyme in blogs and support forums, and by a number of individuals.[138-142] They have used it to help explain what the lack of energy and bone-numbing exhaustion feels like, and why they are unable to engage in everyday activities at a normal pace, complete tasks, attend events, or even get out of bed that day. Employing the use of 'spoons', and becoming a *'spoonie'*, is probably one of the best ways to think about energy management when dealing with invisible illnesses, Lyme-like illnesses, multi-microbial systemic infections, and when having to live with Lyme and/or its co-infections.

References

[1] Walsh, D., in Wilson, A. (2008). *Under our skin*. United States: Open Eye Pictures.

[2] Smith, J., in Wilson, A. (2014). *Under our skin 2: Emergence*. United States: Open Eye Pictures.

[3] Lerche, O. (2016). Lyme disease 'torturous' symptoms make sufferer feel like her body is 'shutting down'. Express. Retrieved from http://www.express.co.uk/life-style/health/696917/Lyme-disease-symptoms-tick-bacteria-fatigue-Sarah-Hook

[4] Dennis, L. (2016). *A stranglehold of victimization*. LinkedIn. Retrieved from https://www.linkedin.com/pulse/stranglehold-victimization-lori-dennis-ma-rp

[5] Rawls, W. (2017). *Unlocking Lyme: Myths, truths, & practical solutions for chronic Lyme disease*. USA: FirstDoNoHarm Publishing.

[6] Muran, P. (2008). Lyme disease – A functional medicine approach. *The Lyme Times, 54*, 3-5.

[7] Oderberg, N. (2009). Managing the stresses of chronic illness: Focused attention affirmations, exercises, and activities promote physical and mental wellness. *The Lyme Times, 55*, 22-23.

8. Rippey, M. (2015). *Episode 27: Lyme expert – Dr. Nicola McFadzean Ducharme – Author, naturopath*. Lyme Ninja Radio. Retrieved from http://lymeninjaradio.com/nicola_ducharme
9. Vaccaro, P. (2007). Peter's story. *The Lyme Times, 50*, 25.
10. Gaudian, M. (2008). Meghan's story. *The Lyme Times, 54*, 18.
11. Blair, R. (2013). Considering anger from a cognitive neuroscience perspective. *Wiley Interdisciplinary Reviews. Cognitive Science, 3*(1), 65-74. doi:10.1002/wcs.154
12. Anonymous, in Wilson, A. (2008). *Under our skin*. United States: Open Eye Pictures.
13. Bridgman, D. in Radulova, L. (2014). Australia's 'hidden epidemic': Woman left unable to walk and speak after her Lyme disease went undiagnosed for 26 years. *Daily Mail Online*. Retrieved from http://www.dailymail.co.uk/news/article-2845997/The-hidden-epidemic-Thousands-Australians-believed-suffering-Lyme-disease-forced-travel-overseas-seek-treatment-government-continues-dismiss-it.html
14. Lorenzetti, R., et al, (2013). Managing difficult encounters: Understanding physician, patient, and situational factors. *American Family Physician, 87*(6), 419-425.
15. Sanchez, S. (2017). *Shame and Illness*. The Path from Lyme Disease to Wellness. Retrieved from http://lymevoice.com/shame-and-illness
16. Halperm, J. (2007). Empathy and patient-physician conflicts. *Journal of General Internal Medicine, 22*(5), 696-700. doi: 10.1007/s11606-006-0102-3

17. Kirk, G. (2017). *Patient empowerment: Don't be afraid to fire your doctor*. Lyme Knowledge: Your Resource for Info on Lyme & Tick-Borne Diseases. Retrieved fromhttp://www.lymeknowledge.com/patient-empowerment-dont-be-afraid-to-fire-your-doctor
18. G. (2017). *I've been failed too many times* ... Personal Communication. September 17.
19. Horowitz, R. (2017). *How can I get better?: An action plan for treating resistant Lyme & chronic disease*. New York: St. Martin's Press.
20. Crystal, J. (2013). Lyme patients blamed for their own illness: Healthcare professionals all too anxious to write off Lyme as all-in-your-head. *The Lyme Times*, 27(2), 6.
21. Rippey, M. (2015). *Op. cit.*
22. Starling, J. (2015). When the fog rolls in: My most frightening and frustrating symptoms are invisible to everyone else. *The Lyme Times, 27*(2), 35.
23. Noelle. (2017). *Severe anxiety, Lyme or leftover PTSD*. LymeNet. Retrieved from http://flash.lymenet.org/scripts/ultimatebb.cgi/topic/1/60542?
24. Glaser, R., & Kiecolt-Glaser, J. (2005). Stress-induced immune dysfunction: Implications for health. *Nature Reviews Immunology, 5*(3), 243-251.
25. Gouin, J., & Kiecolt-Glaser, J. (2011). The Impact of psychological stress on wound healing: Methods and mechanisms. *Immunology and Allergy Clinics of North America, 31*(1), 81-83. doi: 10.1016/j.ac.2010.09.010
26. Kayaklove. *(2015). Lyme disease forums*. Healing Well. Retrieved from http://www.healingwell.com/community/default.aspx?f=30&m=3463643

27. Van Oyen Witvliet, C., Ludwig, T., & Vander Laan, K. (2001). Granting forgiveness or harboring grudges: Implications for emotion, physiology, and health. *Psychological Science, 12*(2), 117-123.
28. Bransfield, R. (2017). *Posttraumatic stress disorder and infectious encephalopathies*. Mental Health and Illness. Retrieved from http://www.mentalhealthandillness.com/Articles/PosttraumaticStressDisorder.htm
29. Schlitz, M. (2005). Meditation, prayer, and spiritual healing: The evidence. *The Permanente Journal, 9*(3), 63-66.
30. Rao, A., et al. (2015). Prayer or spiritual healing as adjuncts to conventional care: A cross sectional analysis of prevalence and characteristics of use among women. *BMJ Open, 5*(6), e007345. doi: 10.1136/bmjopen-2014-007345.
31. M. K. (2017). *A support group*. Facebook. August 12.
32. Panta, P. (2017). The possible role of meditation in myofascial pain syndrome: A New Hypothesis. *Indian Journal of Palliative Care, 23*(2), 180-187. doi:10.4103/0973-1075.204239
33. Luders, E., et al. (2012). The unique brain anatomy of meditation practitioners: Alterations in cortical gyrification. *Frontiers in Human Neuroscience*. doi: 10.3389/fnhum. 2012.00034
34. Luders, E., et al. (2008). Mapping the relationship between cortical convolution and intelligence: Effects of gender. *Cerebral Cortex, 18*(9), 2019-2026.
35. Bhasin, M., et al. (2013). Relaxation response induces temporal transcriptome changes in energy metabolism, insulin secretion and inflammatory pathways. *PLoS One, 8*(5), e62817. doi: 10.1371/journal.pone.0062817

36. Wilson, J. (2014). *Adrenal fatigue: The 21st century stress syndrome*. USA: Smart Publications.
37. Asprey, D. (2016). *Head strong: The bulletproof plan to activate untapped brain energy to work smarter and think faster – In just two weeks*. USA: HarperWave.
38. Horowitz, R. (2017). *Op. cit.*
39. Creswell, J., et al. (2012). Mindfulness-based stress reduction training reduces loneliness and pro-inflammatory gene expression in older adults: A small randomized controlled trial. *Brain, Behavior, and Immunity, 26*, 1095-1101. doi: 10.106/j.bbi.2012.07.006
40. Milton, C. (2017). The unexpected losses and gains of Lyme disease. The Mighty. Retrieved from https://the mighty.com/2017/09/lyme-disease-losses-and-gains
41. Sanchez, S., in Gruenig, M. (2017). Disappearing from society – A Look into Chronic Illness. Documentary. Retrieved from https://player.vimeo.com/video/21888 7760
42. Buttaccio, J. (2015). A life on pause: When Lyme steals everything, you will spend every last cent trying to get well. *The Lyme Times, 27*(2), 34.
43. Ben. (2012). *Lyme disease and Bartonellosis*. Retrieved from http://www.benbrew.com/lb/lb.html
44. Sherr, V. (2015). The agony of Lyme brain: Mainstream medicine misses psychiatric symptoms of Neuroborreliosis. *The Lyme Times, 27*(3), 24.
45. McFadzean Ducharme, N. (2016). *Lyme brain: The impact of Lyme disease on your brain, and how to reclaim your smarts*. USA: BioMed Publishing Group.
46. Global Lyme Alliance. (2017). *Living with Lyme brain*. Global Lyme Alliance. Retrieved from https://globall yme alliance.org /living-lyme-brain
47. Sherr, V. (2015). *Op. cit.*

48. Crystal, J. (2017). *Living with Lyme brain*. Global Lyme Alliance. Retrieved from https://globallymealliance.org/ living-lyme-brain
49. Starling, J. (2015). *Op. cit.*
50. Bransfield, R. (2017). *Lyme Disease and cognitive impairments*. Mental Health and Illness. Retrieved from http://www.mentalhealthandillness.com/Articles/LymeDiseaseAndCognitiveImpairments.htm
51. D. (2017). *I hope that lady that accidentally drank ...* Personal Communication. September 07.
52. Rissenberg, M., & Chambers, S. (1998). Distinct pattern of cognitive impairment noted in study of Lyme patients. *The Lyme Times, 20*, 29-32.
53. McFadzean Ducharme, N. (2016). *Op. cit.*
54. Ross, M. (2017). Brain fog in Lyme disease. You can fix it. *The Treat Lyme Book*. Retrieved from http://www.treatlyme.net/treat-lyme-book/brain-fog-lyme-disease
55. Buhner, S. (2013). *Healing Lyme co-infections: Complimentary and holistic treatments for Bartonella and Mycoplasma*. Vermont: Healing Arts Press.
56. Cho, Y., et al. (2015). Effects of artificial light at night on human health: A literature review of observational and experimental studies applied to exposure assessment. *Chronobiology International, 32*(9), 1294-1310. doi:10.3109/07420528.2015.1073158
57. Bedrosian, T., & Nelson, R. (2017). Timing of light exposure affects mood and brain circuits. *Translational Psychiatry, 7*(1), e1017. doi: 10.1038/tp.2016.262
58. O. (2017). *A support group*. Facebook. September 05.
59. Rettner, R. (2012). *Light at night bad for health, docs say*. LiveScience. Retrieved from https://www.livescience.com/36488-light-night-health.html

60. Chang, A., et al. (2015). Evening use of light-emitting eReaders negatively affects sleep, circadian timing, and next-morning alertness. *Proceedings of the National Academy of Sciences of the United States of America, 112*(4), 1232-1237. doi: 10.1073/pnas.1418490112
61. Van der Lely, S. (2015). Blue blocker glasses as a countermeasure for alerting effects of evening light-emitting diode screen exposure in male teenagers. *Journal of Adolescent Health Care, 56*(1), 113-119. doi: 10.1016/j.jadohealth. 2014.08.0 02
62. Horowitz, R. (2017). *Op. cit.*
63. Wilson, J. (2014). *Op. cit.*
64. D. (2017). *Even when you feel like you can finally get to sleep* ... Personal Communication. September 07.
65. Horowitz, R. (2017). *Op. cit.*
66. Singleton, K. (2008). *The Lyme disease solution*. USA: BookSurge Publishing.
67. Hamilton, D. (1989). Lyme disease. The hidden pandemic. *Postgraduate Medical Journal, 85*(5), 303-308, 313-314.
68. Margulis, L., et al. (2009). Lyme disease & AIDS: Resurgence of the 'great imitator'. *Symbiosis, 47*, 51-58.
69. Rawls, W. (2017). *Op. cit.*
70. Horowitz, R. (2017). *Op. cit.*
71. UMMC. (2005). *Conditions with similar symptoms as Lyme disease*. University of Maryland Medical Center. Retrieved from http://www.umm.edu/health/medical/altmed/condition-symptom-links/conditions-with-similar-symptoms-as-lyme-disease
72. Jenner, L. (2013). *Lyme is often misdiagnosed as other diseases and disorders*. Lyme-Symptoms. Retrieved from http://www.lyme-symptoms.com/Lyme Mimics.html
73. Vaccaro, P. (2007). *Op. cit.*

74. Burrascano, J. (2008). *Diagnostic hints and treatment guidelines for Lyme and other tick borne illnesses,* (16th ed). Advanced Topics in Lyme Disease. Retrieved from http://www.lymenet. org/BurrGuide200810.pdf
75. Marshall, T., & Marshall, F. (2004). Sarcoidosis succumbs to antibiotics – Implications for autoimmune disease. *Autoimmunity Reviews, 3*(4), 295-300. doi: 10.1016/j.autrev. 2003.10.001
76. Purpleyogamat. (2017). *Herx pain ... When is it too much?* Lyme Disease Support Group. MD Junction. Retrieved from http://www.mdjunction.com/forums/lyme-diseas e-support-forums/general-support/2816830-herx-pain-when-is-it-too-much
77. Horowitz, R. (2017). *Op. cit.*
78. Horowitz, R. (2017). *Ibid.*
79. M. (2017). *A support group.* Facebook. August 13.
80. Howenstine, J. (2004). *The Overlooked relationship between infectious diseases and mental symptoms.* News with Views. Retrieved from http://www.newswith views.com/Howenstine/james16.htm
81. Szymanski, J. (2012). *Can an infection suddenly cause OCD?* Harvard Health Publications: Harvard Medical School. Retrieved from https://www.health.harvard. edu/blog/can-an-infection-suddenly-cause-ocd-201202274417
82. Anderson, W., & Gitlin, R. (2014). Interview with Nancy Faass: Lyme neurotoxins, and hormonal factors. *Townsend Letter*. Retrieved from http://www. townsendletter.com/July2014/lymeneuro0714.html

83. University of Cambridge. (2011). *Serotonin levels affect the brain's response to anger*. Science Daily. Retrieved from https://www.sciencedaily.com/releases/2011/09/110915102917.htm
84. Bransfield, R. (2017). *Aggression and Lyme disease*. Mental Health and Illness. Retrieved from http://www.mentalhealthandillness.com/Articles/AggressionAndLymeDisease.htm
85. B., in Taylor. (2017). *Bartonella, the devil of Lyme*. Warriorbook: A Girl's Battle with Lyme Disease. Retrieved from https://warriorbook.wordpress.com/2014/03/13/bartonella-the-devil-of-lyme
86. Mayer, E. (2017). *Lyme rage and irritability*. Now Healing. Retrieved from https://www.nowhealing.com/lyme-rage-and-irritability
87. White, S. (2017). *Ways to combat Lyme rage and irritability*. Lyme and Me. Retrieved from https://www.lymeandme.com/ways-to-combat-lyme-rage-and-irritability
88. Traveler. (2007). *Lyme Disease Forums*. Healing Well. Retrieved from http://www.healingwell.com/community/default.aspx?f=30&m=2534558
89. Lymemomma. (2012). *Lyme disease forums*. Healing Well. Retrieved from http://www.healingwell.com/community/default.aspx?f=30&m=2534558
90. RainStorm. (2017). *Anything to help with Lyme/Bart rage?* Lyme Disease Support Group. MD Junction. Retrieved from http://www.mdjunction.com/forums/lyme-disease-support-forums/general-support/773062-anything-to-help-with-the-lyme-bart-rage

91. Woodarrows. (2017). *Anger and Lyme ...* Lyme Disease Support Group. MD Junction. Retrieved from http://www.mdjunction.com/forums/lyme-disease-support-forums/general-support/10569260-anger-and-lyme
92. Bransfield, R. (2017). *Op. cit.*
93. Strasheim, C. (2015). How amino acid therapy helps to eliminate symptoms of depression in Lyme disease. ProHealth. Retrieved from http://www.prohealth.com/lyme/library/showarticle.cfm?libid=21318
94. Fallon, B., et al. (1992). The neuropsychiatric manifestations of Lyme Borreliosis. *Psychiatric Quarterly, 63*(1), 95-117.
95. Harris, J., et al. (2012). A randomized controlled trial of intensive sleep retraining (ISR): A brief conditioning treatment for chronic insomnia. *Sleep, 35*(1), 49-60. doi: 10.5665/sleep.1584
96. Garakani, A., & Mitton, A. (2015). New-onset panic, depression with suicidal thoughts, and somatic symptoms in a patient with a history of Lyme disease. *Case Rep Psychiatry, 2015*, 457947. doi: 10.1155/2015/457947
97. Horowitz, R. (2013). *Why can't I get better?: Solving the mystery of Lyme and chronic illness.* New York: St. Martin's Press.
98. Horowitz, R. (2013). Are my anxiety and depression due to Lyme disease? Tick-borne illnesses imitate common disorders and worsen psychological symptoms. *Psychology Today.* Retrieved from https://www.psuchologytoday.com/blog/why-can-t-i-get-better/201311/are-my-anxiety-and-depression-due-lyme-disease-0
99. Sherr, V. (2000). Panic attacks may reveal previously unsuspected chronic disseminated Lyme disease. *Journal of Psychiatric Practice, 6*(6), 352-356.

[100] Hilton, L. (2013). *Lyme disease and suicide, an ignored problem*. CNN iReport. Retrieved from http://ireport.cnn.com/docs/ DOC-1037462

[101] Bransfield, R. (2017). Suicide and Lyme and associated diseases. *Neuropsychiatric Disease and Treatment, 13*, 1575-1587. doi: 10.2147/NDT.S136137.

[102] Pandey, G., et al. (2012). Proinflammatory cytokines in the prefrontal cortex of teenage suicide victims. *Journal of Psychiatric Research, 46*(1), 57-63. doi: 10.1016/j.psychires.2011.08.006

[103] Lester, D. (2010). Brain parasites and suicide. *Psychological Reports, 107*(2), 424. doi: 10.2466/12.13.PR0.107.5.424

[104] Lund-Sorenson, H., et al. (2016). A nationwide cohort study of the association between hospitalization with infection and risk of death by suicide. *JAMA Psychiatry, 73*(9), 912-919. doi: 10.1001/jamapsychiatry.2016.1594

[105] Sockalingam, S., Links, P., & Abbey, S. (2011). Suicide risk in hepatitis C and during interferon-alpha therapy: A review and clinical update. *Journal of Viral Hepatitis, 18*(3), 153-60. doi: 10.1111/j.1365-2893.2010.01393.x

[106] Starling, J. (2015). *Op. cit.*

[107] Hilton, L. (2012). *Make the 'double pinkie swear promise' suicide prevention*. What is Lyme Disease? Retrieved from http://whatislyme.com/if-you-ever-feel-suicidal

[108] Evans, J. (2013). Husband killed himself six months after watching his wife die from an overdose because she got Lyme disease from a tick bite. *Daily Mail Online*. Retrieved from http://www.dailymail.co.uk/news/article-2517602/Husband-killed-Lyme-disease-suffering-wifes-suicide.html

[109] U. (2017). *A support group*. Facebook. August 31.

[110] Asprey, D. (2016). *Op. cit.*

[111] Ross, M. (2016). Power up! Energy and mitochondria. *The Treat Lyme Book*. Healing Arts Partnership. Retrieved from http://www.treatlyme.net/treat-lyme-book/power-up-energy-and-mitochondria

[112] Nicolson, G. (2014). Mitochondrial dysfunction and chronic disease: treatment with natural supplements. *Integrative Medicine, 13*(4), 35-43.

[113] Crystal, J. (2015). The debilitating experience of fatigue: Patients know the difference between "Normal Tired" and "Too Tired to Breathe". *The Lyme Times, 27*(3), 19.

[114] Razzie. (2007). *Lyme disease forums*. Healing Well. Retrieved from http://www.healingwell.com/community/default.aspx? f=30&m=1608420

[115] A. (2017). *A support group*. Facebook. September 03.

[116] C., in Gavish, A. (2017). *Finish the sentence – You now you have a chronic invisible illness when ...* Lyme Disease Group. (September 07). Retrieved from https://www.facebook.com/groups/227910764335351/permalink/335350296924730

[117] K. (2016). Personal Communication. June 19.

[118] T. (2017). *A support group*. Facebook. August 23.

[119] Oderberg, N. (2009). *Op. cit.*

120. Niederwerfer, L. (2017). The stages of grief in Lyme disease: A guide to the emotions and feelings that many people with Lyme disease will go through. *The Lyme Times*, Summer. Retrieved from https://www.lymedisease.org/members/lyme-times/2017-summer-patient-matters/grief-stages-lyme-disease
121. Arnold, B. (2009). Lyme's lethal side: Advocates track lives lost to TBD's. *The Lyme Times, 55*, 30-32.
122. Kubler-Ross, E. (2014). On death and dying: What the dying have to teach doctors, nurses, clergy and their own families. USA: Scribner.
123. Kirk, G. (2017). *The six stages to chronic Lyme healing*. Lyme Knowledge: Your Resource for Info on Lyme & Tick-Borne Diseases. Retrieved from http://www.lymeknowledge.com/the-six-stages-of-chronic-lyme-healing
124. Jenner, L. (2013). Healing the emotional pain of Lyme disease. Lyme-Symptoms. Retrieved from http://www.lyme-symptoms.com/Emotion/Index.html
125. Strasheim, C. (2017). Beyond antibiotics: Newer alternative approaches to chronic Lyme disease treatment. *The Townsend Letter, July*. Retrieved from http://www.townsendletter.com/July2017/antibiotics0717.html
126. Kirk, G. (2017). *Op. cit.*
127. Brock, V. (2016). *A window into the isolation of Lyme disease and chronic invisible illness*. Blog Post. Retrieved from https://themighty.com/2016/10/the-isolation-of-lyme-disease-and-chronic-invisible-illness
128. Buttaccio, J. (2015). *Op. cit.*
129. D. (2017). *For me, I see it as a death ...* Personal Communication. September 07.

130. McFadzean, N. (2012). *The beginner's guide to Lyme disease: Diagnosis and treatment made simple*. USA: BioMed Publishing Group.
131. Perry., in Gruenig, M. (2017). Disappearing from society – A Look into Chronic Illness. Documentary. Retrieved from https://player.vimeo.com/video/218887760
132. Leland, R. (2007). Rachel's story. *The Lyme Times, 48*, 3.
133. Hill, A. (2016). *When sick people don't look sick enough, they must be faking it. You can be chronically ill and still feel like cracking a smile once in a while*. Huffington Post. Retrieved from http://www.huffingtonpost.com/entry when-sick-people-don't-look-sick-enough-they-must-be_us_57ae800ae4b0ae60ff02902c
134. Miserandino, C. (2003). *The spoon theory*. ButYouDontLookSick.com. Retrieved from https://butyoudontlooksick.com/articles/written-by-christine/the-spoon-theory
135. Miserandino, C. (2003). *Ibid.*
136. Miserandino, C. (2003). *Ibid.*
137. Brune, J., & Wilson, D. (2013). *Disability and passing: Blurring the lines of identity*. United States: Temple University Press.
138. Jenna's Lyme Blog. (2015). *Lyme disease and the spoon theory*. Blog Post. Retrieved from http://jennaslymeblog.com/lyme-disease-and-the-spoon-theory
139. Fight Lyme. (2013). *My take on the spoon theory*. Blog Post. Retrieved from https://www.fightlyme.org/2013/02/17/my-take-on-the-spoon-theory
140. Fighting Lyme Disease. (2013). *The Spoon Theory*. Blog Post. Retrieved from https://fightlymedisease.wordpress.com/2013/02/16/the-spoon-theory

[141] Lyme 101. (2012). *The spoon theory*. Blog Post. Retrieved from https://lyme101.wordpress.com/2012/09/19/the-spoon-theory

[142] Morales, H. (2017). *The spoon theory*. Facebook status update. Retrieved from https://www.facebook.com/groups/227910764335351/search/?query=spoon%20theory

14. Frequently Asked Questions About Lyme And Its Co-infections

FAQ

Several questions constantly get asked by those who are first diagnosed with Lyme and/or its coinfections. Here are some of the most common questions currently being asked across a variety of social media platforms. Answers are based on the available literature.

Is Lyme disease sexually transmissible?

Sexual transmission of Lyme disease, along with transplacental transmission, has been refuted in animals.[1,2] However, sexually active patients have seen high antibiotic failure rates, leading to speculation of re-infection by a spouse.[3] There has also been some epidemiological evidence that Lyme can spread in the absence of infected ticks with person-to-person transfer implicated.[4,5] Evidence of Lyme spirochetes has also been found in semen and vaginal secretions,[6] as well as in breast milk and urine.[7] Ultimately though, peer-reviewed research is yet to definitively show that live spirochetes can pass between partners or to children and infect them. As there is comparatively little research regarding alternative transmission of the disease among human populations, additional research is required.[8] A more comprehensive overview regarding this particular question can be found on the Lyme Disease, Science, & Society blog,[9] and on various Lyme Disease Society pages.[10]

If we're pregnant can Lyme be passed onto our baby in utero?

Some Lyme disease doctors[11-13] do think that Lyme is congenital and gestational, with there being a possibility of transplacental transmission of spirochete from mother to fetus,[14] but it is also considered unlikely.[15] Nonetheless, a number of case reports do provide evidence for the possibility. In one case, a pregnant lady with untreated Lyme disease in the first trimester gave birth to a stillborn.[16] In another case, a mother with Lyme disease in the first trimester gave birth to a child who died of congenital heart disease during the first week of life.[17] In both cases, the Lyme spirochete was found in the organs of the infants on autopsy, so it is possible for Lyme to pass to a newborn during pregnancy.[18] In a further study,[19] 60% of women who went untreated for Lyme disease went on to have pregnancies with adverse outcomes, compared to 31.6% of those who were treated with oral antibiotics, and 12.1% for those who were treated parenterally.[20] One Lyme pediatric doctor[21] has stated that mothers with Lyme disease have a 50% chance of passing it on in utero if they are left untreated, a 25% chance if they take antibiotics during pregnancy, and a 5% chance if they take two antibiotics. However, these statistics are not supported by any scientific study.[22]

Are the co-infections of Lyme disease sexually transmissible? If we're pregnant, can the co-infections be passed onto our baby in utero?

It is known that *Babesia* can be transmitted via blood transfusion,[23] particularly in the United States,[24,25] and likely from mother to fetus.[26-28] The transplacental transmission of tick-borne relapsing fever (TBRF) has been reported in the Middle East,[29] and in Africa.[30] *Bartonella* can be passed from mother to fetus,[31,32] and possibly between partners.[33] Human granulocytic anaplasmosis (HGA) has been found to be transmissible in utero,[34] and through blood transfusion.[35] The risk of obtaining *Ehrlichia* from organ transplants or from blood transfusions is also probable,[36,37] as is *Rickettsia*.[38] *Mycoplasma*, depending on the strain, can be obtained from sexual contact, contaminated food, or airborne droplets.[39] Some strains, such as those predominantly sexually transmitted like *Mycoplasma hominis* can lead to potentially adverse pregnancy outcomes,[40,41] and can see transmission from mother to child during birth.[42]

Is Lyme disease or any of the co-infections permanent?

If caught early, Lyme and/or its co-infections can be treated with a great measure of success.[43,44] However, if misdiagnosed or left undiagnosed for years, maybe 5 or even 25 years or more, then the issue becomes much more complex. There are blog reports of people with long-term illnesses seeing success with the use of different treatment protocols,[45,46] or even more alternate and perhaps extreme treatment modalities.[47] This means for those without success from treatment, there may be lingering symptoms.[48] At this time, there appears to be no real definitive answer, as Lyme and/or its co-infections impact each person in unique ways,[49] and there is no one-size-fits-all approach to treatment.[50]

What labs test for Lyme and/or its co-infections?

There are a number of good quality labs that you could use for testing. Some are readily available to consumers, while others will need a medical practitioner to approve and sign-off on the test before it can be conducted. Labs to consider might include:

- Armin Labs – Augsburg, Germany[51]
- Australian Biologics – Sydney, Australia[52]
- DNA Connexions – Colorado Springs, USA[53]
- IGeneX – California, USA[54]

Where can I go to get help with Lyme and/or its co-infections?

The resources list has a section dedicated to organizations and associations around the world that provide assistance and support for those with Lyme and/or its co-infections, but unfortunately, these do not exist in all countries.

Can I donate blood if I have Lyme and/or its co-infections?

Individuals that are being treated for Lyme and/or its co-infections might be best advised against donating blood, as blood is not always screened for infections like *Babesia*,[55] or it is screened only under an investigation protocol with donor consent.[56] Besides *Babesia*, it is known that a number of other co-infections can be passed on through transfusion, such as *Anaplasmosis*,[57] *Ehrlichia*,[58,59] and *Rickettsia*,[60] and probably through organ donation, so this is best avoided as well.[61] *Bartonella* may also be transmitted through blood transfusion, and it may not be detected through traditional screening methods.[62]

Can I get disability if I have Lyme and/or its co-infections?

This will depend on the nation that you are living in, and on the criteria used to assess disability applications and payments. The answer is likely to be no, at least on the first application, and maybe even on a third application. Obtaining disability for Lyme certainly will not be easy, and it will probably take multiple attempts, and be very costly.[63] As late disseminated or chronic Lyme and/or its co-infections can lead to a host of other issues, you may find it easier to qualify for disability based on these complications, as opposed to the actual Lyme and/or the co-infections themselves.[64] It would be best to contact support groups for further information, and talk to those who have gone through the application process.

What is the Lyme Cryme?

The Lyme Cryme refers to two issues: the introduction of an ELISA test prior to a Western blot to test for Lyme disease, putting in place a two-tier testing system; and the changing of the case definition for Lyme, and what this means for test results.[65] The changing of the case definition for Lyme at a 1994 conference[66] in Dearborn, Michigan, has been referred to as the 'Dearborn stunt'.[67] The change in case definition also ties in with conflicts of interest[68] surrounding trials of the failed LymeRix vaccine.[69] Ultimately, the result is that bands on the Western blot test designed to detect a low- or no-antibody response from Neuro-Lyme patients have been discluded. This means that today, only those people with a high antibody response, or about 15% of those with the disease, can be officially considered positive for it when using the two-tier testing system, hence the Lyme Cryme.[70] A documentary on YouTube delves into this much further.[71]

Is there a conspiracy about Lyme? What about that lab, and that island?

There well may be a conspiracy, and for someone with late disseminated or chronic Lyme and/or its co-infections who needs help right now, it could have potentially impacted the kind of treatment options that are available. Most certainly, the air of conspiracy has tinged the perception of the disease that medical professionals and the general public have towards it and anyone with it, or anyone who thinks they may have contracted it.[72]

A recent theory is that Lyme disease escaped from Plum Island, which is located off the coast of Long Island, New York, and a few miles off the coast of Lyme, Connecticut. Plum Island was used as a military base during the Spanish-American War (1898), and turned into a government animal disease center in 1954.[73] It is argued[74] that, even though test animals on the island are destroyed to prevent the spread of contagions that are used in experimentation (like for bioweapon development), birds flying between the island and the mainland can spread any disease they might pick up, and any ticks harboring disease could also hitch a ride on them. Carroll[75] explores this theory, and the conspiracy, along with *Lab 257* in his book of the same name. The fire of conspiracy is also fueled for many, because for such an epidemic, they feel that for too long it has been ...

> *[so] weird that no one wants to talk about it, doctors are scared to treat and diagnose it, [and] the government doesn't talk about it* – Fergurson.[76]

The most problematic nature of all of this is when patients start to be viewed as conspiracy theorists by medical professionals. It is here, when the physician, clinician, or other health provider becomes dismissive, then the illness, and concerns of the patient for testing, may not be taken seriously.[77]

Hang on a tick, so what now? What else do I need to know about this thing?

It can be a relief to finally get a diagnosis if you have been very ill for a very long time. However, if the diagnosis is Lyme and/or its co-infections, then that relief can quickly fade. Why? Because research still lags behind that of other diseases such as AIDS,[78] and testing is still problematic.[79-81] As more people are becoming ill, particularly celebrities,[82-85] public awareness of the seriousness of Lyme disease and/or its co-infections is increasing, and with it the realization that much more research, and funding for research, is required. If you have just been diagnosed with *early disseminated, late disseminated* or *chronic Lyme disease*, and/or one of the co-infections, at this time the road ahead will be long, and it will not be easy. You will need support from family, friends, and caregivers, and you may at times need to reach out to organizations and associations that offer help. Lyme and/or its co-infections will change you – and the people around you. Diagnosis is just the beginning.

References

[1] Moody, K., & Barthold, S. (1991). Relative infectivity of Borrelia burgdorferi in Lewis rats by various routes of inoculation. *The American Journal of Tropical Medicine and Hygiene, 44*(2), 135-139. doi: 10.4269/ajtmh.1991.44.135

[2] Woodrum, J., & Oliver, J. (1999). Investigation of venereal transplacental, and contact transmission of the Lyme disease spirochete, Borrelia burgdorferi, in Syrian hamsters. *The Journal of Parasitology, 85*(3), 426-430.

[3] Bach, G. (2001). *Recovery of Lyme spirochetes by PCR in semen samples of previously diagnosed Lyme disease patients.* International Scientific Conference on Lyme Disease.
Retrieved from http://www.anapsid.org/lyme/bach.html

[4] Harvey, W. T., & Salvato, P. (2003). 'Lyme disease': Ancient engine of an unrecognized Borreliosis pandemic? *Medical Hypotheses, 60*(5), 742-759. doi: 10.1016/S0306-9877(03)00060-4

5. Stricker, R., Moore, D., & Winger, E. (2004). Clinical and immunologic evidence for transmission of Lyme disease through intimate human contact. *Journal of Investigative Medicine, 52*, s151. doi: 10.1136/jim-52-suppl1-412

6. Middelveen, M., et al. (2015). Culture and identification of Borrelia spirochetes in human vaginal and seminal secretions. *F1000Research*. Retrieved from https://f1000 research.com/articles/3-309/v3

7. Schmidt, B., et al. (1995). Detection of Borrelia burgdorferi DNA by Polymerase Chain Reaction in the urine and breast milk of patients with Lyme Borreliosis. *Diagnostic Microbiology & Infectious Disease, 21*(3), 121-128. doi: 10.1016/0732-8893(95)00027-8

8. Stricker, R., & Middelveen, M. (2015). Sexual transmission of Lyme disease: Challenging the tickborne disease paradigm. *Expert Review of Anti-Infective Therapy, 13*. doi: 10.1586/14787210.2015.1081056

9. Other, C. (2014). *Part 1: Sexual transmission of Lyme disease – Is there evidence?* Lyme Disease, Science, & Society. Retrieved from http://campother.blogspot.com/2014/03/part-1-sexual-transmission-of-lyme.html

10. Lyme Disease UK. (2016). *Congenital Lyme disease*. Lyme Disease UK: Patient Support. Retrieved from http://lymediseaseuk.com/2016/11/28/congenital-lyme-disease

11. Jones, C., in Scutti, S. (2013). *What is Lyme disease?: Signs and symptoms of the invisible illness*. Medical Daily: Healthy Living. Retrieved from http://www.medicaldaily.com/what-lyme-disease-signs-and-symptoms-invisible-illness-247742

12. Jones, C. (2011). Pregnancy and tick-borne diseases: Gestational Lyme. *ILADS Conference: Making the Difference in the Diagnosis & Treatment of Lyme Disease*, Oct. 28. Toronto, Canada.
13. Horowitz, R. (2014). Co-infections presentation, diagnosis, and treatment. *Symposium on Tick-borne Diseases*. May 17. USA: Maryland. Retrieved from https://www.youtube.com/watch?v=O9a-2Nb2sbk
14. Macdonald, A., Benach, J., & Burgdorfer, W. (1987). Stillbirth following maternal Lyme disease. *New York State Journal of Medicine, 87*(11), 615-616.
15. Lakos, A., & Solymosi, N. (2010). Maternal Lyme Borreliosis and pregnancy outcome. International Journal of Infectious Diseases, 14(6), e494-e498. doi: 10.1016/j.ijid.2009.07.019
16. Macdonald, A., Benach, J., & Burgdorfer, W. (1987). *Op. cit.*
17. Schlesinger, P., et al. (1985). Maternal-fetal transmission of the Lyme disease spirochete, Borrelia burgdorferi.
Annals of Internal Medicine, 103(1), 67-68. doi: 10.7326/0003-4819-103-1-67
18. Weber, K., et al. (1989). Borrelia burgdorferi in a newborn despite oral penicillin for Lyme Borreliosis: Implications for the fetus. *The Pediatric Infectious Disease Journal, 7*(4), 286-289.
19. Lakos, A., & Solymosi, N. (2010). *Op. cit.*
20. Lakos, A., & Solymosi, N. (2010). *Ibid.*
21. Jones, C. (2011). *Op. cit.*
22. McFadzean, N. (2012). *The beginner's guide to Lyme disease: Diagnosis and treatment made simple*. USA: BioMed Publishing Group.

23. LeBel, D., et al. (2017). Cases of transfusion-transmitted Babesiosis occurring in nonendemic areas: A diagnostic dilemma. *Transfusion.* doi: 10.1111/trf.1426
24. Horowitz, R. (2014). *Op. cit.*
25. Marcum, L. (2017). Babesia in the U.S. blood supply. *The Lyme Times.* Summer Issue.
26. Sethi, S., et al. (2009). Probable congenital Babesiosis in infant, New Jersey, USA. *Emerging Infectious Diseases, 15*(5), 788-791. doi: 10.3201/eid1505.070808
27. CDC. (2017). *Tickborne diseases of the United States: A reference manual for health care providers*, 4th ed. U.S. Department of Health and Human Services. Centers for Disease Control and Prevention.
28. Trivino, C. (2017). *Thompson mom passed rare tick borne illness to newborn.* NBC Connecticut. Retrieved from http://www.nbcconnecticut.com/news/local/Thompson-Mom-Passed-Rare-Tick-Borne-Illness-to-Newborn-442057583.html
29. Mahram, M., & Ghavami, M. B. (2009). Congenital tick-borne relapsing fever: Report of a case with transplacental transmission in the Islamic republic of Iran. *Eastern Mediterranean Health Journal, 15*(3), 761-764.
30. Jongen, V., et al. (1997). Tick-borne relapsing fever and pregnancy outcome in rural Tanzania. *Acta Obstetricia et Gynecologica Scandinavica, 76*(9), 834-838. doi: 10.3109/00016349709024361

[31.] Breitschwerdt, E., et al. (2010). Molecular evidence of perinatal transmission of Bartonella vinsonii susbsp. Berkhoffii and Bartonella henselae to a child. *Journal of Clinical Microbiology, 48*(6), 2289-2293. doi: 10.1128/JCM.00326-10

[32.] Horowitz, R. (2017). *How can I get better?: An action plan for treating resistant Lyme & chronic disease.* New York: St. Martin's Press.

[33.] Hirsch, E. (2017). Co-infection Bartonella treatment. *Chronic Lyme Disease Summit 2,* June 21. Health Talks Online. Retrieved from http://chroniclymediseasesummit 2.com/expert/evan-h-hirsch

[34.] Dhand, A., et al. (2007). Human Granulocytic Anaplasmosis during pregnancy: Case series and literature review. *Clinical Infectious Diseases, 45*(5), 589-593. doi: 10.1086/520659

[35.] Jereb, M., et al. (2012). Severe Human Granulocytic Anaplasmosis transmitted by blood transfusion. *Emerging Infectious Diseases, 18*(8), 1354-1357. doi: 10.3201/eid1808.120180

[36.] Rowan, K. (2013). *Ehrlichiosis, rare tick infection, spread to 9-year-old boy via blood transfusion.* Huffington Post. Retrieved from http://www.huffingtonpost.com/2013/04/03/ehrlichiosis-blood-transfusion-tick-infection-9-year-old-boy_n_3009093.html

[37.] CDC. (2016). *Preventing ticks in the yard – Create a tick-safe zone through landscaping.* Centers for Disease Control and Prevention. Retrieved from https://www.cdc.gov/lyme/prev/in_the_yard.html

38. Nicholson, W., & Paddock, C. (2017). Rickettsia (spotted & typhus fevers) & related infections, including Anaplasmosis & Ehrlichiosis. In G. Brunette (Ed.). *CDC Yellow Book 2018: Health Information for International Travel*. USA: Oxford University Press.

39. Rawls, B. (2016). *Understanding Mycoplasma: Mycoplasma, the most common Lyme co-infection*. RawlsMD. Retrieved from https://rawlsmd.com/health/articles/mycoplasma-the-most-common-lyme-co-infection

40. Taylor-Robinson, D., & Lamont, R. (2011). Mycoplasmas in pregnancy. *BJOG, 118*, 164-174. doi: 10.1111/j.1471-0528.2010.02766.x

41. Capoccia, R., Greub, B., & Baud, D. (2013). Ureaplasma urealyticum, Mycoplasma hominis and adverse pregnancy outcomes. *Current Opinion in Infectious Diseases, 26*(3), 231-240. doi: 10.1097/QCD.0b013e328360 db58

42. Chua, K., et al. (1999). Colonization and transmission of Ureaplasma urealyticum and Mycoplasma hominis from mothers to full and preterm babies by normal vaginal delivery. *The Medical Journal of Malaysia, 54*(2), 242-246.

43. Horowitz, R., in Manny, D. (2016). *The Lyme disease debate: Can the condition be chronic?* Fox News Interview. Retrieved from http://www.foxnews.com/health/2016/05/25/lyme-disease-debate-can-condition-be-chronic.html

44. Rippey, M. (2017). *Episode 123: Jean Monro, MD – UK Lyme expert*. Lyme Ninja Radio. Retrieved from http://lyme ninjaradio.com/123-jean-monro-md

45. Cosentino, B. (2015). Success with Wahls Paleo diet for Lyme disease. Real Food Rebel: Natural Solutions for Better Health. Retrieved from http://realfoodrebel.com/wahls-paleo-diet-for-lyme-disease
46. Luminary, V. (2016). Lyme Disease bites – Remission from chronic Lyme!!! Transformational Guide & Animal Whisperer. Retrieved from http://takebackyourpowernow.com/2016/06/lyme-disease-bites-remission
47. McKeon, M. (2014). *Whole-body hyperthermia treatment*. Public Health Alert: Investigating Lyme and Chronic Illness. Retrieved from http://www.publichealthalert.org/-whole-body-hyperthermia-treatment.html
48. Melia, M. & Auwaerter, P. (2016). Time for a different approach to Lyme disease and long-term symptoms. *New England Journal of Medicine, 734*, 1277-1278. doi: 1056/NEJMe1502350
49. Burrascano, J. (2008). *Diagnostic hints and treatment guidelines for Lyme and other tick borne illnesses*, (16th ed). Advanced Topics in Lyme Disease. Retrieved from http://www.lymenet.org/BurrGuide200810.pdf
50. Strasheim, C. (2017). Beyond antibiotics: Newer alternative approaches to chronic Lyme disease treatment. *The Townsend Letter, July*. Retrieved from http://www.townsendletter.com/July2017/antibiotics0717.html
51. Arminlabs. (2017). *Welcome to our laboratory*. Arminlabs Diagnosing Tick-Borne Diseases. Retrieved from https://www.arminlabs.com/en
52. Australian Biologics. (2017). *Three decades of experience*. Australian Biologics Laboratory Testing Services. Retrieved from http://www.australianbiologics.com.au

53. DNA Connexions. (2017). *Lyme Disease Test*. DNA Connexions. Retrieved from http://www.dnaconnexions.com
54. IGeneX. (2017a). *The IGeneX advantage*. IGeneX Inc. Retrieved from https://www.igenex.com
55. Horowitz, R. (2014). *Op. cit.*
56. ARC. (2017). *Infectious disease testing*. American Red Cross. Retrieved from http://www.redcrossblood.org/learn-about-blood/blood-testing
57. Jereb, M., et al. (2012). S *Op. cit.*
58. Rowan, K. (2013). *Op. cit.*
59. CDC. (2016). *Op. cit.*
60. Nicholson, W., & Paddock, C. (2017). *Op. cit.*
61. Vanderhoof-Forschner, K. (2004). *Everything you need to know about Lyme disease and other tick-borne disorders*. USA: John Wiley & Sons.
62. de Piva Dinez, P., et al. (2016). Risk factors for Bartonella species infection in blood donors from southeast Brazil. *PLoS Neglected Tropical Diseases, 10*(3), e004509. doi: 10.137/journal.pntd.0004509
63. Rafik, M. (2016). Disability denied. *The Lyme Times*. Summer Issue.
64. Leland, D. (2012). *Touched by Lyme: Can you get disability benefits for Lyme disease?* Lymedisease.org: Advocacy, Education, & Research. Retrieved from https://www.lymedisease.org/burke-disability-lyme
65. Reliosis, B. (2016). *Lyme cryme: How it all went down*. Blab: The Bad [Lyme] Attitude Blog. Retrieved from https://badlymeattitude.com/2016/08/26/lyme-cryme-how-it-all-went-down

66. Engstrom, S., Shoop, E., & Johnson, R. (1994). *Immunoblot interpretation criteria for serodiagnosis of early Lyme disease*. Proceedings of the Second National Conference on Serologic Diagnosis of Lyme Disease, October, 27-29. Dearborn, Michigan. Retrieved from http://www.action lyme.org/DEARBORN_PDF.pdf

67. Heath, J. (2017). *Overcoming Lyme disease: The truth about Lyme disease and the hidden dangers plaguing our bodies. Secrets to surviving chronic Lyme disease*. Michigan: Positive Healing Publishing.

68. Bernstein, J. (2013). *Lyme disease community blows whistle on corruption within the CDC*. ProHealth. Retrieved from http://www.prohealth.com/library/showarticle.cfm?li bid=18502

69. FDA Vaccine Advisory Committee. (2001). LymeRix vaccine victim's stories and related articles. U.S. Food & Drug Administration. Retrieved from https://www.fda.gov/ohrms/dockets/a c/01/briefing/3680b2_17.pdf

70. Reliosis, B. (2015). *Help wanted: Lyme – AIDS 2.0*. Blab: The Bad [Lyme] Attitude Blog. Retrieved from https:// badlymeattitude.com/2015/08/26/help-wanted-lyme-aids-2-0

71. LymeRix Whistleblower. (2016). *Cryme disease: The Lyme cryme against humanity*. Truth Cures. Retrieved from https://www.youtube.com/watch?v=f8DU1Z6R-ms

72. McAllister, M. P., & Kitron, U. (2003). Differences in early print media coverage of AIDS and Lyme disease. In L. K. Fuller. (Ed.), *Media-Mediated Aids* (43-62). New Jersey: Hampton Press.

73. Homeland Security. (2017). *Plum Island Animal Disease Center*. Science and Technology. Retrieved from https://www.dhs.gov/science-and-technology/plum-island-ani mal-disease-center

74. Carrol, M. C. (2005). *Lab 257: The Disturbing Story of the Government's Secret Germ Laboratory*. USA: William Morrow Paperbacks.

75. Carrol, M. C. (2005). *Ibid*.

76. Ferguson, A., in Dumitru, S. (2017). *Lyme disease on Plum Island: Fringe conspiracy theory or government cover-up?*
Tick Talk. Retrieved from https://sites.newpaltz.edu/t icktalk/social-attitudes/story-by-smaranda-dumitru

77. Lorenzetti, R., et al, (2013). Managing difficult encounters: Understanding physician, patient, and situational factors. *American Family Physician, 87*(6), 419-425.

78. Rippey, M. (2016). *Episode 113: In production – The Lyme trials*. Lyme Ninja Radio. Retrieved from https://lyme ninjaradio.com/113-winslow-murdoch-lindsay-keys

79. Stricker, R. (2007). Let's tackle the testing. *BMJ, 335*(7628), 1008. doi: 10.1136/bmj.39394.676227.BE

80. Horowitz, R. (2014). *Op. cit*.

81. Cook, M. J., & Puri, B. K. (2017). Application of Bayesian decision-making to laboratory testing for Lyme disease and comparison testing for HIV. *International Journal of General Medicine, 10*, 113-123. doi: 10.1128/JCM.43.5080-5084.2005

82. Fox News. (2015). *'In the Lyme light': 10 celebrities diagnosed with the painful tick-borne disease*. Fox News: Outbreaks. Retrieved from http://www.foxnews.com/health/2015/07/31/in-lyme-light-10-celebrities-diagnosed-with-painful-tick-borne-disease.html

83. Edwards, S. (2016). *How Celebrities are changing the way we see chronic Lyme*. Jezebel. Retrieved from http://jezebel.com/how-celebrities-are-changing-the-way-we-see-chronic-lym-176410 9037
84. Mango, A. (2016). *8 celebrities who've struggled with Lyme disease*. Health. Retrieved from http://www.health.com/health/gallery/0,,20981646,00.html#what-is-lyme-disease-0
85. Pfeiffer, M. (2016). *'Quiet plague' claims another celebrity*. The Huffington Post. Retrieved from http://www.huffingtonpost.com/mary-beth-pfieffer/quiet-plague-called-lyme-_b_9578544.html

15. Resources List

Only a small selection of the appropriate resource content is presented here because new information is continually becoming available, and of course, websites can go down, books can go out of print, and other complications can arise that can prevent access to certain content. It has also been kept short so that, like any other resource list, it can be added to, and there is a section to do so at the end of this book. The following content is covered:

- Applications
  - Diet
  - Health support
  - Lighting
  - Medication reminders
  - Symptoms trackers
  - Reminders
- Books
  - Comic
  - Conspiracy
  - Diet
  - General
  - Kids
  - Parents
  - Patient stories
  - Treatment
- Documentaries and films

- Online resources
  - Blogs
  - Facebook support groups
  - Forums
  - Podcasts
  - Symptoms surveys, questionnaires, and checklists
- Organizations and associations
  - Australia
  - Canada
  - Great Britain
  - United States of America
  - Worldwide
- Websites
  - Detoxification
  - General
  - Kids with Lyme
  - Living with Lyme
  - Organizations
  - Treatment protocols
- Video
  - YouTube channels
  - Website video archives

Applications
Diet

CalorieKing is a very easy way to check and record the calories and nutrition values of the food you eat on a daily basis. It has a comprehensive database of over 70,000 foods and fast-food franchise data, with the ability to add your own food and recipes as well. Although primarily a diet application, it can be used to track food and its nutritional values for those who are ill. It is available for iOS devices.

MealLogger is a free photo food journal and nutrition application which provides an easy way to visually journal all the foods that you eat by taking their photographs, and selecting the serving amounts. This enables you to track daily food servings and food categories, and to share the information with others who might be interested, such as a physician or other health professional. It is available for Android, and iOS devices.

Health support

Dminder is an application that can help you track and manage your levels of vitamin D. It will automatically work out the best times for generating vitamin D based on your location, how much can be generated, and how long it will take before you burn. It is available for both android and iOS devices.

SunSmart is an application that provides a sunscreen calculator to help you know how much to apply, and a vitamin D tracker so that you know how much sun exposure that you require. It also includes weather forecast and personalization options. It is available for both android and iOS devices.

F.lux is software for computers that can be installed to automatically adjust the color temperature of displays according to the location and time of day in order to help alleviate eye strain and reduce sleep pattern disruption. It is available for a range of operating systems including Linux, Mac OS, and Microsoft Windows.

Lighting

Philips Hue is a wireless smart lighting system that allows you to control the color emitted by the lights in your home. It consists of an app, a bridge, light bulbs, and light strips. The application allows control of lights and their colors from smart phones, and tablet devices. It is available for both android and iOS devices.

Medication Reminders

Dosecast is a free application to help you track the medications and dosages that you need to take each day. It also allows for scheduling that is flexible to accommodate the type of medication you are taking throughout each day, week, or month. It is available for Amazon, Android, and iOS devices.

Pillboxie is a paid application that allows you to track medications and dosages, and schedule reminders. It is unique in the way that it allows for a 'visual' type management of medications. It is available for iOS.

Symptoms Trackers

Daylio is a daily diary, journal, and mood tracker that allows you to make entries by using emoticons. It also allows for notes to be added, and provides graphical representation of all the data and statistics so that at the end of a month, it is easy to track progress. Daily entries take under ten seconds to complete. It is available for Android, and iOS devices.

Flaredown is a comprehensive symptom and treatment tracker. It allows you to customize all symptoms and treatment options, which makes it easy to visualize your health status over time, and to track daily medications and symptoms. It is an app that can be used for all chronic conditions, and it is easy and fast to use once everything is set up. It is available for Android, and IOS devices.

My Pain Diary: Chronic Pain & Symptom Tracker is a paid comprehensive pain, medication, and event logger. It enables you to track any symptom for a variety of chronic health conditions, and it provides a fully searchable history with color-coded entries for easy visual tracking. It also supports the export of graphs to a pdf. It is available for iOS devices.

Reminders

Due is one of the most useful reminder applications for setting up simple reminders very quickly and with minimal effort. It is available for iOS devices.

Paperless Lite is an application that allows you to make lists of anything and everything, and it is an easy way to keep a reminder or to-do list or just make notes. It is available for iOS devices.

Remember the Milk is a robust reminder and to-do list that can sync with your devices and other applications, allowing you to easily track all daily reminders. It is available for a wide range of online, computer-based, and portable devices.

Books

Comic

Lyme Loonies is the first cartoon book aimed at capturing and illuminating the struggles faced by those with Lyme.

Conspiracy

Lab 257: The Disturbing Story of the Government's Secret Plum Island Germ Laboratory sees an attorney, through this book, present information related to the American government work on biological warfare, and the development of diseases able to unleash destruction on Soviet food supplies.

Diet

The Wahls Protocol: A Radical New Way to Treat All Chronic Autoimmune Conditions Using Paleo Principles explores how a modified version of the Paleo diet can be successfully tailored for individuals to follow.

The Lyme Diet: Nutritional Strategies for Healing from Lyme Disease details a diet for Lyme that is anti-inflammatory, immune optimizing, detoxifying, and gut and hormone balancing. There are also meal suggestions and recommendations for lab work.

General

Cure Unknown: Inside the Lyme Epidemic is a very in-depth look at the controversies and the uncertainties that surround Lyme disease.

Kids

Little Bite, BIG Trouble: A Bird's-Eye View of Chronic Lyme Disease is a great book for children to read, and for parents to read with them, to help them understand Lyme disease and what it means to have an invisible illness. It is written by Sarah Schlitche Sanchez, who together with her husband Aaron produces the LymeVoice podcast (http://lymevoice.com).

Parents

When Your Child has Lyme Disease: A Parent's Survival Guide is a book that offers a great deal of practical information for parents with a newly diagnosed child with persistent Lyme symptoms.

Patient Stories

Confronting Lyme Disease: What Patient Stories Teach Us is a good introduction to Lyme disease, and it talks about how others have dealt with having the disease.

Treatment

Healing Lyme: Natural Healing of Lyme Borreliosis and the Co-infections Chlamydia and Spotted Fever Rickettsiosis is one of three books by Stephen Harrod Buhner. The other two are *Healing Lyme Disease Co-infections: Complimentary and Holistic Treatments for Bartonella and Mycoplasma*, and *Natural Treatments for Lyme Co-infections: Anaplasma, Babesia, and Ehrlichia*. These books outline his protocol for treating Lyme and/its co-infections.

Insights into Lyme Disease Treatment: 13 Lyme-Literate Health Care Practitioners Share their Healing Strategies is a book that discusses the strategies taken by a range of doctors, and the protocols they use in order to heal their patients.

Documentaries and Films

Earthing

Down to Earth is a short documentary introducing the concept of grounding, and the potential health benefits that can come from performing it.
https://vimeo.com/205264910

The Grounded is a documentary that discusses the concept of earthing for health.
https://www.youtube.com/embed/cRW0XO2xWn4?rel=0

Lyme

Disappearing From Society is a short documentary that features four people with chronic Lyme. The short stories capture the daily struggles of those who seem to be falling off the face of the planet, as they spend more and more time in bed. It was written to help people understand the complexities of healing from this opportunistic disease viewed through the lens of the social and emotional losses.
https://vimeo.com/218887760

Lyme Cryme explores what it calls the Dearborn stunt, as well as OspA disease – and who is not allowed to have it.
https://www.youtube.com/watch?v=f8DU1Z6R-ms

The Monster Inside Me explores the realities of having Lyme disease, and its effects on all areas of life.
http://www.imdb.com/ title/tt6714754

Under Our Skin investigates the Lyme disease epidemic, with patient and doctor interviews.
http://www.imdb.com/title/tt1202579?ref_=fn_al_tt_1

Under Our Skin 2: Emergence is a follow-up to *Under Our Skin* that offers hope as it revisits the people interviewed in the first documentary, showing how they have reclaimed their lives.
http://www.imdb.com/title/tttt3735216/?ref_=fn_al_tt_4

EMF and RF Protection

Take Back Your Power focuses on the problems with smart meters and how the frequencies that they use can damage the body.
https://www.youtube.com/watch?v=R3g0P8iWnq0

Online Resources

Blogs

All Things Lyme is a blog by Daniel Cameron, MD, MPH. He is a board-certified internist and epidemiologist, and one of the founders of ILADS (International Lyme and Associated Diseases Society).
http://danielcameronmd.com/daniel-cameron-md-lyme-blog

GoodbyeLyme is a look at clearing Lyme through the use of acupuncture, Chinese herbal remedies, craniosacral techniques, detoxification, energy healing, and essential oils.
http://goodbyelyme.com

Lyme Knowledge is dedicated to providing information sourced from Lyme patients and institutions, focusing on prevention, diagnosis, and symptoms. It also provides updates on the latest treatment protocols.
https://lymeknowledge.wordpress.com

Lymestats is dedicated to providing information and statistics about Lyme and its co-infections.
http://lyme stats.org

Facebook Support Groups

Buhner Healing Lyme and Co-Infections is a group for people using the Buhner protocol for treatment of Lyme and/or co-infections.
https://www.facebook.com/groups/1441091676154216

Cowden *Lyme Protocol and Ideas that Work* is a group where people share what has worked for them in the treatment of Lyme and various co-infections.
https://www.facebook.com/groups/1547743332142929

Lyme Australia & Friends offers support to those with Lyme and associated illnesses. It is open to people who are diagnosed with, or looking at the possibility of having Lyme and/or its co-infections, as well as to family members and carers of those with these illnesses.
https://www.facebook.com/groups/LymeAustraliaandFriends

Lyme Herbals – Cowden, Buhner, Jernigan, Byron White & More is capped at 10,000 members, but it is a group for discussion on various treatment protocols for Lyme and its co-infections.
https://www.facebook.com/groups/263709223729311

Lyme Disease Group supports those around the globe with Lyme disease and associated infections.
https://www.facebook.com/groups/227910764335351

Lyme Success Stories is a group where those that have come close to healing, or have actually defeated Lyme and/or its co-infections, can share their testimonies.
https://www.facebook.com/groups/180457375461056

Forums

LymeNet Europe is a forum built for information
and discussion about Lyme disease.
http://www.lymeneteurope.org/forum

MDJunction Lyme Disease Support Group is an online forum for patients, family members, and friends dedicated to dealing with Lyme disease together.
http://www.mdjunction.com/lyme-disease

Podcasts

Lyme Ninja Radio sees acupuncturist Mackay Rippey interview experts on Lyme and other tick-borne diseases, and discuss the various means of coping with those afflicted.
http://lymeninjaradio.com

LymeVoice is where Aaron and Sarah Sanchez explore the social and emotional impact of Lyme on households where the disease has had an impact. Interviews are conducted with authors, doctors, patients, and other professionals.
http://lymevoice.com

Symptoms Surveys, Questionnaires, and Checklists

Comparison Chart of Lyme Disease and Co-infections Symptoms is an extremely comprehensive comparison chart compiled by Louise Jenner.
http://www.lyme-symptoms.com/LymeCo- infectionChart.html

MSIDS Questionnaire developed by Richard Horowitz MD, is a questionnaire available from his book *How can I get Better?* It is also available online.
http://www.cangetbetter.com/symptom-list

Lymedisaese.org online Lyme Symptoms Survey allows you to check to see if your symptoms are that of Lyme disease.
https://www.lymedisease.org/lyme-disease-symptom-checklist

Lyme Journey Symptom Tracker from the Lyme Ninja Radio podcast provides a monthly means of tracking progress. It takes around six minutes to complete, and provides a single overall score, with a higher score meaning a worse level of symptoms.
http://lymeninjaradio.com/tracker

Organizations and Associations

Australia
Lyme Disease Association of Australia
http://www.lymedisease.org.au

Canada
CanLyme – Canadian Lyme Disease Foundation
https://canlyme.com

Great Britain
Lyme Disease Action (LDA)
http://www.lymediseaseaction.org.uk

Lyme Disease UK
https://lymediseaseuk.com

United States of America
Lyme Disease Association (LDA)
https://www.lymediseaseassociation.org

American Lyme Disease Federation (ALDF)
http://www.aldf.com

International Lyme & Associated Diseases Society (ILADS)
http://www.ilads.org

Worldwide

Global Lyme Alliance
https://globallymealliance.org

Websites
Detoxification
Detoxing Methods is available from the *Tired of Lyme* website, and it provides a comprehensive list of detox methods in alphabetical order.
http:// www.tiredoflyme.com/detox-methods

Lyme Detoxification 101: The basics is a short but comprehensive article from the website of the *Treat Lyme Book*, discussing the fundamental essentials of detox.
http://www.treatlyme.net/treat-lyme-book/lyme-detoxification-101-the-basics

Earthing
EarthConnection is a European-based store selling various earthing and EMF and RF protection products.
https://www.earthconnection.eu

Earthing.com is an American-based store selling various earthing products, with links to a number of documentaries and resources on the topic.
https://www.earthing.com

EarthingOz is an Australian-based store selling various earthing products, with links to a variety of resources on the topic. They also sell various products to protect from EMF exposure.
https://www.earthingoz.com.au

EMF and RF Protection

EarthConnection is a European-based store selling various earthing, and EMF and RF protection products.
https://www.earthconnection.eu

EarthingOz is an Australian-based store selling various earthing products, with links to a variety of resources on the topic. They also sell various products to protect from EMF exposure.
https://www.earthing oz.com.au

No Radiation for You is a website containing information about protecting yourself from EMF and RF radiation exposure. They also link to their store where various products are available for purchase, including meters and RF blocking fabric.
http://www.norad4u.com

General

LymeDisease.org provides news, information, and healthcare policy analysis for those in the Lyme community. In-depth coverage includes: Lyme disease in children and adolescents, integrative medicine, and insurance challenges.
https://www.lymedisease.org

Lyme Handbook is a quick reference guide to things associated with Lyme disease.
https://lyme handbook.com

Kids with Lyme

Children's Lyme Disease Network is the place to go for families with children infected with Lyme disease and experiencing challenges.
http://www.childrenslymenet work.org

Dr. Jones kids is a great resource for information on Lyme and Children. Dr. Jones has treated over 12,000 children, and he is a pediatric tick-borne disease expert.
https://sites.google.com/site/drjone skids/home

The Lyme Times is a newsletter distributed by Lymedisease.org. There are two issues important for kids with Lyme:
- Issue 42, the Children's Treatment Issue https://www.lymedisease.org/lymetimes/childrens-treatment-issue
- Issue 45 the Children's Education Issue https://www.lymedisease.org/lymetimes/childrens-education-issue

Living with Lyme

Living with Lyme Disease is a website that presents information for teenagers living with Lyme. http://www. livingwithlymedisease.org

Organizations

CanLyme is an organization that provides public and medical professionals in Canada with information on Lyme disease and related co-infections. https://canlyme.com

Global Lyme & Invisible Illness Organization provides links to support groups worldwide. It is the group responsible for founding and organizing Red Shoe Day, an annual awareness event for those with Lyme and invisible illnesses.
http://www.globallymeinvisibleillness.org

International Lyme and Associated Diseases Society (ILADS) is an American-based organization that promotes awareness of Lyme and associated diseases and strongly supports health care professionals and physicians in advancing standards of care.
http://www.ilads.org

Lymedisease.org is a patient advocacy group seeking quality healthcare for patients with Lyme and other tick-borne diseases.
https://www.lymedisease.org

Lyme Disease Association of Australia seeks multi-sector recognition and the diagnosis and treatment for Australian patients with Lyme and associated diseases.
http://www.lymedisease.org.au

Treatment Protocols

Buhnerhealinglyme.com is the website of master herbalist, author, and earth poet Stephen Harrod Buhner. Information on his protocol for fighting Lyme and co-infections, with questions and answers, are available.
http://buhnerhealinglyme.com

Guidebook for the Byron White Formulas is a comprehensive site detailing information regarding the product line available for support with bacterial, fungal, and viral conditions.
http://www.gordonmedical.com/unravelling-complex-chronic-illness/services-offered-at-gordon-medical-associates/guidebook-for-the-byron-white-formulas-table-of-contents

Cowden Support Program utilizes a number of Nutramedix herbs, and this webpage details the protocol as well as the primary function of each product used with it.
http://www.nutramedix.ec/ns/cowden-support-program

Video

YouTube Channels

Partners in Lyme is part of the *Know How Things Work* series of videos, and at times see a husband and wife discuss their experiences and the impact of Lyme on their lives.
https://www.youtube.com/channel/UCq9BsSud1OzM6-atLcX81UQ

Lyme Disease Association of Australia YouTube Channel curates and uploads various clips relevant to making changes to how Lyme disease and tick-borne disease sufferers are treated.
https://www.youtube.com/channel/UCVgJglJQhY77iBLbAwJr1IQ

Website Video Archives

LymeTubes is a website with a vast collection of links to videos, podcasts, and other sites related to Lyme disease, its co-infections, and other invisible illnesses.
http://lymetubes.com

16. Appendices

The appendices consist of the following:
A. Symptoms of *Borreliosis* (Lyme Disease)
B. Symptoms of *Babesia, Bartonella, Ehrlichia/Anaplasma, Rickettsia,* and *Mycoplasma*
C. Signs and symptoms tracker – example checklist
D. Western blot – bands and explanations
E. Infographics – data and tables

Appendix A: Signs and Symptoms* of *Borreliosis* (Lyme Disease)

Ears (Hearing)
- Buzzing in ears
- Decreased hearing in one or both ears, plugged ears
- Pain in ears, oversensitivity to sounds
- Ringing in one or both ears

Eyes (Vision)
- Double or blurry vision
- Flashing lights/peripheral waves/phantom images in corner of eyes
- Increased floating spots
- Pain in eyes, or swelling around eyes
- Oversensitivity to light

Cognition
- Difficulty with concentration or reading
- Confusion, difficulty in thinking
- Forgetting how to perform simple tasks
- Going to the wrong place
- Memory loss (short or long term)
- Speech difficulty (slurred or slow)
- Stammering speech

---

* Reproduced with permission from the Lyme Disease Association of Australia, www.lymedisease.org.au

General Well-Being
- Allergies/chemical sensitivities
- Continual infections (eye, kidney, sinus, etc)
- Early on, experienced a 'flu-like' illness, after which you have not since felt well
- Extreme fatigue
- Increased effect from alcohol, possible worse hangover
- Low body temperature
- Pain migrates (moves) to different body parts
- Phantom smells
- Swollen glands/lymph nodes
- Symptoms seem to change, come and go
- Unexplained fevers (high or low grade)
- Unexplained weight gain, loss

Digestive and Excretory Systems
- Constipation
- Diarrhea
- Irritable bladder (trouble starting, stopping), or interstitial cystitis
- Upset stomach (nausea or pain), or GERD (gastroesophageal reflux disease)

Head, Face, and Neck
- Dental problems (unexplained)
- Headache, mild or severe, seizures
- Facial paralysis (Bell's Palsy, Horner's syndrome)
- Jaw pain or stiffness

- Pressure in head, white matter lesions in brain (MRI)
- Sore throat, clearing throat a lot, phlegm, hoarseness, runny nose
- Stiff or painful neck
- Tingling of nose, (tip of) tongue, cheek or facial flushing
- Twitching of facial or other muscles
- Unexplained hair loss

Musculoskeletal System

- Bone pain, joint pain or swelling, carpal tunnel syndrome
- Stiffness of joints, back, neck, tennis elbow
- Muscle pain or cramps (fibromyalgia)

Neurological System

- Burning or stabbing sensations in the body
- Fatigue, CFS (Chronic Fatigue Syndrome), weakness, peripheral neuropathy, or partial paralysis
- Increased motion sickness
- Lightheadedness, wooziness
- Numbness in body, tingling, pinpricks
- Poor balance, dizziness, difficulty walking
- Pressure in the head
- Seizures – often 'atypical'
- Tremors or unexplained shaking

Psychological Well-Being
- Difficulty falling or staying asleep
- Disorientation (getting or feeling lost)
- Feeling as if you are losing your mind
- Mood swings, irritability, bi-polar disorder
- Narcolepsy, sleep apnea
- Over-emotional reactions, crying easily
- Panic attacks, anxiety
- Too much sleep, or insomnia
- Unusual depression

Reproduction and Sexuality
- Loss of libido
- Sexual dysfunction
- Testicular pain
- Unexplained breast pain, discharge
- Unexplained menstrual pain, irregularity

Respiratory and Circulatory Systems
- Chest pain or rib soreness
- Endocarditis, Heart block
- Heart palpitations or extra beats
- Night sweats or unexplained chills
- Shortness of breath, can't get full/satisfying breath, cough

Appendix B: Signs and Symptoms of *Babesia*, *Bartonella*, *Ehrlichia/Anaplasma*, *Rickettsia*, and *Mycoplasma*

Babesia[1-3]

Possible primary complaint:
- Mental and/or emotional

Signs and symptoms can include:
- Air hunger (shortness of breath, constant sighing, yawning attacks)
- Babesia drunkenness
- Blurred vision (intermittent)
- Brain fog
- Concentration difficulties
- Déjà vu
- Dry cough (chronic)
- Depression or anxiety
- Dizziness (light-headed)
- Eye pain or pressure
- Fullness in throat, difficulty swallowing
- Gastro-intestinal issues (gastric motility)
- Headaches or migraines (pressure sensations)
- Heart palpitations
- Insomnia
- Light and/or sound sensitivity
- Neuropathy (burning/pain/numbness)
- Occasional fever
- Profound fatigue

- Rubber band sensations
- Sensations of heat or pain shocks
- Short-term memory loss
- Sleep disturbance (delayed sleep onset, frequent waking, difficulty falling back to sleep)
- Strange dreams or nightmares
- Sweats or chills (night sweats, sometimes day sweats)
- Tinnitus
- Vertigo

Bartonella[4-7]

Possible primary complaint:
- Pain: Muscle, joint, feet (burning and/or numb)

Signs and symptoms can include:
- Acne
- Agitation, irritability, rage, impulsivity, or aggression
- Brain inflammation – brain fog, memory problems, headaches (front or top of head)
- Chemical sensitivities
- Confusion and disorientation that can be transient
- Cough
- Dizziness
- Drowsiness
- Enlarged lymph nodes
- Ear issues – ringing, decreased/increased sensitivity to noise

- Eye issues – pain in eyes, blurred vision, disturbance of depth perception, *conjunctivitis* (pink eye)
- Fatigue
- Fainting
- Fever, low-grade (morning and/or late afternoon)
- Foot pain – typically in morning or evening involving heels and soles of the feet (similar to *plantar fasciitis*)
- Gastrointestinal (GI) tract disorders
- Hallucinations
- Joint pain/stiffness – often symmetrical
- Mood swings
- Muscle pain (especially in calves or shins), spasms and/or weakness
- Nerve issues – numbness, crawling sensations, or burning sensations
- Panic/anxiety attacks
- Polyps in/on major organs
- Rashes – red, purple, or white striae (stretch marks), tender lumps and nodules along sides of legs or arms, and spider veins
- Renal (kidney) disorders
- Seizures
- Sleep issues – difficulty falling asleep, poor sleep quality
- Sweats, morning or late afternoon (sometimes at night)
- Sore throat

- Urinary issues – pain or burning when urinating, urgency to go to the toilet, difficulty in expelling urine
- Urinary tract infections (UTI)

Ehrlichia/Anaplasma[8-11]

- Bloodshot eyes
- Chills
- Confusion
- Fever
- Gastrointestinal symptoms (anorexia, diarrhea, nausea, vomiting)
- Headaches
- Malaise
- Muscle pain
- Rashes (more common in children)

Rickettsia[12,13]

- Digestive problems
- Fever
- Headache
- Nausea
- Muscle pain
- Rash
- Vomiting

Mycoplasma[14]

- Anxiety
- Confusion
- Decreased attention
- Fatigue
- Fever
- Insomnia
- Joint pain, occasional swelling
- Memory problems
- Mood changes
- Muscle pain

References

[1] Anderson, W. (2010). Babesia like Organisms (BABLO): Consideration, Signs, and Symptoms. Gordon Medical. Retrieved from http://www.gordonmedical.com/unravelling-complex-chronic-illness/babesia-like-organisms-bablo-consideration-signs-and-symptoms

[2] Schaller, J., & Mountjoy, K. (2015, July). Advanced 2015 Babesia care: Profound testing defects and preventing disability and death. *Townsend Letter: The Examiner of Alternative Medicine*. Retrieved from http://www.townsendletter.com/July2015/babesia0715html

[3] Fearn, D. (2017). Co-infections: Answers to the most commonly-asked questions. *The Lyme Times Special Issue: Patients Issue*. Retrieved from http://www.lymedisease.org/members/lyme-times/special-issues/patient-issue/lyme-disease-co-infections

4. Schaller, J. (2007). *Ignore Bartonella and die: Trivializing Bartonella is like ignoring TNT*. Public Health Alert: Investigating Lyme and Chronic Illness. Retrieved from http://www.publichealthalert.org/ignore-bartonella-and-die-trivializing-bartonella-is-like-ignoring-tnt.html
5. Singleton, K. (2008). *The Lyme disease solution*. USA: BookSurge Publishing.
6. Forsgren, S. (2015, July). Unravelling the mystery of Bartonellosis. *Townsend letter: The Examiner of Alternative Medicine*. Retrieved from http://www.townsendletter.com/July2015/bartonellosis0715.html
7. Fearn, D. *Op. Cit.*
8. McFadzean, N. (2012). *The beginner's guide to Lyme disease: Diagnosis and treatment made simple*. USA: BioMed Publishing Group.
9. Buhner, S. (2015). *Natural treatments for Lyme co-infections: Anaplasma, Babesia, and Ehrlichia*. Vermont: Healing Arts Press.
10. Cameron, D. (2017). *The role of co-infections*. All Things Lyme. Retrieved from http://danielcameronmd.com/co-infections
11. CDC. (2017). *Tickborne diseases of the United States: A reference manual for health care providers*, 4th ed. U.S. Department of Health and Human Services. Centers for Disease Control and Prevention.
12. Cox, R. (2016). *Rocky Mountain Spotted Fever symptoms in pictures*. OnHealth. Retrieved from http://www.onhealth.com/content/1/rocky_mountain_spotted_fever

[13] CDC. (2017). *Rocky Mountain Spotted Fever (RMSF)*. Centers for Disease Control and Prevention. Retrieved from https://www.cdc.gov/rmsf/symptoms/index.html

[14] Brewer, J. (2007). Tickborne diseases and co-infections. *The Lyme Times*, 48, 20-27.

Appendix C:
Signs and Symptoms Tracker – Example Checklist

The signs and symptoms tracker can be filled in with typical, new, and relieved signs and symptoms each week or month as you progress to full health. One is left blank for you to photocopy and fill in, if you wish; the other is provided as an example.

1. You can mark any changes experienced over a period of time such as a week or a month. This might include stabbing pain changing to dull pain, or to no pain. These can perhaps be marked with an asterisk (*).
2. Description of signs and symptoms can be listed in order of severity, and by type.
3. You can use a numerical scale to compare the severity of the signs and symptoms over a month, or compare the severity of the signs and symptoms to others over the month, perhaps using: 1 for least bothersome/tolerable, 5 for bothersome, 10 for most bothersome/painful.
4. You can use a numerical scale to reflect on the signs and symptoms over time, or over the month if perceptible, and using a numerical scale, perhaps mark them: 1 for getting better, 5 for about the same, 10 for getting worse.

Signs and Symptoms Tracker[1]

	Type[2]	Description[2]	Current Impact[3] 1 2 3 4 5 6 7 8 9 10	Over Time[4] 1 2 3 4 5 6 7 8 9 10
Typical	Fatigue	On couch mostly, overall tired/worn out feeling	☐☐☐☐☐☐☐☐☐☑	☐☐☐☐☐☐☐☐☐☑
	Cognition	Forgetting 2-3 times a day (draw a bath, don't take it)	☐☐☐☐☐☐☐☐☑☐	☐☐☐☐☑☐☐☐☐☐
	Eyes	Aching/overtired, painful orbs (like liquid is freezing)	☑☐☐☐☐☐☐☐☐☐	☐☐☐☑☐☐☐☐☐☐
	Joints	Knuckles/wrists ache, right big toe has dull pain	☐☑☐☐☐☐☐☐☐☐	☑☐☐☐☐☐☐☐☐☐
	Feet	Morning pain (plantar fasciitis), night numbing/burning	☐☐☐☐☑☐☐☐☐☐	☐☐☐☐☑☐☐☐☐☐
	Startle Response	Moderate noises hurt (door slams, timer for medication)	☐☐☐☐☐☐☑☐☐☐	☐☐☐☐☐☐☐☐☐☑
	Muscles	Overall aches, back pain between shoulders	☐☐☐☐☐☑☐☐☐☐	☐☐☐☐☐☐☑☐☐☐
	Insomnia	Middle to bathroom, terminal occasionally	☐☐☐☐☐☐☐☑☐☐	☐☐☐☐☐☐☐☑☐☐
New	Feet	Day dull stabbing	☐☐☐☑☐☐☐☐☐☐	☑☐☐☐☐☐☐☐☐☐
	n/a	n/a		
	n/a	n/a		
Relieved	Insomnia	Early, resolved with blue blockers	n/a	n/a
	Muscles	Calves had icepick like pain	n/a	n/a
	Pain	Food/alcohol (mango and beer) caused back pain	n/a	n/a

Signs and Symptoms Tracker[1]

Relieved			New			Typical								Type[2]	Description[2]	Current Impact[3] 1 2 3 4 5 6 7 8 9 10	Over Time[4] 1 2 3 4 5 6 7 8 9 10
n/a	n/a	n/a															
n/a	n/a	n/a															

Appendix D: Western Blot – Bands and Explanations

Each band has a corresponding explanation.[1-5] The numbers on the Western blot refer to how much a specific part of the bacteria weighs in kilodaltons (kDa).

Band	Explanation
9	Cross-reactive for *Borrelia*.
12	Specific for *Borrelia burgdorferi*.
18	*Flagellin* fragment.
20	May be cross-reactive for *Borrelia*.
21	Unknown.
22	Specific for *Borrelia burgdorferi*, probably really the 23/25 band.
23-25	Osp C, specific for *Borrelia burgdorferi* (can be an early band).
28	Osp D, specific for *Borrelia burgdorferi*.
[23-28]	Potential for CNS involvement.
30	Osp A – substrate binding protein – common in European and one Californian strain (check for Mycoplasma).
31	Osp A, specific for *Borrelia burgdorferi*.
34	Osp B, specific for *Borrelia burgdorferi*.
35	Specific for *Borrelia burgdorferi*.
37	*Fla A* (flagellin) gene product, specific for *Borrelia burgdorferi*.
38	Cross-reactive for *Borrelia burgdorferi*.

41	*Flagellin* protein of all spirochetes. This is usually first to appear after a *Bb* infection, and specific for all *Borrellia*. Can be positive due to relapsing fever, oral spirochetes and syphilis. *Flagella* or tail protein (many bacteria have *flagella*). This is the most common *Borreliosis* antibody.
45	Cross-reactive for all *Borrelia* (sometimes people with Lyme who have a positive on this band have the *Ehrlichiosis* co-infection). Heat shock protein: this helps the bacteria survive fever.
50	Cross-reactive for all *Borrelia*.
55	Cross-reactive for all *Borrelia*.
57	Cross-reactive for all *Borrelia*.
58	Unknown, but may be a heat shock *Borrelia burgdorferi* protein (check for viral infections).
60	Cross-reactive for all *Borrelia*.
66	Oms 66, cross-reactive for all *Borrelia*, common in all bacteria (check for *E-coli*).
83	High molecular mass protein. Specific antigen for the Lyme bacterium. This is the DNA of *Borrelia burgdorferi*. (Same as *band 93*, laboratories can vary in assigning significance between *band 83* versus 93).
93	An immunodominant protoplasmic cylinder antigen, associated with the *flagellum*. Possibly the same as band *83*.
Note:	Bmp – Bacterial membrane protein Fla – *flagellin* Oms – Outer membrane spanning Osp – Outer surface protein

Appendix D: Western Blot | 361

Band Intensity

When reporting bands, they will be marked with a level of intensity which stems from breaking pieces of bacteria into parts and suspending them in a gel, and then using electricity to push antibodies made by the immune system through that gel. The antibodies then attach to the bacteria forming a black band, which is then interpreted on a scale.

Scale	Explanation
-	Negative (not present)
+	Low
++	Medium
+++	High
IND or +/-	Indeterminate (IND) or equivocal (present, but not as intense as a 'low reading')
Note:	Some LLMD may read an indeterminate as a very low positive, or as a weak positive, taking appropriate symptoms into account.[6]

References

[1.] Zoller, L., et al. (1993). Western blot as a tool in the diagnosis of Lyme Borreliosis. *Electrophoresis, 14*(9), 937-944. doi: 10.10002/elps.11501401149

[2.] Schaller, J. (2007). [Lyme] *Western blots made easy*. Public Health Alert: Investigating Lyme and chronic illness. Retrieved from http://www.publichealthalert.org/lyme-western-blots-made-easy.html

3. Ruth. (2014). *How to read an IGeneX Western blot.* Healing Well. Retrieved from http://www.healingwell.com/community/default.aspx?f=30&m=3177270
4. IGeneX. (2017). *Test interpretations.* IGenex Inc. Retrieved from http://www.igenex.com/testing/interprerpretations
5. Jones, C. (2017). *Lab test info.* Children with Lyme & Tick Borne Diseases. Dr. Jones Kids. Retrieved from https://sites.google.com/site/drjoneskids/lab-tests
6. Horowitz, R. (2017). *How can I get better?: An action plan for treating resistant Lyme & chronic disease.* New York: St. Martin's Press.

Appendix E: Infographics – Data and Tables

The statistics and research provided in this book, has been graphically illustrated in the following infographics.

- Medical misdiagnosis
- Annual number of Lyme disease infections in the United States
- Special skills of *Borrelia burgdorferi*
- Possible transmission vectors
- Rate of co-infections
- Tick life cycle
- Steps to avoid a tick bite
- Tick removal
- Time to infection
- Vaccination and prevention
- Symptoms manifesting with Lyme
- The average patient
- Testing
- Initial allopathic treatment
- Long-term treatment options
- Immune Support
- Lyme detox
- Lyme diet
- The spoon theory checklist

Medical Misdiagnosis

50%
psychogenic diagnosis given to patients instead of a physical diagnosis

10%-20%
overall misdiagnosis rate in the United States

7%-17%
diagnostic error rate in hospitals

2.5-7 times longer to reach a real diagnosis once misdiagnosed for those with rare diseases

Appendix E: Infographics | 365

Annual Number of Lyme Disease Infections in the United States

The **CDC reports** that, in the U.S., Lyme disease infects:

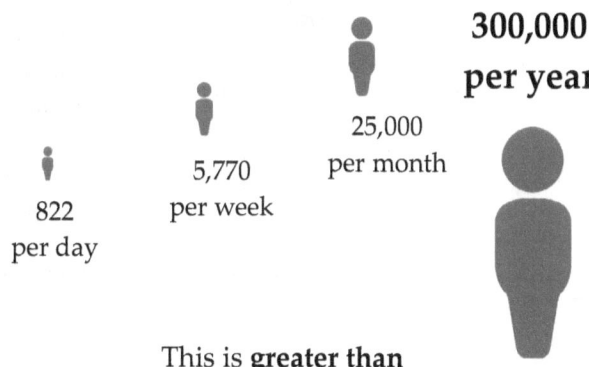

822 per day

5,770 per week

25,000 per month

300,000 per year

This is **greater than** *AIDS, West Nile Virus, and the Avian Flu **combined**.*

Special Skills of *Borrelia burgdorferi*

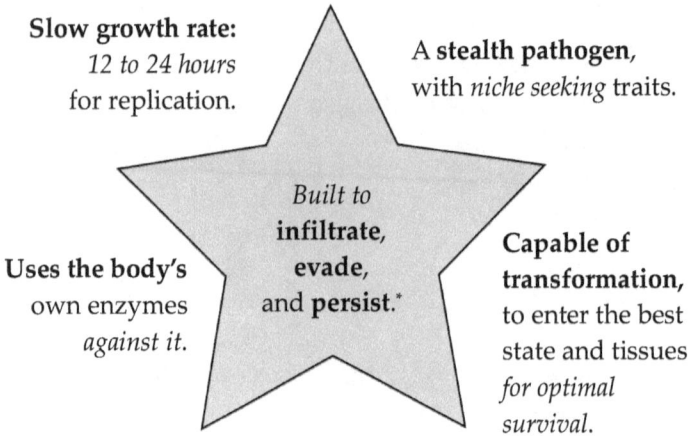

- **Slow growth rate:** *12 to 24 hours* for replication.
- A **stealth pathogen**, with *niche seeking* traits.
- **Uses the body's** own enzymes *against it.*
- *Built to* **infiltrate, evade, and persist.***
- **Capable of transformation**, to enter the best state and tissues *for optimal survival.*

Motility prowess *unforeseen* in the microbial world!

---

* For more information, see Berndtson, K. (2013). Review of evidence for immune evasion and persistent infection in Lyme disease. *International Journal of General Medicine, 6,* 291-306. doi: 10.2147/IJGM.S44114

Possible Transmission Vectors

Ticks can carry
multiple **disease-causing** pathogens.

Transmission of Lyme and its co-infections
may not be limited to ticks.

Other possible vectors are:

Mosquitos   *Fleas*   *Lice*   *Mites*

Rate of Co-infections

None, one, or many co-infections can come with a bite.

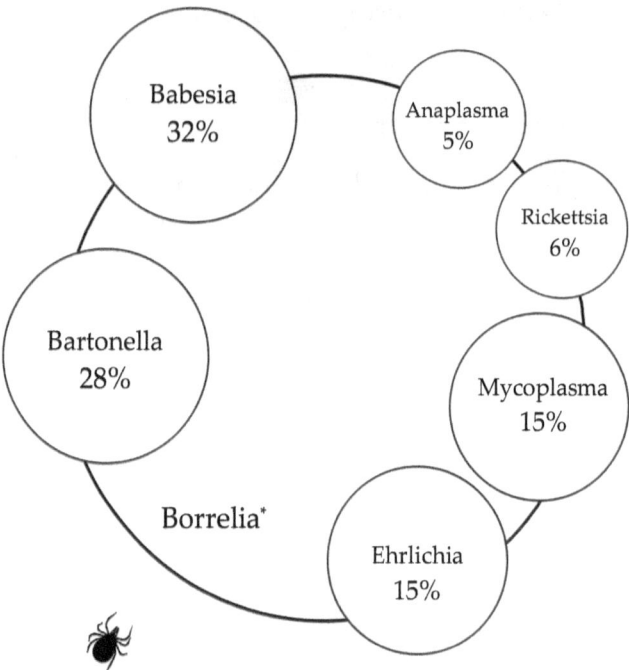

Not *all* ticks carry Lyme and its co-infections.

* Percentages as found in Johnson, L., et al. (2014). Severity of chronic Lyme disease compared to other chronic conditions: A quality of life survey. *PeerJ*, 2, e322. doi: 10.7717/peerj.322

Tick Life Cycle

Year 1

Spring/Summer
1. Eggs hatch into larva in the spring. Larva attach to first host.

Fall/Winter
2. Infected larva molt into nymphs. Nymphs lay dormant during winter.

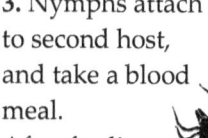

4. Adult ticks attach to third host in the fall/autumn, take a blood meal, mate, and drop off host.
 Female lays eggs.

3. Nymphs attach to second host, and take a blood meal. After feeding, drop off to molt into an adult tick.

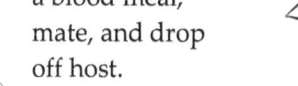

 **Fall/Winter**

Spring/Summer

Year 2

Steps to Avoid a Tick Bite

Clothing
1. Light colored
2. Long sleeves/pants
3. Closed-toe shoes
4. Spray with repellant
5. Tuck pants into socks/boots

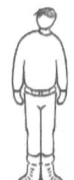

Checking
1. Check for ticks (scalp, ears, armpits, groin, behind knees)
2. Remove the tick properly
3. Keep the tick for testing if bitten
4. Check pets as well

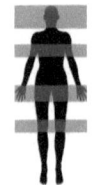

Hiking
1. Stay mid-trail
2. Avoid tall grass
3. Take off clothes before entering car/home
4. Use dryer to kill ticks

Landscaping
1. Barriers around yards (gravel, mulch, wood chips)
2. Remove leaf litter
3. Employ chemical/natural deterrents

Tick Removal

Follow advice like the CDC and ASCIA guidelines, for example:

1. *Freeze* tick

2. Remove tick with *fine-tipped tweezers*

3. Grab tick *close to mouth*

4. *Pull upward* (do not twist)

5. *Clean and disinfect* bite area

6. *Keep tick* for testing

7. *Watch for rash* and other symptoms

   Note: Not every tick bite causes Lyme.

   *If you are having difficulty,
   then seek medical attention.*

Time to Infection

Likely 16 to 24 hours

No minimum transmission *time* confirmed

	3 days	4 days
One Tick	**31% infection** rate	**57% infection** rate
Two Ticks	2 Days **100% infected**	**Instant Infection** when *spirochetes are in the mouth parts of ticks* with a systemic infection.

Median infective dose

18 spirochetes in salivary gland extract, 251 spirochetes in midgut extract

Vaccination and Prevention

Vaccine trials are underway.

No current vaccine.

A preventative injectable is *in development*.

Symptoms Manifesting with Lyme

Early Localized	Early Disseminated	Late Disseminated
>1 month of infection	1-4 months of infection	4+ months of infection

Affects Multiple Body Systems

- Rash
- Flu-like Illness
- Muscle pain
- Stiff neck
- Tender glands
- Sensitivity to light
- Sound sensitivity
- Temperature sensitivity
- Unexplained fatigue
- Cognition
- Psychological well-being
- Ears (hearing)
- Eyes (vision)
- Head, face, and neck
- Respiratory and circulatory systems
- Digestive and excretory systems
- Reproduction and sexuality
- General well-being
- Neurological system
- Musculoskeletal system

The great imitator – Lyme mimics 250+ diseases.

The Average Patient

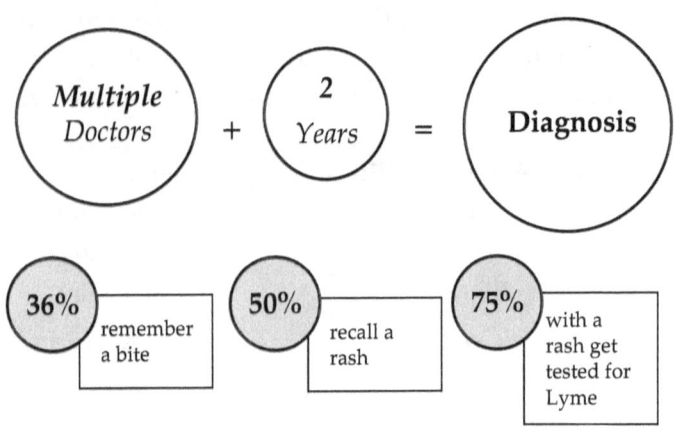

Testing

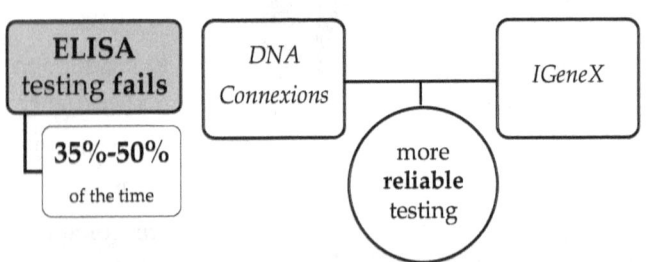

Negative test results do not rule out a Lyme diagnosis.

Initial Allopathic Treatment

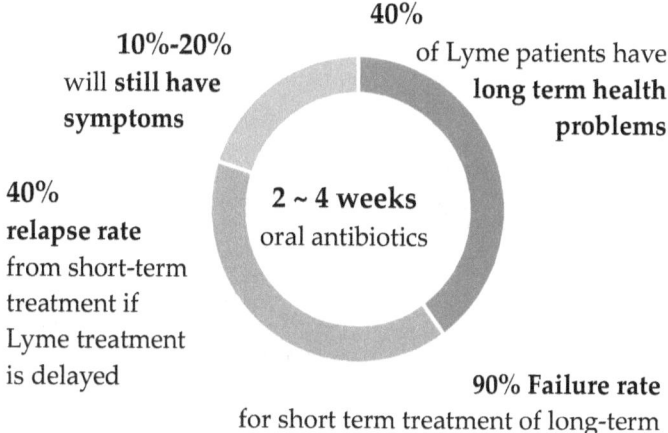

40% of Lyme patients have **long term health problems**

10%-20% will **still have symptoms**

2 ~ 4 weeks oral antibiotics

40% relapse rate from short-term treatment if Lyme treatment is delayed

90% Failure rate for short term treatment of long-term infected patients

Long-Term Treatment Options

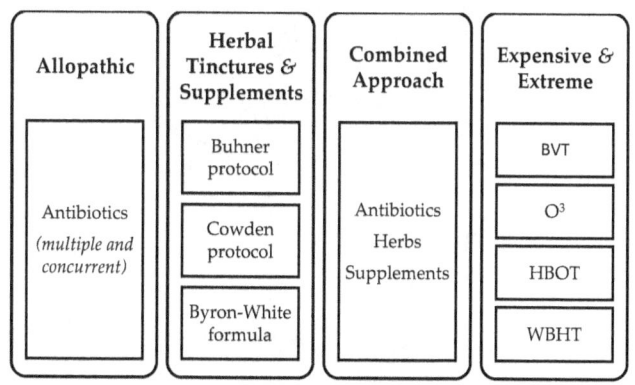

Allopathic	Herbal Tinctures & Supplements	Combined Approach	Expensive & Extreme
Antibiotics *(multiple and concurrent)*	Buhner protocol	Antibiotics Herbs Supplements	BVT
	Cowden protocol		O^3
	Byron-White formula		HBOT
			WBHT

Immune Support

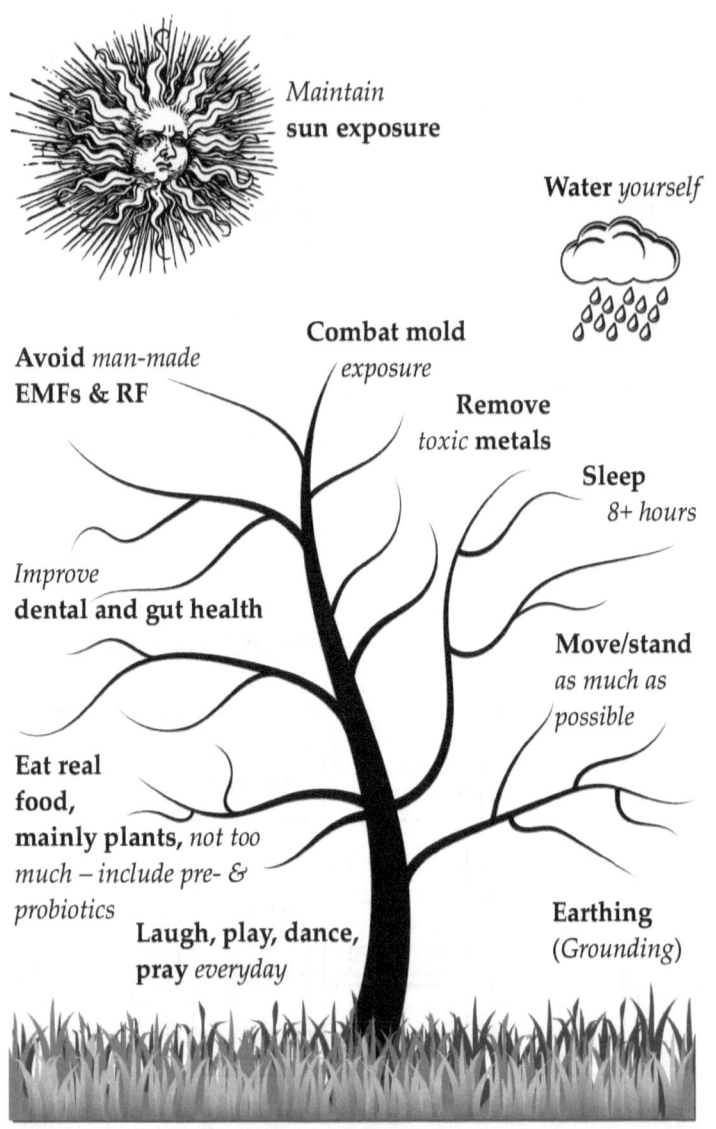

Lyme Detox

Alleviate a Herx

A herx, or reaction to toxins and die-off, can occur
48 to 72 hours after treatment

Detox can help *alleviate Herxheimer reactions* and help *remove toxins* from the body

The Horowitz Herx Relieving Drink
Relief in less than 2 hours for 70% of people.

Take	1,500mg	Liposomal glutathione
Mix	2 tablets	Alka-Seltzer Gold
	2oz (60mls)	Lemon Juice
	8oz (240mls)	Water
Sip	Over several minutes	

Detox Methods

Cupping Therapy
Herbal Tinctures
Lemon Water
Supplements
Epsom Salt
Massage
Exercise
Sauna
Clays

Etc.

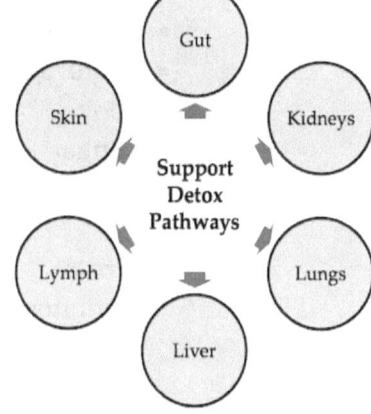

Do what you can when you can!

Lyme Diet

Many things you cannot control when ill –
diet you can control!

EAT TO

- Reduce inflammation
- Boost the immune system
- Reduce body burdens

AVOID

- Foods that provoke allergies/sensitivities/intolerance
- Caffeine
- Dairy
- Gluten
- GMOs
- Hydrogenated fat/oils
- Soy
- Sugar

Hydrate
continuously throughout the day

Appendix E: Infographics | 379

The Spoon Theory Checklist

Every day you wake up
with a *different number* of spoons.

Today you have **12 spoons**. It's a good day!

Yesterday, you had **3 spoons**. It was a bad day. ☹

Okay, spoonie, how will you use your spoons today?

1 Spoon	**2 Spoons**	**3 Spoons**	**4 Spoons**	**5 spoons**
☐ Get out of bed	☐ Get dressed	☐ Do the laundry	☐ Visit the doctor	☐ Go to the grocery store and return home
☐ Brush your hair	☐ Take a shower	☐ Put the laundry away	☐ Socialize	☐ Go to work and return home
☐ Clean your teeth	☐ Cook dinner	☐ Clean something	☐ Read a book	☐ Drop off the kids at school
☐ Count out pills	☐ Eat breakfast	☐ Check the mail box	☐ Walk or drive somewhere	☐ Pick up the kids from school

Glossary

AAD	Antibiotic-associated diarrhea
AC	Alternating current
ADD	Attention deficit disorder
ALA	Alphalinolenic acid
ALCAR	Acetyl-L-carnitine
AMD	Age-related macular degeneration
ASCIA	Australasian Society of Clinical Immunology and Allergy
ATP	Adenosine triphosphate
BBB	Blood-brain barrier
CBC	Complete blood count
CBS	Cystathionine beta synthase
CDC	Centers for Disease Control and Prevention - *headquartered near Atlanta, Georgia in the United States*
CDSA	Comprehensive digestive stool analysis
CFS	Chronic fatigue syndrome
CFU	Colony forming units
CNS	Central nervous system
CT/CAT scan	Computerized axial tomography scan
DEET	N,N-Diethyl-meta-toluamide
DHA	Docosahexaenoic acid
DMSO	Dimethyl Sulfoxide
DNA	Deoxyribonucleic acid

DSCATT	Debilitating syndrome complexes attributed to ticks
DVT	Deep vein thrombosis
ECG	Electrocardiography
EEG	Electroencephalograph
EMG	Electromyography
EHA	Eicosapentaenoic acid
EHA	Electromagnetic hypersensitivity
ELISA	Enzyme-linked immunosorbent assay
EM rash	*Erythema migrans* rash
EMF	Electromagnetic field
EMR	Electromagnetic radiation
ENT	Ear, nose, and throat specialist
ERMI test	Environmental relative moldiness index test
ES	Electrosensitive
EZ water	Exclusion zone water
FCC	Federal communications commission
FOS	Fructooligosaccharides
GERD	Gastroesophageal reflux disease
GI	Gastrointestinal
GM	Genetically modified
GP	General practitioner
HBOT	Hyperbaric oxygen therapy
HCL	Hydrochloric acid

HEPA filter	High efficiency particulate air filter
Herx	*Short for* Jarisch-Herxheimer reaction *which occurs when dead or dying bacteria release toxins into the blood and tissues at a high rate causing inflammation and pain. Also known as* JHR *or* herxing.
HGA	Human granulocytic anaplasmosis *(formerly* HGE – human granulocytic ehrlichiosis*)*.
HIV	Human immunodeficiency virus
IARC	International Agency for Research on Cancer
IBS	Irritable bowel syndrome
IDSA	Infectious Disease Society of America
IFA	Indirect immunofluorescence assay
ILADS	International Lyme and Associated Disease Society
IoT	Internet of things
LED	Light emitting diode
LDAA	Lyme Disease Association of Australia
LLMD	Lyme literate medical doctor

ISDA	Infections Disease Society of America
Lymie	A slang term for those with Lyme
MARCoNS	Multiple antibiotic resistant coagulase negative *staphylococci*
ME	Myalgic encephalomyelitis
MRI	Magnetic resonance imaging
MS	Multiple sclerosis
MSM	Methylsulfonylmethane
MSIDS	Multiple systemic infectious disease syndrome
MTHFR	Methylene tetrahydrofolate reductase
NRQZ	National radio quiet zones
OCD	Obsessive compulsive disorder
OTC	Over-the-counter
PCR	Polymerase chain reaction
PTLDS	Post-treatment Lyme disease syndrome
PTSD	Post-traumatic stress disorder
RF	Radio frequency
RMSF	Rocky Mountain spotted fever
rRNA	Ribosomal ribonucleic acid
SAD	Seasonal affective disorder
SAR	Specific absorption rates
SIBO	Small intestinal bacterial overgrowth

SNP	Single-nucleotide polymorphism
SFG	Spotted fever group
SST	Serum separating tube
Spoonie	A person with a chronic illness that uses the spoon theory to explain the need for energy rationing.
SuOx	Sulfite oxidase
UTI	Urinary tract infection
UV	Ultraviolet
VCS test	Visual contrast sensitivity test
WBHT	Whole-body hyperthermia treatment
WHO	World Health Organization

Notes

Notes

About the Book

So, you or a loved one has (or thinks they have) Lyme disease. Now what? This book was written to answer just that question, and to serve as a starting point for those inflicted with Lyme (*Borreliosis*) and/or its co-infections such as *Babesia* and *Bartonella*.

The book will also provide family, friends, and caregivers a unique perspective into what being ill with Lyme and/or its co-infections can feel like, and an insight into understanding the diseases better. It is hoped that after reading this book, that they can start their Lyme journey with you.

A background of Lyme disease and its co-infections, their transmission, tips for preventing infection, steps for tick removal, a listing of symptoms, testing preparation and approaches, as well as potential treatment options are all covered. Methods of immune support and detox, what to eat and not to eat, and what it is like living with Lyme and/or its co-infections are also included, along with a listing of useful resources, a symptoms tracker, details of the bands of the Western blot, and infographics summarizing the major points of the book.

Lyme and its co-infections will change you and those around you, and it can be a very long journey if not treated early.

Diagnosis is just the beginning!

About the Author

David Kent holds a doctorate with a specialization in technology, education, and research from Curtin University in Australia, and the skills acquired while undertaking these unique specializations have proven useful in the development of this book. He has presented at international conferences as well as published a number of peer-reviewed journal articles, books, and book chapters in his areas of expertise, and a number of his publications have been translated into other languages.

www.ingramcontent.com/pod-product-compliance
Lightning Source LLC
Chambersburg PA
CBHW020632230426
43665CB00008B/146